The New Age:
A Christian Critique

The New Age:
A Christian Critique

Ralph Rath

Greenlawn Press

ISBN 0-937779-15-6

Library of Congress Catalog Card Number 90-80211

Printed in the United States of America.

First Printing.

To Patricia Lewsen Rath

Table of Contents

Introduction

There is good news and bad news regarding the New Age movement. The good news is that New Agers are hungry for religious experience and searching for a deeper meaning in life. The bad news is that they are coming up with the wrong answers.

Instead of learning about a loving Creator who made them and all creation and who wants them to live with him in sublime happiness in heaven, New Agers have come to believe that God is a heartless charge of superhuman force that compels them to be reincarnated over and over again until they atone for someone else's sins committed in a previous life. Instead of relying on the loving power of the true God to work wonders in their lives, New Agers are putting themselves under the influence of demonic spirits. They are in sad, sad shape.

Fortunately, a number of evangelical Protestants have been writing books and magazine articles on the New Age and have been witnessing to New Agers in other ways. They have developed television and radio programs and special research centers. They have set up some telephone referral switchboards.

I am grateful for the ongoing work of these evangelical Protestants as well as for the research done by Roman Catholics and mainline Protestants. I am appreciative of the comments and help given by the editors of Greenlawn Press. I am especially grateful to Kay TePas for her comments and careful research graciously provided to me when she was a doctoral student in theology. This is a much better book thanks to Kay.

A word of caution. The New Age is not the true religion, but it sometimes seems very close to the true faith. You might want to begin by reading Chapter 15 of this book, which summarizes basic Christian beliefs. Be sure you know the truth before you read about errors.

A word of warning. The New Age is energized by powerful demonic spirits. Pray for God's protection before studying the New Age.

Part 1

New Age— What Is It?

In this first section of the book, we'll treat the basic New Age teachings, the roots of New Age thinking, and a few of the major New Age organizations. You'll become familiar with some New Age terminology. The New Age movement is a large and diverse phenomenon, but these are the basic facts a Christian should know.

Chapter 1

The New Age

What is the New Age movement? It is a noxious mixture of pantheism and occultism that is spreading like a virulent plague throughout the country. It has contaminated big-grossing movies, best-selling books, popular personnel-training programs and some nontraditional medical practices. It is destroying faith in God and putting many people under the influence of demonic spirits.

The New Age is not "new." It has disentombed religious perversions and malevolent practices that go back to the beginnings of humanity. As Christianity has lost its traditional influence, evil has crawled out from under every rock. Much of this evil is energizing the New Age movement, but many Christians are unaware of this.

F. LaGard Smith, a Christian writer about the New Age, tells about the time he was going to debate a supporter of the New Age ideas of Shirley MacLaine at a Minneapolis television studio. In the audience warm-up, the program host asked the 140 persons in the audience how many were New Agers. About 130 put up their hands. Then he asked how many were Christians. Again, nearly all put up their hands. Many members of the audience considered themselves Christians *and* New Agers and apparently did not have any problems with this.[1]

I find nothing good in the New Age religion as such. On the other hand, I have a great respect for the major non-Christian religions of the world. I see these as attempts by human beings of intelligence and good will to probe the meaning of life and to search for religious truth. I think the Christian should engage in constructive dialogue with sincere followers of major non-Christian religions. This should involve sincere mutual respect.

This is not the attitude I take with the insidious New Age movement. New Agers are disguising themselves as angels of light while they try to undermine Christianity. I oppose New Agers on every front.

As a Christian, I believe in a loving God who created me—and everything else—out of nothing and sent his only Divine Son to redeem me. New Agers believe in an impersonal force as the ultimate reality; it is neither good nor bad. They also, somewhat paradoxically, believe in a higher self—Christians would say an inner demonic spirit—that tells them all sorts of nonsense.

I believe the loving God cares for me and has prepared a place in heaven for me to enjoy his presence for all eternity. God allows evil to happen, but will make good come out of it—in this life and the next—through his providence. New Agers believe they are gods and that any good or evil befalling them is their own doing because they create their own reality. They believe that they are doomed to a nearly endless cycle of reincarnations to pay off all the bad debt (karma) they have accumulated in life.

I am so happy I am a Christian!

God Within

The New Age is pantheistic. It says everything is god. We are god. We create our own reality. The New Age also has us looking inside to find a higher self to instruct us and guide us. The New Age wants us to experience our god-power.

Typically, a false religion like the New Age mimics the true religion, Christianity. God dwells in the Christian in a special way. Christians are imbued with the Third Person of the Trinity, the Holy Spirit. We can call on the Holy Spirit to guide us. Through prayer and through the sacraments, we are united to Jesus in a very intimate way. We can operate with God's power.

St. Augustine, in his *Confessions*, talks about his personal search for God:

> Everywhere, O Truth, you give hearing to all who consult you, and at one and the same time you make answer to them all, even as they ask about varied things. You answer clearly, but all men do not hear you clearly.

> Too late have I loved you, O Beauty so ancient and so new, too late have I loved you! Behold, you were within me, while I was outside: it was there that I sought you, and, a deformed creature, rushed headlong upon these things of beauty which you have made. You were with me, but I was not with you. They kept me far from you, those fair things which, if they were not in you, would not exist at all.[2]

Though Augustine says he found God inside himself, it is clear that Augustine is a Christian and not a New Ager. In this passage, Augustine states clearly that God is exalted Truth and Beauty, that Augustine himself is a creature, that God seeks to draw all persons to himself, that God dwells patiently in a person even if that person chases around trying to find happiness in God's creatures.

Another of the early Christian writers, Gregory of Nyssa, talks about human beings as being a reflection of God.

Thus all the harmony that is observed in the universe is rediscovered in the microcosm, i.e., in human nature, and it corresponds to the whole by virtue of its parts, as far, at least, as the whole can be obtained by the parts.

The Divine Nature, whatever it may be in itself, surpasses every mental concept for it is altogether inaccessible to reasoning and conjecture, nor has there been found any human faculty capable of perceiving the incomprehensible.

If a man's heart has been purified from every creature and unruly affections, he will see the image of the Divine Nature in his own beauty . . . . It is indeed within your reach; you have within yourselves the standard by which to apprehend the Divine. For he who made you did at the same time endow your nature with this wonderful quality. For God imprinted on it the likeness of the glories of his own nature, as if molding the form of a carving into wax. But the evil that has been poured all around the nature bearing the Divine Image has rendered useless to you this wonderful thing, that lies hidden under vile coverings. If, therefore, you wash off by a good life the filth that has been stuck on your heart like plaster, the divine beauty will again shine forth in you.[3]

The Christian can look inside himself to find God, but the Christian clearly realizes he is not God. The greatest goodness and beauty the creature can attain are only a faint shadow of the divine beauty. There is a profound difference between Christian teachings and New Age teachings.

Basic Differences

What is the basic Christian teaching? God is an infinite spiritual personal being who created everything out of nothing. God created powerful spiritual beings, angels, some of whom rebelled against God and are now known as Satan and demons. God created humans with a mortal body and an immortal soul. God destined humans to live in eternal happiness in heaven, but humans sinned and lost their chance of achieving this heavenly destiny. Though there is only one God, there are three Persons in God: the Father, the Son and the Holy Spirit. The Son of God became man nearly 2,000 years ago as Jesus of Nazareth. He died and rose from the dead, thereby redeeming mankind. Humans can be saved today by repenting of sin and accepting Jesus as Lord and Savior of their lives. They can have their sins forgiven. They are immortal. Each person is unique and will live for all eternity in either heaven or hell. The Bible and the Christian church are the principal sources of Christian teaching.[4] (See Chapter 15 for a more complete exposition of basic Christian teaching.)

What is the basic New Age teaching? The New Age embodies all the principal errors about the nature of God and the nature of humans that have been dreamed up since the beginning of recorded history. The errors are mixed together in the New Age and served up in a manner that is sometimes nonreligious (it is then termed "scientific") and sometimes heavily occultic. Often, seemingly contradictory elements are lumped together. There is no God; there is only a gigantic charge of electricity, as it were, enlivening everything. There are very powerful and very wise ascended masters and other entities that we must listen to and invite inside our personalities. There is no objective reality; all is illusion. We can create any reality we desire because we ourselves are gods. The individual person is not immortal. Reincarnational recycling is operative whether you like it or not. Nothing is objectively good or objectively evil. Christianity may be an exception to this last dictum. New Agers often say that Christianity is bad.

Adherents see the New Age as a religious movement replacing Christianity. Here's what *A Complete Guide to the Tarot* says:

The Christian religion, as we have known it, is felt by many to be losing vitality, and the new Aquarian religion has not yet been revealed. Many have predicted a new savior who has already been born in the East and who will lead us into a universal religion that all present faiths can join in proclaiming. Tarot and astrology both show the necessity of combining and balancing force and form, and their followers will probably be among the first to recognize and follow the religion of the dawning Aquarian Age.[5]

Here are some of the things Christian researchers are saying about the New Age.

Elliot Miller

"The New Age movement is best understood as a *network*—or, to be more exact, a *metanetwork* (network of networks)," Elliot Miller wrote in the first of a six-part series of articles on the New Age.[6] "Networks tend to be decentralized, often having no single leader or headquarters, and with power and responsibility widely distributed," Miller explained. New Agers cannot be easily stereotyped. They come with many different belief systems and lifestyles. Also, they are everywhere. This loosely structured network of organizations and individuals, Miller continued, is "bound together by common values (based in mysticism and monism—the worldview that 'all is one') and a common vision (a coming 'new age' of peace and enlightenment, the 'Age of Aquarius')." Nevertheless, there are some differences within the New Age movement itself.

> New Agers may differ over such questions as when the New Age begins, whether it will be preceded by a worldwide cataclysm, how it will be politically structured, whether there will be a Christ-figure governing it, or who the true avatars (god-men) or messengers from the spirit world are

(if there are any). Nonetheless, they agree that they can hasten the new order that they *all* await by cooperating to influence developments in our culture's political, economic, social, and spiritual life.[7]

Under the New Age umbrella of networks there are hundreds of smaller (but sometimes individually very large) networks and movements. Some of these are completely New Age and some are tangentially New Age. For example, some New Age people are active in the ecology and peace movements, though these movements are not New Age. Some cults can be considered part of the New Age movement and others clearly cannot. "The consciousness movement, the holistic health movement, the human potential movement, all have contributed generously to the New Age movement, as have the followers of many Eastern gurus and Western occult teachers," Miller stated. "However, participation in one of these movements does not always indicate conscious or actual participation in the New Age movement—remember that networks have fuzzy borderlines."[8]

I believe, like Miller, that the New Age phenomenon is a loosely structured movement. It is not a tightly structured cult or conspiracy. Some people, on the other hand, think it is a tightly structured conspiracy. (See Chapter Six for their views.)

Brooks Alexander

Religious cults are on the decline, but the church, because of the New Age movement, is facing an anti-Christian on-slaught of "such historical magnitude that we can never get leverage on it," Brooks Alexander said in an interview.[9] With the cults on the decline, "the real issue increasingly is New Age thinking and New Age practices influencing the church."

Alexander warns, however, that satanic cults and witch-craft are on the rise today. "It's very difficult to be optimistic about the future," he said. "The worldview is changing to the one that prevailed in the declining side of the Roman Empire—to paganism and a pseudo-scientific form of pantheism."[10]

The February, 1988, issue of *Eternity* featured several articles on New Age. Alexander wrote one of them in which he described the New Age movement as "a modern version of the pantheistic dream, a godless religion that makes a god of man." He said its common denominator is a "worldview of occult mysticism, articulated in secular terms." He went on to trace the movement from the "beatniks" of the 1950s and their infatuation with Zen through the hippie movement and the occult revival of the 1960s and the human potential movement of the 1970s. "In the 1980s," Alexander wrote, "all these strands came together, mingling in new and fanciful ways."[11] The result is a widespread movement that can be very dangerous.

> Beyond the diversity of the New Age movement we see a common theme and a common impact on people. The theme is that our godhood can only be unleashed by restructuring the way we think; the impact is that this always involves shutting down our rational, critical mind. New Agers say that as long as our critical intellect insists on dividing up reality and making distinctions (e.g., between "true" and "false"), it fragments the vision of oneness that reveals our true divine nature. New Age "empowerment" comes only to those whose rational, critical filter has been removed or disabled.
>
> The end-product of New Age spirituality, therefore, is a person incapable of distinguishing truth from falsehood, and programmed to ignore the issue up front.[12]

Douglas Groothuis

In his book, *Confronting the New Age,* Douglas Groothuis lists nine beliefs or doctrines that summarize the basic

worldview of the New Age movement. We should remember that some of these doctrines on the surface may seem
very close to authentic Christian doctrines. We need to pay
close attention always to separate the true from the false.
Here is Groothuis's list:

1. *Evolutionary optimism.* The New Age movement
teaches that we are poised on the edge of a quantum leap in consciousness as evolution surges
upward. We face a great time of both planetary
crisis and opportunity.

2. *Monism.* All is one. One is all. . . . The New Age
viewpoint, in a sense, seeks to return to the form-
less and empty primeval soup and sinks therein. It
must dismiss the diversity of creation—which we
must presuppose in order to perform philosophical tasks such as counting (above one) and kissing
(someone else)—as somehow unreal.

3. *Pantheism.* The great Oneness of Being is thought
to be "God." All that is, at metaphysical root, is
God . . . . Self-deification is now as popular as it is
unbiblical and unrealistic. The New Age takes the
truth that we are made in God's image and warps
it to mean we are all gods.

4. *Transformation of consciousness.* It is not enough
merely to believe New Age teachings. They must
be experienced. New Agers are often encouraged
to be initiated, not just interested. Many mystical
means serve the same exotic end, whether they be
non-Christian meditation techniques, drugs, yoga,
martial arts, the use of crystals or spontaneous experiences such as near-death encounters. The end
is a feeling of oneness with everything that is, and
the realization of one's own divinity, sometimes
called the "Higher Self."

5. *Create your own reality.* The phrase "create your own reality" is often intoned in New Age circles as a basic premise. The idea is that we are not under any objective moral law. Rather, we all have different ways to realize our divine potential. And since "all is one" (monism), we can't slice up life into categories like good versus evil. That is too dualistic; we must move "beyond good and evil" in order to realize our full potential.

6. *Unlimited human potential.* If we are all God, it is thought that the prerogatives of the deity pulsate within us. We are endowed beyond measure. We are miracles waiting to happen. Untethered from such old-age fables as human finitude, depravity and original sin, we in the New Age are free to explore the luminous horizons of godhood. Ignorance is our only problem.

7. *Spirit contacts.* There is a galaxy of masters, entities, spirits, extraterrestrials and other talkative types who communicate (by either automatic writing or vocalization) through mediums—who are more recently called "channelers" (an apt title for the television age).

8. *Masters from above.* In much of New Age thought the distinction between the extraterrestrial and the spiritual is blurred when UFO sightings and even encounters ("of the third kind") become mystical experiences. UFOs (and their passengers) are sometimes claimed to exhibit paranormal phenomena.

9. *Religious syncretism.* New Age spirituality is a rather eclectic grab-bag of Eastern mysticism, Western occultism, neopaganism and human potential psychology. But New Age spokespeople tend to view the true essence of all religion to be one . . . . If externals appear different—say, be-

tween Hindu pantheism and Christian theism—
an appeal is made to a supposedly mystical core
that unites all religions: All is one, all is God, we
are God, we have infinite potential, we can bring in
the New Age. This mystical method rides rough-
shod over the express teachings of the nonpanthe-
istic religions, but the New Age claims that the
supposedly "esoteric" elements in these religions
have been suppressed.[13]

Statistics

Many surveys and statistics document how widespread
the New Age movement is. Groothuis cites a poll by sociologist Andrew Greeley and colleagues at the University of
Chicago's National Opinion Research Council[14] as reporting
that more Americans are claiming to have experienced the
paranormal in one form or another. In 1973, 27% of those
polled claimed contact with the dead; in 1984, 42% did. In
1973, 58% claimed they had experienced ESP (extrasensory
perception); in 1984, 67% did. In 1973, 24% claimed to
experience clairvoyance; in 1984, 31% did. In 1973, 58%
claimed to experience *déjà vu*; in 1984, 67% did.

Roughly 30 million adult Americans—about one in four—
now believe in reincarnation, reports Russell Chandler, religion writer for the *Los Angeles Times*.[15] He also said 14% of
adults endorse the work of spirit mediums or channelers.
Chandler noted that a 1978 Gallup poll indicated that 10
million Americans were engaged in some aspect of Eastern
mysticism and 9 million in spiritual healing. (The results did
not distinguish between pantheistic, occultic and Christian
healing.) The Gallup organization also found that between
1978 and 1984 belief in astrology had risen from 40% to 59%
among schoolchildren. Chandler cited a 1987 survey conducted by Northern Illinois University that reported that
67% of American adults read astrology reports and 36%
believe that the reports are accurate.

Karen Hoyt cited similar statistics in the Introduction to

The New Age Rage.[16] As she wrote in 1987, 23% of Americans believed in reincarnation; 23% believed in astrology; 25% believed in a nonpersonal energy or life force. The December 17, 1987, *Daily Herald* of Palatine, Ill., said that 42% of persons polled in a University of Chicago study reported having had contact with the dead.[17] An article in the June, 1988, *Intercessors for America Newsletter*[18] reported that a poll of unchurched Americans taken by Doug Self revealed that 57% believed in pantheism. In the 1985 edition of his book, *The Kingdom of the Cults,* Walter Martin estimated that there were "around 60 million cultists and another 60 million Americans who dabble in the occult in the United States today."[19]

Time reported that the National Science Foundation in 1986 stated that 43% of the U.S. citizenry believe it "likely" that some of the UFOs reported "are really space vehicles from other civilizations." The same *Time* article noted that the number of New Age bookstores had doubled in the previous five years, to about 2,500. "A surprising number of successful stockbrokers consult astrological charts . . . . A yuppie investment banker who earns $100,000 a year talks of her previous life as a monk."[20]

Thousands of New Age believers met on August 16 and 17, 1987, at more than 350 so-called sacred sites around the world for what was termed a Harmonic Convergence. In ceremonies that received wide press coverage, people hummed, chanted and held hands in an attempt to "synchronize the earth with the rest of the galaxy" and bring about an age of peace. The worldwide total turnout was estimated at 20,000.[21]

Psychic fairs are popular. The May 13-15, 1988, "Whole Life Expo" in the Pasadena Civic Center drew more than 20,000 persons.[22] Do you want to market your product to New Agers? The New Age Mailing Lists company of Berkeley can help you. Their summer and September, 1988, catalogs listed 2.3 million names on 70 general New Age lists, 4.6 million names on 22 New Age health lists, and 5.9

million names on 42 New Age educational lists.

Monkey Business

New Agers believe that thoughts create reality and they believe that, if enough people get together and think the same thing, it will happen. This is the idea behind the Harmonic Convergence event mentioned previously: if enough people around the globe would get together and think good thoughts about peace, it would happen.

For many years, New Agers thought they had scientific proof for this thesis in the so-called "hundredth monkey" phenomenon. The story has to do with some Macaque monkeys on Japanese islands in the 1950s. The New Age fable has it that one monkey learned a new behavior, washing sweet potatoes in water before eating them. Other monkeys on the island learned this behavior by observation. When 100 monkeys learned this behavior, however, something marvelous and magical happened. Other monkeys on other islands learned this action through some sort of paranormal thought transference. Books and articles about this so-called scientific proof spread rapidly throughout the New Age community.

Unfortunately for them, further studies were done and the whole "scientific" theory fell apart. It was documented that one particular monkey swam from the first island to another island and it was also documented that monkeys fairly frequently swam between the islands. "The activity of monkey missionaries would explain the situation better than recourse to the paranormal,"[23] Groothuis commented dryly.

Good Points

The New Age movement has its good points. New Agers are promoting some very worthwhile causes. Karen Hoyt mentioned 10 of them.

    1. Emphasizing cooperation instead of competition.

2. Working to protect creation, instead of overexploiting and destroying the earth's resources.

3. Encouraging spontaneity and creativity.

4. Promoting the cause of peace in the world.

5. Calling for radical transformation and a total change of mind—even though the Christian idea of needed change is very different from that of the New Age movement.

6. Promoting the importance of the body and its care and emphasizing such things as exercise and healthy food.

7. Developing human potential and a positive self-image.

8. Backing the global village concept—a crisis in one country affects the whole world.

9. Working for a nontoxic environment.

10. Networking.[24]

Elliot Miller commended New Agers for occupying what he calls a "service void" by meeting needs in areas the church has neglected. New Agers have been in the forefront of reforms in health care, education and business personnel-training. "They have also led the way in such social innovations as food co-ops (providing alternatives to overpriced, chemically overtreated foods), hospices for the dying (which allow for a more humane environment than traditional institutions), local bartering systems and 'skills banks,' and women's 'health collectives' aimed at protecting women from medical abuses (e.g., unnecessary hysterectomies and mastectomies)," Miller wrote. "Thus, people in need must often go to New Agers for help, and in the process are exposed to Aquarian influences."[25]

Dangers

It's nice that the New Age movement promotes a lot of nice things, but it is also a very dangerous and, at times, a nasty movement.

It is decidedly anti-Christian. It repudiates and holds as worthless such basic Christian tenets as the Creator God, the immortality of the human soul, sin, judgment, salvation, heaven, hell, Jesus as the unique Savior. New Age author David Spangler dismissed Christianity by saying: "We can take all the scriptures and all the teachings, and all the tablets, and all the laws, and all the marshmallows and have a jolly good bonfire and marshmallow roast, because that's all they are worth. Once you are the law, once you are the truth, you do not need it externally represented for you."[26]

The above quotation is from Russell Chandler's book. He also quoted George Craig McMillan, describing laya yoga and enlightenment in the New Age magazine, *Life Times,* as saying: "Belief in God or nonbelief in God means nothing because you are part of that process (of enlightenment), generating, organizing, destroying, continually."[27]

Where is God? Inside us. Chandler quoted New Age-allied psychiatrist Scott Peck as saying: "If you desire wisdom greater than your own, you can find it inside you . . . . To put it plainly, our unconscious is God . . . . The goal of spiritual growth (is) . . . the attainment of godhead by the conscious self. It is for the individual to become totally, wholly God."[28]

A warning about this new ideology was sounded by Baptist Carl F.H. Henry of Arlington, Va., a leading Evangelical theologian, during a series of lectures in the summer and fall of 1987. Chandler said the basic theme of the lectures was that "Western civilization, nurtured by biblical notions of moral absolutes, purpose, and the ultimate triumph of good over evil, is now wallowing in a swamp of neopaganism." "The West has lost its moral compass," Henry charged. The culture is thus sinking in a neopagan naturalism that says that "nature alone is real, that man is essentially only a complex animal, that distinctions of truth and good are temporary and changing."[29]

"We face a growing secularism that tries to exclude God and religious truth from human affairs," Pope John Paul II said in a September 18, 1987, address at St. Mary's Cathedral in San Francisco.

> . . . We face an insidious relativism that under-
> mines the absolute truth of Christ and the truths of
> faith and tempts believers to think of them as
> merely one set of beliefs or opinions among others
> . . . . All these attitudes can influence our sense of
> good and evil at the very moment when social and
> scientific progress requires strong ethical guid-
> ance. Once alienated from Christian faith and
> practice by these and other deceptions, people
> often commit themselves to passing fads, or to
> bizarre beliefs that are either shallow or fanatical.[30]

Demonic Powers

New Age dangers are not only philosophical; demonic powers are being unleashed. (See Chapter Eight for more on satanism and Chapter 15 for the Christian teaching on Satan and demonic spirits.) Anticult writer Walter Martin has often warned about the dangers of dabbling in occultic practices such as Ouija boards, the Tarot, channeling, the serious study of astrology, magic and so forth. "You're knocking at the unopened door," he said in an interview. "The knob is on your side. But when you've opened Pandora's box, you don't know what will come through."[31]

The New Age is opening all sorts of doors to the demonic world, although New Agers ordinarily do not talk about Satan and demonic spirits as such. They talk about the higher self or the divinity within a person or about so-called ascended masters. Still, the perceptive Christian understands that New Agers are often talking about listening to demonic spirits, getting power from demonic spirits and allowing oneself to come under the dominion of demonic spirits.

Satanists often will ask Satan directly to come in and take over. New Agers in general will often seek the same ends, but will use less precise terminology. They want to be divine; they want supernatural power. They don't really care where this power comes from and they can be very vague when talking about it.

We should remember that not every paranormal New Age occurrence is demonic. Some are due to psychic powers and some phenomena are only hallucinations. Nevertheless, some paranormal occurrences are demonic and New Agers don't seem to care that this is the source of the power. According to Chandler, New Agers talk about an individual "actualizing his or her divine nature and achieving union with the Ultimate Unifying Principle by applying a plethora of consciousness-changing techniques, or 'psychotechnologies,' to body, mind and spirit."[32] Chandler continued:

> Some examples of what [Marilyn] Ferguson calls "intentional triggers of transformative experiences" are: meditation, yoga, chanting, mood-altering music, mind-expanding drugs, esoteric systems of religious mysticism and knowledge, guided imagery, balancing and aligning "energies," hypnosis, body disciplines, fasting, martial arts, mechanical devices that measure and alter bodily processes, and mental programs ranging from contemporary psychotherapies to radical seminars designed to obliterate former values and inculcate the New Age mind-set.[33]

Many people who practice martial arts or chanting or who engage in guided imagery or in many of the techniques mentioned above never get involved in the New Age at all. Many may remain good, practicing Christians. Many others will get involved in the New Age movement without ever coming under the influence of demonic spirits. However, some people will come under the influence of demonic spirits through some of the New Age activities mentioned above. If you open the door to the world of demonic spirits, you never know what will come through. (Chapters Seven and Eight will have some accounts of demonic activity in the cults, to develop this point further.)

Not every New Age phenomenon is caused by demonic spirits, but many of them are. James W. Sire has an interesting paragraph on this point.

A major difficulty in the New Age worldview comes with what it borrows from animism—a host of demigods, demons and guardians who inhabit the separate reality or the inner spaces of the mind. Call them projections of the psyche or spirits of another order of reality. Either way they haunt the New Age and must be placated by rituals or controlled by incantation. The New Age has reopened a door closed since Christianity drove out the demons from the woods, desacralized the natural world and generally took a dim view of excessive interest in the affairs of Satan's kingdom of fallen angels. Now they are back, knocking on university dorm-room doors, sneaking around psychology laboratories and chilling the spines of Ouija players. Modern folk have fled from grandfather's clockwork universe to great-great-grandfather's chamber of Gothic horrors.[34]

Sacramental churches have rescued much of the natural and consecrated it to Christian supernatural ends. The sacraments all have natural elements elevated by divine power: the water in baptism, bread and wine in the Eucharist, oil in the anointing of the sick, for example. These natural symbols are directed properly toward God; New Age symbolism is undirected or directed toward the demonic.

There are other dangers in the New Age besides dangers from demons. An advocate of yoga warned: "Yoga is not a trifling jest if we consider that any misunderstanding in the practice of yoga can mean death or insanity."[35] Practitioners of yoga often warn of the power of the kundalini energy, represented as a serpent coiled at the base of the spine. Groothuis noted, "The purpose of many forms of yoga is to 'awaken the kundalini' and release its energy upward through the seven chakras (energy centers) of the body. But the yogis themselves caution that this is no child's play. One might get burned (literally!) by the serpent's hot breath—or go insane."[36]

Is there physical power being tapped that is unknown to Western science and medicine? Are there chakras? Does the kundalini have a basis in reality? Very careful research by thoroughly orthodox and knowledgeable Christians is needed. Reckless experimentation by the novice would be rash indeed.

What Is True?

From a Christian perspective, there are four possible explanations for real or apparent paranormal phenomena.

1. *God and his angels* are the cause. In this case, the phenomena lead directly to the glorification of God the Father or Jesus. The Bible is supported and never contradicted. We are talking here about authentic miracles, spiritual gifts and divine revelations.

2. *Satan and other demonic spirits* are the cause. Very often, the ideas or phenomena are good or at least neutral even if caused directly by demonic spirits. The demonic spirits often are trying to entrap, not terrify. They may be trying to promote false teaching or gradually to lead the individual into serious evil. The key point is that the demonic phenomena do not give glory to God. They often contradict the Bible and other sound Christian teaching. If mediumistic spirits talk of the life after death as meandering through a blue haze, then where are Jesus and the angels and saints? If death is "revealed" as a peaceful transition into a bright light, then where is the divine judgment for sin? (See Chapter Three for a fuller treatment of near-death experiences.)

3. *Undiscovered psychic powers* are the cause. Do we nat-

urally have ESP, extrasensory perception? Do we have natural psychic healing powers to heal ourselves by positive imaging or to heal others by the laying on of hands? Is there a sound physical or psychological basis for the chakras? I believe that we probaly have some sort of psychic powers, but that these are often exaggerated by enthusiasts. Fraud and demonic spirits may also be the cause of some apparent psychic phenomena.

4. *Fraud and deception* are rampant in the paranormal field. It is also probably true that people with real psychic powers or who at times are in contact with demonic spirits may resort to fraud to back up their act. If the channeler cannot be sure he will go into a trance on cue and give a message to the crowd who have paid good money and assembled at a particular time and place, the channeler may fake the message. Sometimes the message may come from a demonic spirit and other times it may be acting. Neither is good, of course.

It is maddening the way New Age savants can declare there is no difference between right and wrong, between truth and falsehood. This is an assertion they claim is true and they would deny that the opposite is true. Also, to say there is no morality is a moral statement. New Agers are bewilderingly inconsistent, to put it mildly.

"The most serious error underlying New Age mythology is the unwarranted assumption (based in monistic subjectivism) that there are no truths 'out there' that we need be concerned about," Elliot Miller wrote in the fourth of his series of articles. "If, as Christians argue, the Bible is a trustworthy divine revelation, such thinking is grievously false, for God is an objective, not subjective, reality as far as humanity is concerned. Therefore, certain propositions are objectively true, and others objectively false."[37]

"In 1908 G.K. Chesterton observed in *Orthodoxy* that 'of all conceivable forms of enlightenment the worst is what . . . people call the Inner Light. Of all horrible religions the most horrible is the god within,'" Douglas Groothuis noted. "That

Jones shall worship the god within him turns out ultimately
to mean that Jones shall worship Jones."[38] (We must note
again that Groothuis is talking about the New Age view of
the indwelling pantheistic god. There is a perfectly legiti-
mate way for Christians to acknowledge God dwelling in
them.)

Back in the early years of the Spiritual Counterfeits
Project (SCP), Brooks Alexander wrote a paper on "The
Coming World Religion" that appeared in the July/August,
1974, issue of *Right On*. It was reprinted in the winter, 1984,
issue of *SCP Journal* and was called at that time one of the
"foundation papers of the SCP ministry."[39]

"Humanity is experiencing a rekindling of its deep-
seated desire for unification," Alexander wrote. The human
race is dreaming again about a world at peace and having
common religious ideals, a world "in which the petty divi-
sions that plague humankind are vanished in the universal
light of a Truth so great none can doubt it." This has long
been a dream of humanity. "The most ancient traditions of
our world agree in their expectation of just such a time of
peace, truth and spiritual harmony," Alexander wrote. "The
concept may be Millennium, Age of Aquarius, the Age of
Enlightenment, the 'next step in human evolution,' the New
Age, or the coming Transformation."[40]

The Bible also speaks of a great age of truth that is to
come, but, according to Alexander, the book of Revelation
adds a sobering chapter. It talks about a time toward the end
of history when "our race will be brought together in a
common expression of humanistic spirituality." The coming
world religion "will offer itself to us as the ancient wisdom
and hidden truth underlying all the religious forms of history." However, it will not be an underlying truth, it will
simply be a lie. Alexander talks about this great deception,
applying to it the book of Revelation's figurative condemnation of ancient Rome.

The book of Revelation—Chapter 17—refers to
this false religious system in its final configuration

as Mystery Babylon . . . .

Occult illumination is precisely the opposite of a God-centered orientation to reality. It is radically human-centered, and thus becomes the perfected expression of the great lie through the logical necessity of its own presuppositions, which discount God and exalt humankind in the classical fashion of falsehood . . . .

This (false) wisdom is the *samadhi* of yoga and the "illumination" of classical occultism. It is the "Christ consciousness" of countless cults, and it is the "It" of *est*. It is the cornerstone of Mystery Babylon, and the experiential basis of the coming world religion.

Mystery Babylon is more than an experience or an idea. It is preeminently a religious system—one that reflects widespread participation, as well as deception and control. God bluntly calls this religious deceiver a whore and declares that its end will be in accord with its character: "Her plagues shall come in a single day, pestilence and mourning and famine, and she shall be burned with fire, for mighty is the Lord God who judges her" (Rev. 18:8).[41]

Chapter 2

East Coming West,
Hinduism, Yoga,
Contemporary Hinduism,
Buddhism, Zen,
Other Roots, Pantheism

Philosophy ─────

In this chapter, we will examine the roots and origins of the various ideas which New Agers use. Many of these ideas come from the age-old religions of mankind, particularly Eastern religions and pantheism. Other ideas are not religious at all, but arise from philosophical monism, the occult and paganism. Since the New Age borrows concepts from Eastern religions such as Buddhism and Hinduism, it is important to understand how these religions differ among themselves, and how the New Age beliefs differ from them all. The major world religions represent the genuine, heartfelt strivings of human beings to reach God, and are not the issue here. Our interest involves the use New Agers have made of these religions' tenets. J. Isamu Yamamoto, a writer/editor with the Spiritual Counterfeits Project, used a classic metaphor from each of three major world religions to illustrate some differences.

> * In the Shankara tradition which pervades most of contemporary Hinduism, the raindrop is pictured

as the symbol of the individual self and the ocean as the symbol of the universal soul. The absorption of the raindrop into the ocean is symbolic of the absorption of the person into the impersonal universe. After people attain enlightenment, they lose their identities and become one with the all. Absorption is the goal of the monist Hindu.

* The candle flame is a Buddhist image for the individual; it is the light of life that flickers in the darkness of sorrow. The quest of ardent Buddhists is to extinguish their own flame. They seek not merely a physical death but a death that will deliver them from both the physical and the spiritual life. Extinction is the goal of the traditional Buddhist.

* Jesus tells the parable of the forgiving father who embraces his prodigal son after the son returns from a period of immorality. Jesus paints a picture of a loving God who seeks to restore a personal relationship with each one of us. God is a person and we are people. Jesus promises that we will enjoy an eternal, loving relationship with our Creator if we believe in him and commit our lives to his teachings. Relationship is the goal of the orthodox Christian.[1]

Yamamoto concluded his essay by saying it "is inconceivable that ultimately a person will become one with an impersonal universe, extinguished, and involved in a personal relationship eternally with Christ. Either one or none of the three will occur, and that is a significant reason why Hinduism, Buddhism and Christianity are different."[2]

Christianity is based on the real, the historical. Faith tells the Christian that Jesus of Nazareth, who lived and died and rose again nearly 2,000 years ago, is God. The Apostle Paul wrote that, if Jesus had not risen from the dead, then the faith of the Christian would be foolish. To the Eastern mind, however, as James W. Sire has described it, historical facts are not important. If yesterday's facts have a here-and-now meaning,

> ... then their facticity as history is of no concern. The Eastern scriptures are filled with epigrams, parables, fables, stories, myth, songs, hymns, epics—but almost no history in the sense of events recorded because they took place in an unrepeatable space-time context. If history is valuable, it will be so as myth and myth only, for myth takes us out of particularity and lifts us to essence.[3]

East Coming West

In years past, a discussion of Eastern religions would have only been of interest to Western Christians who were planning to go to the Orient as missionaries, but times have changed. Eastern philosophy is spreading rapidly in the West. As it comes, it is being westernized. "As Eastern and occult ideas are propagated to Occidentals on a mass scale, they are filtered through the pervasive secularism of our culture," Alexander explained. "In this way, they are demystified without changing their essential content. The basic components of [a pantheistic/occult] worldview are recast in forms of expression that are naturalistic, scientific, and humanistic in orientation. Occult philosophy is being secularized and psychologized with increasing refinement. In such forms, its fundamental concepts are easily adopted and easily applied by contemporary intellectuals."[4] Thus, Westerners are adopting religious practices without the corresponding religious faith.

The Maharishi Mahesh Yogi came to the United States in 1959 to spread his brand of Hinduism. He gave his U.S. organization a religious title—the Spiritual Regeneration Movement. Basically, it flopped. Americans were not interested in becoming Hindus. So the Maharishi went back to

India, rethought his strategy and came back and founded the International Meditation Society and the American Foundation for the Science of Creative Intelligence. Note the progressive secularization of titles. The Maharishi was teaching the same old Hindu stuff, but the American people were more interested in buying it the more it became nonreligious. (See Chapter Seven for more on the Maharishi and Transcendental Meditation.)

Historic Hinduism is world-denying. Elliot Miller has noted, "In traditional Hinduism the earthly is set in direct conflict with the spiritual, so that those who are serious about seeking God and salvation are expected to renounce the world of temporal pleasures and responsibilities."[5] Most Westerners are not interested in giving up everything, shaving their heads and retreating to monasteries. They want enlightenment along with the good life. Whereas the world is *maya* (illusion) for the Hindus, New Agers affirm the value of temporal realities: people, nature, culture, education, politics, even science and technology. "In fact," Miller continued, "contemporary New Age thought represents an effort to graft the fruits of higher learning onto the various branches of mystical tradition."

To be completely fair, we should note that there is some ambiguity in Eastern religions. While proclaiming that all is illusion and advocating extreme asceticism, there is also a practical side to their beliefs. Hindus, for example, have put a high priority on peace efforts and Buddhists teach the value of a virtuous life. "The Buddha's teaching is meant to carry man to safety, peace, happiness, tranquillity, the attainment of *nirvana*," Walpola Rahula has written. "The whole doctrine taught by the Buddha leads to this end. He did not say things just to satisfy intellectual curiosity. He was a practical teacher and taught only those things which would bring peace and happiness to men."[6]

As we discuss these Eastern religions individually, you will recognize many terms and concepts which have been incorporated into today's New Age movement.

Hinduism

Hinduism is "more like a tree that has *grown* gradually than like a building that has been *erected* by some great architect at some definite point in time," explained K. M. Sen.[7] In his book, *The New Cults,* Walter Martin stated that modern-day Hinduism is the product of a 5,000-year gradual evolution. Hindus refer to their religion as the "eternal system," or *sanatana dharma.* The term "Hindu" was coined by the Persians after the "Indus" or "Sindu" River. "Orthodox Hinduism encompasses a variety of sects with diversified beliefs, practices, and traditions," Martin wrote. "In keeping with Hinduism's monistic worldview, these sects are not considered by Hinduism to be wrong or heretical, but merely to be different perspectives of the *sanatana dharma.*"[8]

The oldest of the Hindu scriptures, the Vedas, were composed over a 1,000-year period, beginning about 1400 B.C. There are a number of these vedic wisdom books, each one having three parts: 1) the *mantras,* hymns of praise to the gods; 2) the *brahmanas,* a guide for practicing rituals; and 3) the *upanishads,* teachings on religious truth.[9] "The Upanishads teach that every aspect of the universe, both animate and inanimate, shares the same essentially divine nature," Martin explained. "There is only one Self in the universe. Approximately 700 B.C. a system for interpreting the Vedas, called Vedanta, was established, and it remains the leading school of Hindu philosophy in India today."[10]

In his book, *Christ and the New Consciousness,* John P. Newport defined some of the key Hindu terms.

> **Brahman (god).** Ultimate or absolute reality for Hinduism is known as *Brahman.* Brahman or god is absolute existence, absolute consciousness, and absolute bliss. It is impersonal. It is above all distinctions and is beyond thought.
>
> **Maya (the nature of the world).** If Brahman or Unity alone is real, then what about the ordinary world we know? For Vedanta Hinduism, it is a

dream. The dreamer (god) is real, but his dream is
unreal. This dream world is called *maya*. The world
of science and everyday existence is illusion, ignorance, and shadow. It is a world where individu-
ality and diversity are *thought* to be real but actually they are not. Only those of us who are ignorant
consider the world to be real. When you are enlightened, you will realize the world is illusory and
only Brahman is real.

Atman (man's nature). For Hinduism, the body
and mind, like other material objects, are merely
illusory appearances. When this is realized, the
only reality that remains is *atman* or self. The self
is nothing other than Brahman or god .... The *true
self* is god. The *I* which I consider myself to be is in
reality the *not-self*. This not-self is caught in a
world of illusion, ignorance and bondage. Yoga is
the liberation of the not-self to allow it to be absorbed back into god .... You must lose your personal ego-consciousness into god. You must say,
"I am Brahman."

Karma (law of retribution). *Karma* is the Hindu
teaching that one's present life is the result of a past
action in a former existence. It is related to the idea
of reincarnation .... It may take many rebirths
through centuries to be finally reabsorbed into
Brahman, but a soul or self will never pass into
nonexistence .... No man in the sense of an individual or person survives death. Atman or soul
survives, but atman is impersonal. When atman is
reincarnated, it becomes another person.

Guru (spiritual teacher). The *Upanishads* teach
that true progress toward self-realization is not
possible without the guidance and help of a guru.
He alone is qualified to grant initiation and prescribe the spiritual discipline (sadhana) needed for

each seeker. A person must completely submit to his guru's direction.

Avatar (god appearing as man). A reform movement in the 12th century developed the idea of Hindu gods as personal. Loving devotion to one or more of these gods is called *bhakti,* or adoration. From time to time, when the need is great, these gods descend to earth in terms of an avatar or incarnation.

Sad-Guru (Perfect Master). While the divine may "descend" into the human level (as an avatar), a human may also "ascend" into the divine. This is done through mastery over his nature and an achieved union with god. When man thus becomes god he is called Sad-Guru or Perfect Master.

Sadhana (spiritual discipline). Each guru prescribes a discipline for his followers. If faithfully followed, this discipline should lead to god-realization, or *samadhi* (a mystic trance). Steps such as restraint, observances, posture, breath regulation, concentration, and meditation are utilized to lead to this god-realization.

Mantra (sacred sound). For certain Hindus, the world is created and maintained by the utterance of certain sounds. These sacred sounds are called mantras . . . . A mantra is not just a formula or prayer. It is an embodiment in sound of a particular god. It is god itself . . . . The frequent repetition of the mantra will gradually transform the personality of the worshiper into that of the deity worshiped.[11]

Yoga

In a leaflet entitled *Yoga,* Indian philosopher Vishal Mangalwadi stated that salvation in Hinduism consists in "the realization, perception or experience of our so-called 'true nature.' This realization takes place when we are able to alter our consciousness and attain what is called a 'higher' state of consciousness." How do we alter our consciousness? "Through the manipulation of our nervous system because the consciousness is dependent upon the nervous system."[12] Numerous techniques have been developed to manipulate the nervous system. These are generally called "yoga."

Other writers talk about yoga without talking about a manipulation of the nervous system. "Yoga is a method or training designed to lead to integration or union," Huston Smith has written. "The yogas that do concern us (spiritual yogas) are those designed to unite man's spirit with God who lies concealed in its deepest recesses."[13]

"Yoga can be understood as a broad term including any aspect of Hinduism leading to self-liberation or god-realization," John P. Newport noted. "It is a practical system of self-culture developed by the ancient religious leaders of India. It is probably the world's oldest science of physical and mental self-development. It is the spiritualization of all of life. The various postures and breath controls are aids to spiritual realization. It seeks to make man's physical and emotional systems into instruments of spiritualized realization."[14]

Mangalwadi has described some of the more popular yoga techniques:

> **Hatha yoga: salvation through physical exercises.**
> By physiological manipulation of one's body, the nervous system can be affected and consciousness altered. The problem with Hatha yoga is that it is a long and tedious process requiring much discipline and a competent teacher. The question is frequently asked whether a Christian can practice Hatha yoga . . . . It seems to me that if a person is practicing certain exercises developed in India for health reasons, he should not say he is practicing yoga. For the physical exercises become yoga only when they are practiced to alter consciousness, or

to merge into god. For yoga means union of soul with god.

Japa yoga: the "mechanical path" to salvation. Japa is the repetition or chanting of a mantra, usually a name for god or an evil spirit . . . . Constant repetition of a sound eliminates all other stimuli, thus concentrating the mind and eventually itself becoming a nonstimulus. This induces a state where the mind is aware or conscious, but is not aware or conscious of anything or any thought. One may say that it is only conscious of consciousness. This is what is called pure consciousness or transcendental consciousness.

Surat-Shabd yoga: the path of sound and light. In the Divine Light Mission, these techniques are taught. In order to see the divine light, the initiator asks the devotee to close his eyes; then he places his middle finger and thumb on his eyes and, starting from the corner of the eyeballs, he presses the eyeballs up from the bottom, so that in actual fact if the eyelids were open the center of the pupils would be looking at the point between the two eyebrows on the forehead just above the nose, which is supposed to be the location of the third eye. If the initiate concentrates on this point he can see a light. Some people see only a small point, others see a blinding light, some others see a psychedelic movie of moving patterns and brilliant colors, and some do not see anything at all . . . .

Kundalini yoga: salvation through the "serpent power." Hindu psychology teaches that in the human body three centimeters above the rectum and three centimeters below the genitals at the base of the spine is a beautiful triangle in which lies the *Kundalini Shakti,* or the "Serpent Power." . . . It is also described as "coil power" or the "creative

sex energy." Normally, it is taught, the Kundalini
lies coiled and dormant, but when it is awakened,
it arises and begins to travel upward. In its journey
from the base of the spine to the top of the head, it
passes through six psychic centers called *chakras*.
When it passes through a chakra it gives various
psychic experiences and powers. When at last it
reaches the top chakra, called the *sahasrara chakra*,
one can supposedly attain the power to perform
miracles and achieve liberation.

Many means are used to awaken the Kundalini.
They range from breathing exercises, like *Prana-
yam*, to the homosexual handling of the genitals.
The most influential guru (in recent times) who
preached Kundalini yoga was Swami Muktananda . . . . Kundalini yoga has not been very popular in India because many of the experiences it
gives are what William James calls "diabolical
mysticism." It gives pain, makes people depressed,
and even produces madness.

Tantra: salvation through sex. Tantra is often said
to be the opposite of yoga, but they both aim at the
same end. It is the opposite of Hatha yoga because
the latter is the path of great discipline and effort,
whereas Tantra is the way of free indulgence . . . .
Tantra is, in part, a system of techniques of pro-
longing orgasm in order to experience god or unity
consciousness.

Before the spread of Christianity in India and the
consequent Hindu renaissance, Tantricism had
sunk to such levels of crudity and cruelty, witchcraft and superstition, that in any sophisticated
society the descriptions would appear unthink-
able. But now that the Christian influence has diminished in India, the old Tantric cult is coming
back openly on the surface. The number of centers

in India where Tantra is being taught and practiced is rapidly increasing. In its crudest forms, it
includes worship of sex organs, sex orgies which
include the drinking of blood and human semen,
black magic, human sacrifice, and contact with evil
spirits through dead and rotting bodies in crema-
tion grounds. In its more sophisticated forms, it is
being advocated by the gurus like Bhagwan Shree
Rajneesh .... In his lectures, Rajneesh asserts that
Jesus taught the way of salvation was through
sex.[15]

Contemporary Hinduism

Hinduism has been blamed for many of India's current
woes. One should not help a neighbor in need because his
poverty or illness is his karma (fate) and helping him in this
lifetime will only make his karma worse in his next reincarnation. On the other hand, one should do good acts such as
helping other people to use up some personal bad karma.
(Confusing, isn't it?) Everything is *maya* (illusion) anyhow,
so why try to change things? The caste system and the
degradation of the lowest caste, the Untouchables, are tied to
Hindu teachings that the Untouchables were created from
the feet of Brahma while the Brahmins (the highest caste)
sprang from Brahma's face. "The Hindu has inoculated
himself against any empathy for his fellow man," wrote Bob
Larson. "All of the universe is *lila*, God's cosmic game. And
pain and pleasure are not absolutes but an illusion."[16]

Basically, what Larson said is true, but he was also being
overly harsh. Gandhi, a Hindu, writing on pacifism, did not
consider the world an illusion. "I am an irrepressible opti-
mist," he wrote. "My optimism rests on the belief in the
infinite possibilities of the individual to develop nonvio-
lence. The more you develop it in your own being, the more
infectious it becomes till it overwhelms your surroundings
and by and by might oversweep the world."[17]

Gandhi gave more practical advice: "Action is my domain. What I understand, according to my lights, to be my duty, and what comes my way, I do." He also said: "One's life is not a single straight line; it is a bundle of duties very often conflicting. And one is called upon continually to make one's choice between one duty and another."[18]

Many Hindu gods are simply disgusting. Shiva, wrote Larson, in his disguise as *Bhairava* is "the patricidal god of terror using his father's skull for a bowl." Shiva is also described as "wandering naked about the countryside on his white bull *Nandi*, overindulging in drugs, and encouraging starvation and self-mutilation. The innermost sanctuaries of Shiva temples always feature a *lingam*, the stylized erect phallus which symbolizes his rampant sexuality."

Shiva's consort, *Shakti*, is no better. According to Larson, she "encourages orgies and temple prostitution. She is also credited with originating *sutee*, the sacrifice of widows throwing themselves into the fire of their husband's funeral pyre." Shakti, in her manifestation as *Kali*, is pictured as standing on a beheaded body, wearing a necklace of human skulls. Animals are sacrificed at Kali temples. Every year in India, 100 human sacrifice murders are reported, all in honor of Kali.[19]

Larson catalogued other bizarre outgrowths of Hinduism. At the famous Car Festival of Jugannath in Puri, some devotees suicidally throw themselves in front of a huge chariot bearing a deity's image. "In some villages, temples care for and feed sacred rats at a cost of $4,000 a year," Larson wrote. "Such vermin dispose of 15% of India's grain. The cobra, which is also worshiped, kills 20,000 Indians each year. Females, which Hindu legends relegate to a decidedly inferior state, are so despised that some Indian mothers deliberately strangle their girl babies. Sadhus (holy men), in the name of religious devotion, have been known to sit on a bed of nails and not speak for years, grow their hair into seven-foot braids, stand on a leg like a stork for months, or hold an arm outstretched until it has atrophied."[20]

Cows are held sacred in India, and there are 159 million

of them, 20% of the world's total. "Since the cow is believed to be the mother-goddess of life, its urine is drunk to purify the soul," noted Larson. "They freely roam the streets of urban centers like Bombay and Calcutta, depositing dung everywhere. Aged holy cows are even provided with rest homes called *gosadans*."[21]

Tal Brooke talks about another Hindu custom which he calls the "fish-bait phenomenon." He gives this eyewitness account: "One of the gods in a village temple will tell the village priest that it is time for another sacrifice and the god tells him who the victim will be. So the village teams up, goes to the guy with something like a huge fish pole, and baits his skin, running the entire length of his back, on something that resembles a massive fishhook. Then they go trotting around the village with the fellow hanging in agony from the fish pole." You can still see the scars today of the few who have survived this torture in order to appease some god, Brooke said. The British pretty well stamped out these and similar barbaric practices, he noted, "but they still make one consider the origin of the ideas as well as a system that can so readily absorb and justify them."[22]

Not all writers look at Hinduism so negatively. Huston Smith, in his book, *The Religions of Man*, talks about the influence of Indian religious thought on Henry David Thoreau and Arthur Schopenhauer and many relatively modern thinkers and writers. "Only in our generation has there developed in the West a widespread presentiment of a spiritual greatness in India which we have yet to comprehend and from which we might indeed draw profit."[23]

Buddhism

Unlike Hinduism, which developed gradually over many centuries, Buddhism was founded by one man, Gautama Buddha. Reference works disagree somewhat on the exact place and date of his birth, and his life is filled with legendary details. According to David G. Bradley, to take one account, the founder of Buddhism "was born about 567 B.C. in the town of Kapilavastu in southern Nepal, about 100 miles north of Benares. His father was a petty ruler of the Kshatriya class. The Buddha-to-be was named Siddhartha, and since he was of the Gautama clan he often is called Gautama."[24]

Though wealthy, Gautama decided to abandon his life of luxury and become a mendicant monk. He studied the Upanishads with the best teachers of his day, but was dissatisfied. He tried extreme asceticism and found this lacking.

The night of his 35th birthday, under a full moon, as Bob Larson has told the story, Gautama "sat down under a pipal tree in a forest near Buddh Gaya and declared: 'Until I have attained understanding, I will not rise from here.' That night he entered a trance state and, according to legend, remembered his previous incarnations. His 'divine eye' was quickened, and he was able at last to extinguish all his ignorance and desires. When he arose from the foot of the Bodhi ("wisdom") tree, Siddhartha had become Buddha. Life's problems were no longer an enigma to him."[25]

Buddha began preaching about his new insights and soon numbers of people began following him. His ideas are very complicated and intricate, though seemingly simple on the surface. Larson summarized Buddha's basic discovery "in these three premises: 1) existence is suffering; 2) desire causes suffering; and 3) ridding all desire ends suffering. These three precepts led to a fourth conclusion: desire can be eradicated by following what the Buddha called the Eightfold Path. Buddha's spiritual insights became known as the Four Noble Truths, a so-called middle way between asceticism and hedonism."[26]

Buddha's dharma ("way" or "doctrine" or "work") was aimed at ending the cycle of suffering in successive reincarnations. "Escape from the sorrow of existence would be possible by reaching 'nirvana,' a condition of infinite bliss likened to an extinguished flame. Nirvana, meaning 'blow out,' would be the result of reaching a state where all desire is eradicated," Larson explained. The only way to get to that state is along the Eightfold Path.

1) Right Belief—correctly understanding the Four Noble Truths free of illusion and superstition;

2) Right Resolve—maintaining pure motives;

3) Right Speech—speaking truthfully;

4) Right Conduct—living peacefully and honestly;

5) Right Livelihood—choosing an occupation that harms no one;

6) Right Effort—seeking knowledge with self-control;

7) Right Thought—keeping an active self-critical mind;

8) Right Concentration—practicing meditation and raja yoga with earnest zeal.[27]

These are the basics, but Buddhism is a very complex religion. In addition to the Four Noble Truths and the Eightfold Path, there are 29 more precepts to be followed by the devout Buddhist, five obstacles to one's approach to enlightenment, 227 regulations for Buddhist monks, 10 commandments, and three principles guiding the Buddhist in his search for nirvana.

There is also a tantric Buddhism, a cult devoted to idols and magic and belief in occult sexual power derived from tantric Hinduism. "The union of the individual with the divine is accomplished by ritual sexual intercourse," Larson explained. "Coitus is said to combine the opposite forces of the universe—positive masculine and negative feminine—resulting in the cohabitant's ability to perform supernatural acts."[28]

A major Tibetan Buddhism text, *The Tibetan Book of the Dead*, has been popular among American youth, especially those involved with drugs. "The volume is an occult guide to aid one's traverse through the existence of *bardo*, the dreamlike realm between death and reincarnation," Larson noted. "In the 1960s, some who experimented with LSD reported hallucinogenic visions paralleling experiences in *The Book of the Dead*, stirring Western interest in this exotic faith. Tibetan Buddhists believe that the demons, spirits, and powers of witchcraft encountered in *The Book* are real forces to be avoided and appeased."[29]

Zen

Buddhism came to Japan from China by way of Korea in the early sixth century, A.D. Over the centuries, streamlined versions of Buddhism developed. One of these, Zen Buddhism, appealed "because of its unpretentiousness, its lack of elaborate ritual, and its verbal simplicity," John Newport explained. "The virtues of Zen, such as perfect self-control and indifference to fear or death,"[30] were also appealing.

"Zen," a Japanese word meaning meditation, has helped shape New Age thought and bears the marks of the traditional Chinese religion of Taoism. Fundamental to Taoism is the belief that "in and behind the phenomenal world lies the Tao, the eternal unchanging principle," wrote Chandler. "The Tao is the original source of everything in the universe; it spontaneously produces everything through harmonious interplay of two forces, *yin* (the principle of passive receptivity) and *yang* (the principle of activity)."[31]

According to Taoism, the human body is a microcosmic organism that needs to be balanced with the macrocosm of the universe in order to achieve physical well-being. "Taoism teaches that when events and things are allowed to exist in natural harmony with the macrocosmic forces, peace will result,"[32] Larson explained.

"Zen may be defined as concentration with an empty mind."[33] The Zen practitioner stares at an empty wall or a stone for hours or meditates on an illogical puzzle such as: "What is the sound of one hand clapping?" The payoff for these practices is, allegedly, a sudden awakening to truth or enlightenment. "Experiencing the immediate perception of truth is known as *satori*, a condition in which the meditator realizes all reality as one (pantheism)," Larson observed. "In such a state, there is no such thing as right or wrong, only subjective reality pervades the consciousness."[34]

Practicing Zen is not easy. Practitioners must sit rigidly

for hours, emptying their minds. Sometimes instructors beat
distracted students. Things do happen, though. "Hallucinogenic visions and demonic apparitions are common occurrences to persistent Zen meditators," Larson said.[35] And, of
course, the practitioner comes to realize that all is one, that
there is no eternal Creator God and there is no objective
authority for morality.

The Zen Buddhist would make a good neighbor. Since
all are one, the Buddhist believes we must love one another
as ourselves and serve one another as we would serve ourselves. The realization of one's true nature includes the
realization that one must be moral and selfless.

Concerning the coming of Zen Buddhism to America,
philosopher Jacob Needleman wrote: "From the East had
come an approach that turned askew all our concepts of
religion. No talk of morality, God, immortality, love, duty,
faith, sacrifice or sin. No prescriptions, no commandments,
no judgments. Only the constant and unfathomable call for
man to see into his own nature."[36]

Other Roots

Other roots of the New Age movement include gnosticism, occultism, paganism and pantheism. "Gnosticism
emanated from Pythagorean metaphysics, neoplatonism,
and various occult or mystery schools," Chandler has noted.
"Modern Gnostic historian Robert Anson Wilson traces 'higher intelligence' back through the Rosicrucians, the Renaissance magic societies, medieval witchcraft, the Knights
Templar, European Sufis, etc., to Gnosticism and thence
back to the Eleusinian mysteries and Egyptian cults."[37]

The transcendentalist movement of the 19th century, led
by such authors as Henry David Thoreau and Ralph Waldo
Emerson, brought Eastern ideas to America. Emerson's
"Over-Soul" was the "mystic force within all nature and
human personality" governed and brought into existence by
Mind.[38]

Spiritualism and spiritual healing are other ingredients

making up the New Age philosophical stew. The disciples of Austrian physician Franz Anton Mesmer brought the ideas of healing through hypnosis to America in the early 19th century. Psychic healer Phineas Parkhurst Quimby and one of his pupils, Mary Baker Eddy, developed the idea that disease was caused by false beliefs and not physical disorders. From this came Christian Science, Divine Science, Science of Mind, Religious Science and the Unity School of Christianity. Spiritualism and seances became popular after the Fox sisters in Hydesville, N.Y., in 1848 began alleged communications with the spirit of a murdered peddler by means of raps.[39]

Madame Blavatsky (1831-1891), an eccentric Russian noblewoman, was originally involved in spiritualism, and then founded the Theosophical Society in 1875 with Colonel Henry Steel Olcott (1832-1907). The two of them moved to India for a while where they became steeped in Hinduism and Buddhism. Blavatsky's extremely esoteric and elaborate writings have been described by Robert J.L. Burrows as a "dizzy blend of Western occultism and Eastern mysticism." She added a new dimension to spiritualism, explained Burrows. "Her spirits were not simply those of the departed; they were ascended masters, highly evolved beings who had moved up the spiritual hierarchical ladder and now supervened in human affairs, dispensing knowledge and power to the worthy."[40]

Nina Easton, writing in the *Los Angeles Times Magazine*, said Blavatsky might well be called "a godmother of the New Age movement" because, in the words of Blavatsky's biographer, Marion Meade, she "paved the way for contemporary Transcendental Meditation, Zen, Hare Krishnas; yoga and vegetarianism; karma and reincarnation; swamis, yogis and gurus."[41] Of course, she did not directly introduce these ideas and movements, but she helped prepare the American mind to accept them.

Blavatsky's successors—Annie Besant (1847-1933), Guy Ballard (1878-1939) of the "I AM" Activity, and Alice Bailey

(1880-1949)—continued theosophy's messianic vision of a coming new world religious teacher, inspired by channeled prophecies from a hierarchy of ascended masters. Bailey seems to have coined the phrase, "New Age," which recurs throughout her writings.[42]

Several attempts at putting forth a flesh-and-blood messiah or ascended master have failed. Annie Besant, in collaboration with C.W. Leadbetter, founded the Order of the Star in 1911 to promote the young Indian Jiddu Krishnamurti as the avatar of the dawning new order. In 1929, however, Krishnamurti repudiated his messianic status and denounced the movement. The idea is not dead. In 1982, British esotericist Benjamin Creme ran full-page ads in several newspapers predicting the reappearance of Lord Maitreya, the Christ. Maitreya didn't show.[43] (See Chapter Six for a fuller account of this incident.)

A number of prominent gurus have come to the U.S. in the past 100 years. Swami Vivekananda (1862-1902) made a favorable impression on the World Parliament of Religions held in 1893 at the Chicago World's Fair. He stayed in this country and formed the Vedanta Society. At the beginning of this century, the Sufi master Hazrat Inayat Khan brought the teachings of this brand of Islam to the West. Paramahansa Yogananda arrived in 1920 to attend the International Congress of Religious Liberals and went on to establish the Self-Realization Fellowship. The silent, self-avowed avatar Meher Baba came to the United States in the early 1930s. More recent arrivals include Swami Muktananda, Maharishi Mahesh Yogi, Maharaj Ji and the Bhagwan Shree Rajneesh.

Psychoanalysts Sigmund Freud and Carl Jung helped pave the way for the New Age. So did the proponents of transpersonal and humanistic psychology and of neopaganism and Native American religion. While not directly connected with the New Age movement, these men and ideas prepared the ground for New Age thinking. There are many more influences, many discussed in other parts of this book.

"The New Age movement owes much to the traditions that preceded it, but has combined and expressed the teachings and practices of those traditions in novel and innumerable ways," Burrows said in summary. "The strands of the ancient wisdom that came before the emergence of the New Age movement are now all aswirl, one virtually indistinguishable from the next, and all drawing on one another."[44]

We are experiencing a "paradigm shift," New Age enthusiasts say. "New perspectives give birth to new historic ages," Marilyn Ferguson wrote in her seminal book, *The Aquarian Conspiracy*. "Humankind has had many dramatic revolutions of understanding—great leaps, sudden liberation from old limits. We discovered the uses of fire and the wheel, language and writing. We found that the earth only *seems* flat, the sun only *seems* to circle the earth, matter only *seems* solid. We learned to communicate, fly, explore. Each of these discoveries is properly described as a 'paradigm shift,' a term introduced by Thomas Kuhn, a science historian and philosopher, in his landmark 1962 book, *The Structure of Scientific Revolutions*."[45]

The coming of the New Age and the dawning of the Age of Aquarius are ideas that are linked. According to astrological theory, there are so-called star ages which last for about 2,000 years and during which the earth and its inhabitants are exposed to certain astral influences that mold social and cultural life. "Believers in this theory," *Christianity Today* observed, "argue that for the past 2,000 years, the earth has been influenced by the sign of Pisces, the fish. This sign is identified with Christianity because the symbol of the fish was one of the marks of identification adopted by the early church. Astrologers say the Piscean Age was a 'watery' one in which the occult knowledge was undervalued and occult powers were in decline. But now we stand on the threshold of the Age of Aquarius, (an age) of humanism, brotherhood, and occult happenings."[46]

Also central to New Age belief is "a spiritualized doctrine of evolution, the conviction that personal transformation leads to planetary transformation," Elliot Miller wrote. "The New Age movement views its ideas and programs as the wave of the future (not without some good cause), and considers that it need only achieve a 'critical mass' (not a majority) of public support to overturn the cultural strongholds of secular humanism and traditional religion."[47]

Pantheism

If I had to sum up the basic thrust of the New Age Movement, I would say that fundamentally it is rooted in pantheism, remembering that any such simplified statement is inadequate for such a broad-based and varying movement. According to the New Age worldview, as Brooks Alexander and Robert Burrows have explained, "ultimate reality—god—is one and impersonal. Being one, it contains no distinctions, is undifferentiated, without qualities or attributes. It cannot be personal, since personality is a by-product of differentiation and distinction." In outline format in a 1988 magazine, Alexander and Burrows compared New Age and biblical worldviews on 13 key points. Talking about creation, they noted that New Agers believe that "god *emanates*—not creates—the cosmos out of its own being. There is no distinction or discontinuity between god and the cosmos: all is one. God is creation."[48]

Pantheism is extolled by New Agers as a new revelation, a decided step up philosophically from Christianity. C.S. Lewis saw it otherwise. "So far from being the final religious refinement, pantheism is in fact the permanent level below which man sometimes sinks, but above which his own unaided efforts can never raise him for very long," Lewis wrote in *Miracles*. "It is the attitude into which the human mind automatically falls when left to itself. No wonder we find it congenial. If religion means simply what man says about God, and not what God does about man, then pantheism almost *is* religion. And religion in that sense has, in the long run, only one really formidable opponent, namely, Christianity."[49]

Chapter  3

Reincarnation,
Near-Death Experiences,
Channeling

Problems

After considering Hinduism and Buddhism and pantheism and occultism and other points of theological and philosophical background to the New Age movement, I think it might be helpful to consider several key problem areas. People, in general, are not buying books on Hinduism and Buddhism. They are buying books on reincarnation and channeling and crystals and astrology and other themes in conflict with basic Christian teaching.

Reincarnation

Reincarnation is a key tenet of the New Age movement. This does away with the finality of death and with the judgment of a just God. It asserts that we just keep being reborn again and again in a nearly endless cycle, trying to work off the debt of karma we have accumulated. Eventually, if we are really selfless, we will work off our karma and rise to a higher plane of existence above the cycle of reincarnation.

I have always wanted to ask a reincarnationist this question: "If there is a nuclear holocaust and all living things are killed, into what will you be reincarnated?" The death of every living thing on earth through nuclear war is certainly possible, though it would be a tragedy of such a scale as to dwarf all previous tragedies of human history. Still, it would not be the end for human beings according to the Christian vision. There still would be heaven and there still would be hell. God can also recreate the world, if he chooses, as he can recreate our bodies for the final resurrection. The reincarnationists, I am afraid, would not have a living body to flee to.

There is also a mathematical problem to reincarnation. The population of the world is growing rapidly, but reincarnationists tell of current people having lived many lives before. It simply does not work out mathematically. In 1650, according to *The World Almanac*,[1] there were 550 million people on earth. This figure grew to 1.6 billion in 1900 and 2.5 billion in 1950. In 1987, the world population passed the 5 billion mark and it continues to grow. There simply were not enough people living in previous generations for the 5 billion people today to have lived multiple previous lives.

In his book, *Past Lives, Future Lives*, Bruce Goldberg, a Baltimore dentist/hypnotist and reincarnationist, tackles this problem of the paucity of people in previous generations by proposing the theory that "a soul is able to occupy more than one body at a time."[2] Thanks a lot! That means that if I am hypnotized and come to suppose that I was a mute slave in Ethiopia, a leper in Latin America and a prostitute in ancient Rome, I cannot even claim these existences as my special heritage. Dozens of people living today are also these people. Are we all working off the same karma? If one of my contemporary soul-mates lives a bad life today, does that mean that I am burdened with more bad karma? If you hold reincarnation up to the light of common sense, there are insuperable problems.

Eastern religions talk about reincarnation into and out of the plant and animal world. This, at least, would account for the expanding population problem. However, I have rarely seen a New Age reincarnation story that deals with past lives as a gnat or a toad or a palm tree. As a matter of fact, I have rarely seen a New Age reincarnation story about a previously dull and boring existence as a field hand or scrub lady. Most of the previous incarnations are exotic and exciting.

Reincarnation is also very cruel. According to Goldberg,[3] if our house is burglarized today, it is because we stole in a previous life. If a person today is the victim of rape or murder, it is because the person was a rapist or murderer in a previous existence. Dick Sutphen, in his book *Pre-Destined Love*,[4] also blames present miseries on misdeeds in a past life. A woman suffers from migraine headaches today because previously she hit a lover over the head and killed him. A man today is blind because, as a Roman soldier, he purposely blinded Christian prisoners. A disfiguring birthmark is a carry-over from a terrible burn in the past life. A workaholic is driven by the subconscious memory of being unable to feed his family in an existence centuries before. In one life, a man is hot-tempered; in the next life, he hits people; in this life, he is born as a baby with no arms.

What is particularly cruel about reincarnation is that the people today are, in reality, completely innocent of the crimes for which they are supposedly being punished. They are suffering for something which they never did. It's one thing to suffer for sins you know you've committed, but to be told you're suffering for sins you're unaware of—that's cruel.

Some argue that one can look at karma more positively. After all, Buddhists have a whole series of exhortations to live just and upright lives. Human beings are supposed to be climbing up a trail to *nirvana* (nothingness) by living more and more virtuous lives in each reincarnation. However, one has to ask, has the age-old belief in reincarnation produced a more and more virtuous and moral society in the countries where it has held sway for thousands of years? There is little evidence that this has happened.

In fact, reincarnation appears to discourage one from helping another in need. The poor and the sick and the homeless are simply working out their karmic debt, so leave them alone. "Is it any wonder that health care and social services are seldom seen in the East, except where Christian missionaries have brought a healing hand?," Bob Larson asked. "To be a Good Samaritan, according to reincarnation, would only interfere with the divine order of karmic punishment."[5] "India has immense economic and social problems," observed Norman L. Geisler and J. Yutaka Amano. "The relationship between India's doctrine of karma and rebirth and its socio-economic problems can be seen as going hand in hand."[6]

Reincarnation has also been used by New Agers to justify abortion. Who cares if the unborn child is killed? The soul will just hop into the next available fetus that comes along.

However, this reincarnationist justification of abortion seems to be simply a phenomenon of the West. In the East, at times, there has been an extreme defense of the sanctity of all life. In Jainism, an offshoot of Hinduism, adherents take the vow of *ahimsa*, not to harm any living creature. Jain monks will sweep a path or a chair with a soft brush before treading or sitting upon it to avoid harming even the tiniest insect. Hospitals for maimed and sick rats have been maintained.[7]

High-minded Buddhists use reincarnation as a reason for being kind to all humans one comes in contact with. "Realize that it is not easy to find a being who has not formerly been your mother, or your father, your brother, your sister or your son or daughter,"[8] wrote Hammalawa Saddhatissa.

"According to the doctrine of karma, future happiness is a direct result or continuation of the maintaining of a satisfactory standard of conduct in the present," Saddhatissa has written. "The best that can be done to gain secure and lasting well-being is to cut down the evil actions and increase the good ones."[9] He quoted the Buddha as saying: "Amass good deeds for the other world; for men, everything in the other world rests on merits."[10]

Walpola Rahula described one who has attained Buddhist perfection. "He is free from selfish desire, hatred, ignorance, conceit, pride and all such 'defilement'; he is pure and gentle, full of universal love, compassion, kindness, sympathy, understanding, tolerance. His service to others is of the purest for he has no thought of self. He gains nothing, accumulates nothing, not even anything spiritual, because he is free from the illusion of 'self,' and the 'thirst' for becoming."[11]

Reincarnationists in the West usually attempt to discover past lives through hypnosis. Someone can hypnotize them or they can hypnotize themselves, often using special tapes or books that teach self-hypnosis. This can be dangerous, not only because hypnosis can do psychological damage, but because a hypnotized person is particularly open to outside spiritual influences. "The greatest danger in using hypnosis to verify reincarnation is the subject's spiritually vulnerable condition, in which a trance-state could be manipulated by demonic forces," wrote Larson. "The information about another life being impressed upon the mind may come from an alien spiritual source."[12]

In the 1950s, a book about reincarnation, *The Search for Bridey Murphy,* was a big hit. It told the story of Virginia Tighe, a 33-year-old homemaker who, under hypnosis, assumed the personality of what was presumed to be a 19th-century Irish woman. A few years later, the truth came out. It was discovered that, as a girl, Tighe had been tutored by an Irish grandmother who spoke Gaelic to her and who read her history books about Ireland. The hypnosis had brought to the surface these long-buried memories.

Most of the incidents of hypnotized people seeming to recall events and buildings and languages of long ago and far away can be explained away as the result of a fertile imagination or the recalling of something heard or read a long time ago. Sometimes, however, there seems to be no logical explanation except that the person actually lived a previous life in that situation. There is one other explanation from a

Christian standpoint. This so-called remembering of past events could be the result of demonic activity. Demons were present when things happened in the past. They could be prompting the subject to reveal them now. In any case, we know that divine revelation clearly teaches that there is no reincarnation.[13]

Some reincarnationists believe that there was a conspiracy by Christians in the past to discredit the belief. "Since the espousal of reincarnation and karma by the wisest spiritual and philosophical sages, the people of the East have remained in awe of the relentless revolutions of the 'wheel of life,' " noted Joe Fisher breathlessly. "Not so their counterparts in the Western Hemisphere where reincarnation was buried 14 centuries ago. The conspiring undertakers were the church and the state, fearful that their authority could be challenged by a doctrine that made individuals responsible for their own salvation. Since A.D. 553, when the 'monstrous restoration' of rebirth was denounced by Emperor Justinian, the faithful have been taught to believe in eternal life while ignoring immortality's spiritual sister, reincarnation."[14]

Fisher's main problem is that he does not understand Christianity and the exalted joy of living as an individual for all eternity in heaven in the presence of a loving God. This is much more exciting than the cruel myth of reincarnation, in which we are fated to pay for the sins of someone else who had our soul in a past life. (Someone may object to my saying that someone else has to pay for the negative karma generated in a person's lifetime. Eastern religionists don't believe this; they believe that it is the same person in various reincarnations who pays the karmic debt. I just can't buy this. If I don't know anything about the bloke who had my soul in a previous incarnation, how can you seriously say I am the same person?)

Shirley MacLaine has stated that there was a conspiracy by Christians to change the church's teaching on reincarnation. She charged: "I read that Christ's teachings about reincarnation were struck from the Bible during the Fifth

Ecumenical Council meeting in Constantinople in the year A.D. 553."[15]

Sorry, Miss MacLaine, you're wrong. The New Testament canon was developed in the second and third centuries and received its final form in the fourth century, not the sixth. The earliest versions of the New Testament texts do not differ appreciably from those that date after the sixth century. Furthermore, as Russell Chandler has shown, the Council of Constantinople "never considered reincarnation; it simply was not of great concern to the church fathers. The council *did* discuss—and reject—the idea of the preexistence of the soul, a view which had been held by the church theologian Origen (c.185-254). Origen believed human souls preexisted their physical bodies, but he did not believe in reincarnation. In fact, in his writings he specifically rejected reincarnation as contrary to the Christian faith."[16]

An article on this subject in the *Christian Research Journal* concluded: "Reincarnation was certainly not suppressed by the church in the sixth century or at any other time. It has been explicitly rejected by church leaders since the middle of the second century, and never taken seriously as a belief that might be adopted by Christians. Origen's belief in preexistence of souls was treated as a novel aberration by the church fathers and councils which came after him."[17]

There are many texts in the Bible that explicitly contradict reincarnation and instead talk about judgment and resurrection. Here are some of the more explicit ones.

> When the Son of man comes in his glory, and all the angels with him, then he will sit on his glorious throne. Before him will be gathered all the nations, and he will separate them one from another as a shepherd separates the sheep from the goats . . . . And [the goats] will go away into eternal punishment, but the righteous into eternal life (Mt. 25:31, 32, 46).

> Truly, I say to you, today you will be with me in

Paradise (Lk. 23:43).

I am the resurrection and the life; he who believes
in me, though he die, yet shall he live, and whoever
lives and believes in me shall never die (Jn. 11:25-
26).

And as they were stoning Stephen, he prayed,
"Lord Jesus, receive my spirit" (Acts 7:59).

But if Christ is in you, although your bodies are
dead because of sin, your spirits are alive because
of righteousness. If the Spirit of him who raised
Jesus from the dead dwells in you, he who raised
Christ Jesus from the dead will give life to your
mortal bodies also through his Spirit which dwells
in you (Rom. 8:10-11).

For if the dead are not raised, then Christ has not
been raised. If Christ has not been raised, your
faith is futile and you are still in your sins. Then
those also who have fallen asleep in Christ have
perished. If for this life only we have hoped in
Christ, we are of all men most to be pitied. But in
fact Christ has been raised from the dead, the first
fruits of those who have fallen asleep (1 Cor. 15:16-
20).

It is appointed for men to die once, and after that
comes judgment (Heb. 9:27).

The biblical texts that reincarnationists cite to "prove"
their position are taken out of context. When Jesus tells
Nicodemus (Jn. 3:3) that he must be "born again," it is clear
that Jesus is talking about a spiritual birth and not reincarnation. When Herod heard of the wonders Jesus was working,
he said: "This is John the Baptist, he has been raised from the
dead; that is why these powers are at work in him" (Mt. 14:
1-2). This cannot be reincarnation because Jesus was only a
few months younger than his cousin, John, who was killed

after Jesus was an adult.

When Jesus says (Mt. 11:14) that John the Baptist is "Elijah who is to come," Jesus is not talking about reincarnation. "To say that John the Baptist was a reincarnation of Elijah," Larson explained, "is to ignore his own answer to those who raised this possibility. 'I am not,' he emphatically declared (Jn. 1:21). Luke plainly records that it was in the 'spirit and power,' the *style* of Elijah's ministry, that John came (Lk. 1:17)."[18]

Near-Death Experiences

Whereas reincarnation is clearly against Christian teaching, the jury is still out concerning near-death experiences. The phenomenon was popularized in the 1975 book by Raymond A. Moody, Jr., *Life After Life*. It sold three million copies. Another popular book, *Life at Death: A Scientific Investigation of the Near-Death Experience* by Kenneth Ring (William Morrow & Co.), gives statistics and seeks to probe the impact the experiences have on a person's life. A 1988 article by Jane E. Brody reported that a 1982 Gallup poll indicated that some eight million American adults and an unknown number of children have had a near-death experience. In this experience, she said, summarizing Ring's research, people may:

> Feel peaceful, tranquil, serene and free of pain;
>
> Have an out-of-body experience in which they leave their body and are able to view it from above;
>
> Find themselves in a dark tunnel or void where they encounter a presence and review their life;
>
> See a brilliant, but warm, loving and accepting light;
>
> Enter, merge with or be enveloped by a light and perhaps reunited with deceased relatives, only to be told that they must return to their physical bodies.[19]

Buzzing or ringing sounds are also often reported. "Interestingly," wrote Bruce Goldberg, "there is rarely any form of correlation between a person's religion and his or her experience of death. In other words, it doesn't seem to matter whether the patient is an agnostic, atheist, Christian, Jew, Hindu, or [professes] any other belief; the experiences reported to me are similar."[20]

"The studies have shown a remarkable similarity in the characteristics of these experiences and in their profound and lasting impact on people," Brody continued. "Although details may vary among people of different cultures, the overall pattern of the experience and its aftermath seem to be shared worldwide. Moreover, recent research increasingly indicates that in virtually all cases, people are permanently and often dramatically changed by a near-death experience. People adopt new values, change careers, abandon materialism and question relationships."[21]

This seems, on the surface, to be a serious challenge to the Christian teaching about death. Certain facts should be kept in mind, however.

1) The chief writers about near-death experiences—Moody, Ring and Goldberg—are all New Agers. They were, consciously or unconsciously, filtering data through their New Age bias. Their writing was based on several dozen alleged occurrences while the Gallup poll indicated there were some eight million occurrences to draw from.

2) The Gallup poll talked about the number of experiences, not about the content of the experiences. How would these eight million people describe their experiences? We don't know.

3) Brody's article was written from a New Age perspective. The people she quoted for descriptions of the contents of the near-death experiences were New Agers.

An article in a Christian magazine reports that the publicized near-death experiences are not like Christian conversion experiences. "Modern near-death visionaries are not converted to a particular religious faith," Rodney Clapp wrote in *Christianity Today*. "Instead, they tend to become suspicious of religious 'sectarianism,' and, rather than fleeing to a monastery, more typically take up new voluntary-service duties in a hospital, nursing home, or such. The modern visionaries' conversion is not to an austere spirituality, but to one that affirms joy and laughter."[22]

Clapp reported that Ring, a psychologist at the University of Connecticut, goes so far as to assign near-death survivors a heightened consciousness that makes them the vanguard of the New Age. "Near-death experiences," Ring said, "collectively represent an evolutionary thrust toward higher consciousness for humanity as a whole . . . . To my thinking, the emergence of this new strain of human being, if this hypothesis is right, on the planet now, signals a possibility that the dawning of the New Age is indeed upon us."[23]

Some near-death experiences, however, do confirm Christian beliefs in the afterlife. In his book, *The Beautiful Side of Death*, Floyd C. McElveen recounted some very different experiences.

Thomas Welch nearly died after a fall at an Oregon lumber mill. He recalled an experience of standing near a shoreline of a great ocean of fire. "This is the most awesome sight one could ever see this side of the final judgment," he recounted.[24]

A woman who considered herself to be an average Christian had this experience: "The next thing I remember was entering this gloomy room where I saw in one of the windows this huge giant with a grotesque face that was watching me. Running around the windowsill were little imps or elves that seemed to be with the giant . . . . Then, for some reason the giant turned me loose and sent me back. I felt I was being spared."[25]

A regular church member who nearly died said he found himself "descending through a tunnel lined by fire in its lower half, which opened into a huge, fiery world of horror. He saw some of his old friends from the 'good old days' who exhibited blank stares of apathy [and] who were burdened with useless loads . . . . Complete darkness outskirted the milieu of pointless activity."[26]

A 14-year-old girl who tried to commit suicide by taking an overdose of aspirin said in her delirium while being treated: "Mama, help me! Make them let go of me!" Later she explained what she meant: "Them, those demons in hell . . . . They wouldn't let go of me . . . . They wanted me."[27]

A 54-year-old woman who tried to commit suicide with an overdose of Valium described her experience this way: "I remember going down this black hole, round and round. Then I saw a glowing red-hot spot getting bigger and bigger until I was able to stand up. It was all red and hot and on fire. The earth was like slimy mud that sank over my feet, and it was hard to move. The heat was awful and made it hard to breathe. I cried, 'Oh, Lord, give me another chance.' I prayed and prayed. How I got back, I'll never know."[28]

Now, whose near-death experiences are you going to believe?

Of course, New Agers not only rely on near-death experiences, they supposedly have communications "from the other side," from people who have died. These communications show no hint of the love of God and the eternal joy of the blessed in heaven seeing God face to face. After the medium Arthur Ford died, he allegedly communicated to the world through Ruth Montgomery's automatic writing. Here is what Ford supposedly said about the afterlife, as recorded in Montgomery's book, *A World Beyond.*

> We welcome a newcomer with love and open arms . . . . He hungers and we produce food. It is a thought pattern, but as real to him as that which once used to sustain his physical body . . . . He asks about loved ones whom he does not see around him. Some are still in physical body, some here, some already progressed to a higher state or gone back into another earthly body. We tell him to wait, that within a short time he will understand

more, and that meanwhile he is to do whatever suits his fancy. Some will explore the countryside, gasping in awe at the brilliant colors and lush foliage. Others may wish themselves in a big city and immediately will be there, soaking up the sounds and dodging traffic as excitedly as if they needed to do so. For a time we let them do exactly as they choose. It's up to them. But we are ever within call, and the day comes that they tire of this way and begin to wonder more about their present circumstances. If of a studious nature they will want to join classes, for we have them here. Others may join groups who are experimenting with earthly contact.[29]

This is a nice scene—in fact, it is much nicer than most spiritistic views of the afterlife—but it is not nearly as exciting as an eternity face to face with an infinitely loving God.

Channeling

Channelers are modern-day mediums. They go into a trance and an entity speaks through them. The mediums of a century ago tried to get in touch with the spirit of a departed loved one to get assurances that the departed still had some sort of existence and was happy to some extent. Nowadays, the message often comes from some mythic entity which is thousands of years old and may never have existed as a human being at all or which may have existed as a number of reincarnated humans in various periods of history.

The message from the channelers is pure New Age: there is no Creator God; we are all gods; we create our own reality; there is no death; there is reincarnation; knowledge of self is salvation and power.

Channeling is big business. In 1986, the *Los Angeles Times* estimated that there were more than 1,000 professional channelers in the Los Angeles area, whereas there were only two professional channelers there a decade before.[30] It will cost you $275 to spend a weekend listening to the entity Lazaris, channeled by Jach Pursel. With 600 to 800 other persons at the same weekend seminar, Pursel rakes in an average of $190,000 or more a weekend. (Lazaris apparently gets no cut.) According to an article by Brooks Alexander,[31] Pursel/ Lazaris had a two-year waiting list for private consultations at $93 per hour. Or you can contact Lazaris by phone at $53 per half-hour, billed to your charge card. Audio tapes of Lazaris go for $20 per set and videotapes for $60. Pursel is co-owner of the Illuminarium Gallery in Corte Madera, Calif. It specializes in expensive crystal jewelry and visionary paintings and grosses $5 million a year.

Other channelers are well paid, too. J.Z. Knight charges $400 per person for a group session and Kevin Ryerson charges $250 per session. Bargain hunters, on the other hand, can be instructed by entities such as Merlin and the Spiritual Hierarchy, who conduct group sessions once a month at the Sherman Oaks, Calif., Women's Club for only $12 per person.[32]

In a 1987 article,[33] Alexander noted that the major New Age/occult bookstore in Berkeley had seven shelves of channeled material for sale. Three of those shelves held the older books: *The Urantia Book, The Aquarian Gospel,* the works of Edgar Cayce and so on. The remaining four shelves held more recently published material. Those four shelves outsold the rest of the bookstore.

Jonathan Livingston Seagull, which topped the best-seller lists for two years, was allegedly dictated to Richard Bach by an entity that appeared in the form of a bird.

Russell Chandler listed a number of the popular channelers in addition to Jach Pursel (Lazaris entity) and J.Z. Knight (Ramtha entity). He also noted that when Sharon Gless won an Emmy for her role in "Cagney and Lacey" she announced in her September, 1987, acceptance speech that she owed her success to Lazaris.[34]

Kevin Ryerson, the medium on Shirley MacLaine's television miniseries, channeled such other-worldly entities as

John, a Middle Eastern scholar from Jesus' day, and Tom McPherson, an Irish pickpocket who served in the English diplomatic corps during the Shakespearean era. In Los Angeles, Gerry Bowman channeled John the Apostle every Sunday night on the radio. Penny Torres-Rubin channeled a highly evolved "entity from the seventh dimension" named Mafu who last incarnated in A.D. 79 as a leper in Pompeii. Darryl Anka channeled Bashar, an extraterrestrial humanoid from Essassani, a civilization "roughly 500 light-years in a future timeline in the direction of the Orion constellation." The Rev. Neville Rowe, a graduate electrical engineer, channeled dolphins as well as Soli, an off-planet being from the Pleiades.

Brazilian Luiz Antonio Gasparetto has a weekly psychic television show and claims to channel about 50 "Old Master" artists, including Renoir, Picasso, Goya, Van Gogh and Toulouse-Latrec. They reputedly mix the colors, put them in Gasparetto's hands, and rapidly move his arms and hands over the paper or canvas while he paints furiously—with his eyes tightly shut.[35] (He also performed for Shirley MacLaine. See Chapter Four.)

In reading channeled books, however, it's hard to see what all the fuss is about. *Seth Speaks*[36] is one of the first of the modern channeled works that was widely circulated. The 1972 work consisted of 500 pages of material dictated by Seth, described by the channeler Jane Roberts as an "energy personality essence no longer focused in physical form." The book was rambling, disconnected and boring. The ideas were pedestrian. It is hard to believe that anyone would take the work seriously if it were not for the supposition that it was dictated by a higher entity. Here are some samples of Seth's philosophical puree.

> I am primarily a personality with a message: you create the world that you know. You have been given perhaps the most awesome gift of all: the ability to project your thoughts outward into physical form (p. 6).

There are better places than others to build houses or structures—points where health and vitality are strengthened, where, other things being equal, plants will grow and flourish and where all beneficial conditions seem to meet (p. 76).

The soul knows that good and evil are but different manifestations of a far greater reality (p. 99).

A belief in hell fires can cause you to hallucinate Hades' conditions. A belief in a stereotyped heaven can result in a hallucination of heavenly conditions. You always form your own reality according to your ideas and expectations . . . . The boredom and stagnation of a stereotyped heaven will not for long content the striving consciousness (p. 141).

The crucifixion of Christ was a psychic, but not a physical event (p. 243).

You may have noticed how, in these quotations, Seth contradicts many basic Christian teachings: God created everything; good is the opposite of evil; heaven and hell are objectively real; heaven is supreme happiness; Jesus physically died on the cross.

A more interesting book, probably because it is edited, was *Ramtha*,[37] based on tape recordings of the channeled sayings of Ramtha, allegedly a 35,000-year-old former warrior and now ascended entity who speaks through J.Z. Knight. The first part of the book was pretty good science fiction. Ramtha was a tough dude back in prehistoric times who wiped out some peoples on the way to conquering three-quarters of the known world. He got religion and was able to become an ascended master through only one incarnation. His teachings, however, are vintage New Age and definitely anti-Christian.

The Life Force that you term the Father does not even have the *ability* to judge you. For Life does not possess a personality with an ego that can perceive any part of itself as being what is called good or evil, right or wrong, perfect or imperfect (p. 30).

Yeshua ben Joseph, whom you call Jesus of Nazareth, is a great god, just as you are a great god. But he is not the only son of God; he is a son of God. He was a man who *became* God, just as you will become God (p. 36).

You are the one who is wholly responsible for all you have ever done, been, or experienced. You, who have the power to create the magnificence of stars, have created every moment and every circumstance of your life. Who you are, you chose to be. What you look like, you created. How you live, you *wholly* designed and destined. That is the exercise and privilege, if you will, of being God-man (p. 45).

I don't suppose I will have to point out how consistently anti-Christian these New Age comments are.

"What is the nature of the channeled entities?,"[38] Brooks Alexander asked. He said there are four possibilities.

1. The entities are real and they are telling the truth about themselves.

2. The entities are real and they are lying about themselves.

3. The entities are a "dissociative reaction," a mental dysfunction unrecognized as such. They are like part of a split personality.

4. The entities are a conscious fraud for the purpose of gain.

Number 1 is not true because the entities contradict biblical truths, but the other three possibilities could be true. It could be that numbers 2, 3 and 4 are true in one and the same channeler. The channeler could come under the influence of demonic forces and could relate things demons communicated. This could trigger serious psychological problems, like a split personality. Sometimes the demons could be speaking and sometimes the split personality could be speaking. When a crowd of people have paid thousands of dollars to listen to a demon or a split personality, perhaps the channeler is forced to resort to fraud and imaginative acting to give them their money's worth. Some channelers may be frauds from start to finish.

Elliot Miller reported the doctoral research on channeling done by Margo Chandley at the International College, Westwood, Calif. According to Chandley's study, childhood traumatic experiences were reported by 12 of the 13 channels she researched. "The experiences ranged from epileptic seizures, a shock from a fall, sexual or emotional abuse, neglect or abandonment by parents or peers. She said the channels withdrew into an interior life," Miller observed, referring to a *Los Angeles Times* article for documentation. "Also they all had had abnormal or mystical experiences—always when they were alone—between the ages of 3 and 11, Chandley said. Most had been raised Catholic."[39] Miller added that his research showed that in nearly all cases some form of trance-inducing or occult activity was engaged in prior to the alleged contacts from the channeled entities.

"It is interesting to note that channeling forerunner Alice Bailey said that 85 percent of channeled material comes from the personal subconscious of the channels,"[40] Miller observed. "Many of today's channelers would substantially agree. Channel Joey Crinita of Canada believes that channeling is often nothing more than a form of self-hypnosis in which the imagination creates its own characters."[41]

Demonic influences cannot be discounted. The unanimous way channeled teachings directly contradict basic Christian beliefs strongly suggests a demonic source. The New Age position that we are not sinners and do not need a Savior keeps people from seeking salvation through Jesus. The core New Age/channeling doctrines, "You can be as God" and "You shall not die," were first uttered by the serpent in the Garden of Eden (Gen. 3:4-5). "Embraced then, this 'gospel' produced all of the world's misery," Miller commented. "Embraced now, it will make all that God has done in Christ to remedy the situation of no avail to the individual in question."[42]

The Roman Catholic Church has repeatedly condemned all forms of spiritism and divination. On April 26, 1917, the Vatican formally replied "no" to all points in the following inquiry: "Whether it is allowed either through a so-called medium or without one, and with or without hypnotism, to assist at any spiritualistic communications or manifestations, even such as appear to be blameless or pious, either asking questions of the souls or spirits, or listening to their answers, or merely looking on, even with a tacit or express protestation that one does not want to have anything to do with evil spirits?"[43]

The article by Edward A. Pace on "Spiritism" in the 1909 *Catholic Encyclopedia* saw a probable demonic influence in spiritistic phenomena because "the alleged communications antagonize the essential truths of religion such as the divinity of Christ, atonement and redemption, judgment and future retribution, while they encourage agnosticism, pantheism and a belief in reincarnation."[44]

The Second Plenary Council of Baltimore (1866), Pace reported, "while making due allowance for fraudulent practice in spiritism, declare[d] that some at least of the manifestations are to be ascribed to satanic intervention, and warns the faithful against lending any support to spiritism or even, out of curiosity, attending seances." He also noted that a Vatican decree of March 30, 1898, "condemn[ed] spiritistic practices, even though intercourse with the demon be excluded and communication sought with good spirits only."[45]

The Bible has explicitly forbidden the consulting of mediums and it also instructs us to test all spirits.

> When you come into the land which the Lord your God gives you, you shall not learn to follow the abominable practices of those nations. There shall not be found among you any one who burns his

son or his daughter as an offering, any one who practices divination, a soothsayer, or an augur, or a sorcerer, or a charmer, or a medium, or a wizard, or a necromancer. For whoever does these things is an abomination to the Lord; and because of these abominable practices the Lord your God is driving them out before you (Dt. 18:9-12).

Beloved, do not believe every spirit, but test the spirits to see whether they are of God; for many false prophets have gone out into the world. By this you know the Spirit of God: every spirit which confesses that Jesus Christ has come in the flesh is of God, and every spirit which does not confess Jesus is not of God. This is the spirit of antichrist, of which you heard that it was coming, and now it is in the world already (1 Jn. 4:1-3).

Chapter 4

Astrology,
Crystals,
Pyramids, UFOs,
Shirley MacLaine

More Problems ─────

In this chapter, we will continue the discussion of popular religious or cultural beliefs in conflict with the Christian faith. These non-Christian beliefs are rooted in pantheism and occultism. New Agers take these beliefs seriously.

Astrology

Astrology is very ancient and it is very New Age. It is something taken for granted in many New Age circles. Recently it made headlines across the country.

A stir was caused in the United States in May, 1988, when it was reported that President Ronald Reagan may have used astrology in making key policy decisions. The president did not deny that he read horoscopes and Nancy Reagan's press secretary confirmed that, since the 1981 attempt on the president's life, the first lady had often consulted "a friend that does astrology"[1] in San Francisco to seek reassurance of the president's safety.

The *Philadelphia Inquirer* reported that Nancy Reagan, after consulting an astrologer, insisted that the president sign the U.S.-Soviet nuclear missile treaty at 1:33 p.m. on

December 8, 1987. Reagan, who signed the treaty with Soviet leader Mikhail Gorbachev at exactly that time, later denied making policy decisions based on astrology.[2]

In his book, *For the Record*, Donald T. Regan said: "Virtually every major move or decision the Reagans made during my time as White House chief of staff was cleared in advance with a woman in San Francisco who drew up horoscopes to make certain that the planets were in a favorable alignment for the enterprise." The astrologer, Regan continued, "had become such a factor in my work, and in the highest affairs of the nation, that at one point I kept a color-coded calendar on my desk (numerals highlighted in green ink for 'good' days, red for 'bad' days, yellow for 'iffy' days) as an aid to remembering when it was propitious to move the President of the U.S. from one place to another, or schedule him to speak in public, or commence negotiations with a foreign power."[3] *Time* identified the astrologer as San Francisco socialite Joan Quigley.[4]

What about astrology? Does it work? Is it something a Christian should be involved in?

A Gallup poll reported that 32 million persons—one in five adult Americans—believe in astrology and that eight of 10 Americans can name the sign under which they were born. Nearly 2,000 newspapers carry a daily horoscope, according to a book on the cults by Bob Larson.[5]

Science writer Lawrence E. Jerome claimed that at least 1 billion people around the globe "believe in and follow astrology to some extent."[6] Bernard Gittelson, a New Age human-behavior researcher, has estimated the total circulation of newspapers and magazines carrying astrological columns in the United States, Europe, Japan and South America to be more than 700 million.[7] John Ankerberg and John Weldon reported that the estimates of the number of astrologers range as high as 10,000 full-time and 175,000 part-time.[8] They also noted that a 1984 Gallup poll revealed that 55% of teen-agers (aged 13-18) believed in astrology. This figure was up from 40% in 1978.

Numerology is an occultic belief system with ties to astrology. *Parade Magazine*, which is carried in millions of Sunday papers, had a two-page ad for numerology thinly disguised as an article. (The word "advertisement" appeared on the top of each page in small print.) If you would send in your name and your date of birth and $14, they would send you a numerology profile which would give you a complete description of your personal characteristics.[9]

The claims of astrologers, however, are supported by no scientific or statistical evidence. Russell Chandler has reported that the Committee for the Scientific Investigation of the Claims of the Paranormal issued a statement which said that dozens of rigorous tests in recent years by scientists have found that horoscopes "fail completely in predicting future events." In one test, according to Andrew Fraknoi, an astronomy professor at San Francisco State University, two scientists examined more than 3,000 predictions by astrologers and found them to be correct less than 10% of the time.[10]

In 1975, 192 leading scientists, including 19 Nobel Prize winners, publicly disavowed astrology, according to John Ankerberg and John Weldon. These authors looked at a good deal of research which astrologers claimed gave scientific and statistical support for astrology, but they found this research "both disappointing and questionable."[11] The material they evaluated was principally provided to them by the largest and most scientifically oriented astrological society, the American Federation of Astrologers in Tempe, Ariz. The organization offers nearly 1,000 books and more than 600 tapes for sale and claims that for 50 years it has been the leader in astrological education and research. Ankerberg and Weldon stated, moreover, that a week-long visit to the July, 1988, AFA convention revealed that many of the astrologers had spirit guides and practiced other forms of the occult. The president and first vice-president of the AFA are both spiritists.

A book by Josh McDowell and Don Stewart reported that Paul Couderc, an astronomer at the Paris Observatory, concluded after examining the horoscopes of 2,817 musicians that "the position of the sun has absolutely no musical significance."[12] The musicians were born throughout the entire year on a chance basis. No sign of the zodiac or fraction of a sign favors or does not favor them.

Astrology: True or False? A Scientific Evaluation, a book by two American astronomers, Roger B. Culver and Philip A. Ianna, analyzed and discredited hundreds of astrological claims. In the preface to the revised edition, written in August, 1988, the authors stated that finding "a 5,000-year-old superstition in the White House in any form other than for entertainment is quite incredible and more than a little frightening." They said it was their hope "that if this book does nothing else it will at least bring home the point that astrology is not now and has never been a science in any way, shape, or form."[13]

At the end of their book, Culver and Ianna challenged astrologers to demonstrate their astrological ability through any of several tests, "all of which should be well within the framework of the claims made in the astrological literature." Promotheus Books volunteered to pay the astrologers' total fees for any tests that were passed. Here are some of the tests of astrological ability.

> * Given the times, dates, and places of birth of 60 individuals, half of whom are violent criminals and the other half are peaceful, law-abiding citizens, identify at least 27 of the 30 violent criminals.

> * Given the times, dates, and locations of birth of 60 couples who have been married, but half of whom are now divorced, identify at least 27 of the 30 divorced couples. The time and date of the marriage will also be given to the astrologer in this case.

> * Predict the date to within one day of the high point, low point, largest advance, and largest

decline in the Dow-Jones Industrial Average over a one-year interval of time.

* Predict at least 30 days in advance the occurrence of an earthquake or any other natural disaster such as a flood, tornado, etc. in which the loss of life exceeds 100 or more individuals, specifying the nature of the disaster, its exact time to within 24 hours and its location on the earth to within 100 miles.[14]

Do you think any astrologer will take up this challenge? Don't bet on it.

This is how Ankerberg and Weldon described the basic concepts of astrology.

The *zodiac* is an imaginary "belt" of sky containing the 12 astrological signs or constellations around which the ancients built imaginary human and animal figures. (The zodiac and the constellations are both imaginary geometric configurations.)

The *signs* are the "signs of the zodiac," also known as "Sun-signs." Everyone is born under one of these 12 signs or constellations. (Pisces the fish, Leo the lion, Gemini the twins, Taurus the bull, etc.)

The *houses* are the 12 sections of the zodiac which together symbolize every aspect of life. The planets move through the houses; thus, when a planet falls into the sphere of the given house, it comes under its respective influence. The astrologer plots all these factors and more on a chart. This chart is called a *horoscope*.

The *horoscope* is a "map" of the heavens at the moment of the birth of a person or any specific time thereafter. On this chart, an astrologer plots the positions of the "planets," "signs," and "houses" for a given moment. The chart is then interpreted by numerous complex rules, many of which vary greatly from one astrologer to another.[15]

Here are some of the principal arguments against the validity of astrology.[16]

* Because astrology is based upon an erroneous, geocentric concept (the sun circling the earth), its suppositions and conclusions have no scientific basis.

* The earth has an uneven wobble as it spins on its axis. As a result, there has been a shift in the zodiac. Today, the sun's rays actually enter each of the constellations about one month earlier than they did centuries ago when the present astrological charts were finalized. This means that current horoscope readings are inaccurate by a factor of 30 days.

* For several weeks out of the year, no planet assigned to the zodiac is visible north of the Arctic Circle. The babies born there at that time would have no horoscope.

* Some astrologers contend that there are eight zodiac signs rather than 12, while others argue for 14 or even 24 signs of the zodiac.

* Most astrological charts are based upon the assumption that there are seven planets in our solar system, including the sun and the moon. In ancient times when the original astrological charts were developed, the planets Uranus, Neptune and Pluto were ignored because they were unobservable with the naked eye.

* What about twins? They have the same horoscopes, but they often turn out to have completely different personalities.

* The important horoscope is the one in effect, astrologers say, when the baby draws its first breath, but what about the horoscope at the time of conception? Shouldn't that be more important?

* For various medical and other reasons, mothers today can often pick the day and hour they give birth. They can choose the baby's horoscope, as it were. If astrology were true, the mother—with the help of the doctor—could influence significantly the personality of her child.

* Astrology is a universal practice in pagan religions, but these do not agree on the attributes for each sign. If you were to have your horoscope read by a Hindu in India, it would read much differently from one prepared by a Buddhist in Thailand.

In brief, astrology is totally unscientific and totally illogical. This doesn't seem to faze the faddists. I checked out of the library a few books on astrology by astrologers. You have to check your brains at the door before reading them. They are written in a world completely different from the world of logic and right reason, not to mention completely different from the world of revealed Christian truth. They make one mind-numbing ridiculous statement after another in a pompous and arrogant way. They quote the Bible out of context. They are obviously false, but they are frightening, too.

Yet, somehow, at times, astrology works. Sometimes these unscientific, essentially meaningless charts have meaning. The astrologer's intuition in looking at the charts reveals details and particulars about the subject's life that cannot be explained naturally. What is the answer? Demonic influence is the only reasonable answer.

Charles Strohmer, a former astrologer, has written a book about his experiences, including his conversion to Christianity.[17] In a review of this book, Brooks Alexander made this key point: "Strohmer shows that the horoscopic chart is a mediumistic point of interaction through which demonic spirits make a psychic connection with the thought processes of those who have committed themselves to belief in the astrological system . . . . [D]emons energize occult phenomena."[18] From the relatively harmless dabbling with horoscopes in the newspapers, undoubtedly thousands of people have been led into occultic practices and come under demonic influences. This is the way Strohmer summed it up.

> It took a revelation of Christ to make it clear that astrology is part of the kingdom of darkness. I now

understand that whenever I accurately interpreted someone's horoscope, it was due to deceptive and powerful spiritual beings informing my mind, not because of the reasons taught in astrology books, such as "planetary influences." . . . I am now convinced that only the power of the Holy Spirit and the gospel were capable of delivering me from as evil a delusion as astrology, and bringing me to faith in Christ.[19]

I am not saying that a casual reading of the daily horoscopes in the newspapers or some chitchat about one's astrological signs will put a person under demonic influence, but I am saying that this could be the first step in an evil practice that could lead to demonic influence.

The Bible strongly condemns astrology in many places.

And beware lest you lift up your eyes to heaven, and when you see the sun and the moon and the stars, all the host of heaven, you be drawn away and worship them and serve them (Dt. 4:19).

Those who divide the heavens, who gaze at the stars, who at the new moons predict what shall befall you, . . . behold, they are like stubble, the fire consumes them (Is. 47:13-14).

Thus says the Lord: "Learn not the way of the nations, nor be dismayed at the signs of the heavens because the nations are dismayed at them, for the customs of the peoples are false" (Jer. 10:2-3).

Daniel answered the king, "No wise men, enchanters, magicians, or astrologers can show to the king the mystery which the king has asked, but there is a God in heaven who reveals mysteries" (Dan. 2:27-28).

Crystals, Pyramids
Crystals are a hot item now. They are doing big business.

Why, for heaven's sake, you may ask. Here's one answer—
a rhapsodic quote from the popular book, *The Crystal Connection*.

> Crystals serve for many as keys to unlocking the
> access-windows of awareness to horizons of Light
> previously unimagined . . . . Crystal matrices am-
> plify and transform the crystalline codes of con-
> sciousness, thereby serving to interconnect the
> personal and planetary spheres with the encoded
> crystallinity of the greater domains of Universal
> Light—this is the "crystal connection."
>
> Reality is crystalline in nature. Herein abides cre-
> ation's most essential ordering principle. For all
> Light, all Life, all Intelligence is coded crystallin-
> ity. The overriding importance of the "crystal con-
> nection" is its universal interconnecting proper-
> ties . . . . Quartz crystals and other precious stones
> are matrixed means by which the crystalline codes
> of personal and planetary consciousness are con-
> nectively interlinked with the higher Light-dimen-
> sions in an amplified, coherent manner.[20]

Take a deep breath now and tell yourself: They're talking
about a hunk of rock! Fine. Now you're back in reality. You
will also note that the authors called reality "creation." Was
this a slip of the pen? Do they really believe in a Creator?
If so, it surely can't be God the Creator as revealed in the
Bible. This crystalline gobbledygook is certainly not the
Christian message. But wait, there's more. Here's a quote
from another crystal book, *Crystal Enlightenment*.

> Quartz crystals represent the sum total of material
> plane evolution. The six sides of the quartz crystal
> symbolize the six chakras with the termination
> being the crown, that which connects one with the
> infinite. Most quartz crystals have a flat base which
> was their roots to the earth. Oftentimes quartz are

cloudy or milky at the bottom and gain more clarity as they reach the terminated peak. This also symbolizes a similar growth pattern in which the cloudiness and dullness of consciousness is cleared as we grow closer to the point of union with our infinite self . . . . Clear quartz radiates with divine white light and by seeing, touching, wearing, using or meditating with these crystals one can actually work with that light in a physical form . . . .

When the mineral kingdom and the human kingdom link their forces together, new worlds of consciousness unfold. As the healing essence of quartz crystals vibrates the soul of humanity, vast horizons of hope and joy appear.[21]

It is sad that people believe this drivel and spend lots of money buying these books and buying crystals. A *Time* cover story tells of Tina Lucia of Stone Mountain, Ga., who uses crystals in healing. She uses amethyst, rose and blue quartz, black onyx and obsidian. She gave a crystal wand to Annette Manders, who reported positive results: "I healed a fungus under my toenail with my wand and I had a stomach problem that doesn't bother me any more."[22]

"The crystal-conscious hang the rocks of ages around their necks and suspend them from their ceilings; they wear them on their fingers and in body pouches; they place them on their coffee tables and window ledges and around their pets' necks; they stash them in their pockets, purses, and briefcases; drop them in their toilet tanks and bathtubs; affix them to their carburetors and bedposts; and use them for meditating and relaxing, focusing energy, and finding soul mates," Russell Chandler reported. "Some true believers even drink powdered rock crystals in an energizing elixir dubbed the 'gem and tonic.' And they want you to know that crystals can cure toothaches, allergies, face wrinkles, and toenail fungi."[23]

With all the crystal jewelry being worn and all the crystals decorating homes and offices, it is good that quartz is the most common mineral on the planet, comprising about 12% of the earth's crust.[24] Because of the great demand, the price is going up, however. New York-based Crystal Resources said Americans in 1988 were spending $100 million a year on crystals, and the company's owner Richard Berger predicted the figure could hit $250 million by 1991. Prices for crystals run from a few dollars to $150,000 for museum-quality crystals. That's as much as 1,000% more than 10 years ago.[25]

In an article in *Cornerstone*,[26] Eric Pement noted that a pound of crystals that sold for $10 in 1983 was selling for $500 four years later. He told of a rancher in Texas who bought a load of crystals to keep flies away from his cattle and of a woman in Philadelphia who kept a cluster of crystals in her refrigerator to reduce her electric bill. A New Age teacher in California suggested that a crystal pendant might offer added protection from AIDS and a clothing manufacturer in California sewed crystals in the pants right above the base of the spine.

Fortunately, crystals can be recycled or cleansed. Brett Bravo—psychic counselor, teacher, healer, jewelry designer and organizer of "Emerald City spiritual spa"—told how this could be done at a 1987 San Francisco lecture. Bravo, who said she had had a relationship with rocks since she was five and who once analyzed drilling cores for Shell Oil Company, gave five ways of cleansing a crystal:

a) Burying the crystal for a week;

b) Washing it in sea water;

c) Giving it a smoke treatment (a sage smudge is a favorite of Native Americans);

d) Running a degmagnetizer over it;

e) Putting it on our forehead and adjuring, "Clear!"[27]

It is hard to see how anyone can take this seriously. Wendell Wilson, editor of *Mineralogical Record*, said he was "disgusted" at the claptrap being promoted by modern crystal fanciers, according to Pement's article. George Harlow, curator of gems and minerals at the American Museum of Natural History, was staggered at how naive we have become concerning basic science: "All this baloney only proves that we have failed, and failed miserably, in the teaching of science.... There is simply no evidence that there is any measurable effect [moving] from crystal to human, or as [promoting] any kind of healing."[28]

If they're not wearing a crystal ring or necklace or headband, perhaps the New Agers are wearing a pyramid. J.Z. Knight said she had on a paper pyramid hat when she first had contact with the 35,000-year-old Ramtha. Chandler told of observing a customer at a pyramid booth at a psychic fair in California trying on wire pyramids until he found the right one. Pop-together open-frame portable pyramids kits could be purchased for under $100 from Universal Mind, complete with a compass for proper alignment with magnetic north. According to assorted pyramid promotions, Chandler reported, "the objects are acclaimed for such things as sharpening razor blades, stimulating exceptional plant growth, purifying water and killing bacteria, preserving and dehydrating foods, mellowing inexpensive wines, lowering electric bills, heightening awareness, raising vibrational levels, and amplifying thought, meditation, and astral projections."[29]

At a Celebration of Innovation in San Francisco, Chandler observed that Paradyne Systems of Laguna Beach offered a choice of five wire pyramids for sale. The highest-priced Powerdome pyramid was billed as being "omnidirectional" and "100 times higher than a normal pyramid" in power. Other advertised benefits and selling points of the Powerdome included:

* Increases attention span and high concentration;

* Decreases appetite;

* Expands psychic ability;

* Stronger detoxifier;

* Negative ion effect for euphoric feeling;

* Increases vitamin absorption.[30]

This is a rhetorical question: Does greed have anything to do with the spread of such fads as crystals and pyramids?

UFOs

Unidentified Flying Objects—UFOs—do they exist? Russell Chandler noted that a 1987 Gallup poll showed that 50% of Americans believe UFOs exist—the same percentage who think extraterrestrials are real—and one in 11 reported they had seen something they thought was a UFO.[31]

Christian anticult researcher Bob Larson described four categories of close encounters with UFOs:

1. Observation of a UFO within 500 feet or less;
2. Physical traces left behind;
3. Actual contact with the occupants;
4. Abduction or examination by these beings.

Larson concluded, "The evidence concerning all four kinds of encounters is overwhelming and, in some cases, irrefutable."[32] Larson admitted that most UFO sightings are easily dismissed as mistakenly identified planets, rocket launchings, weather balloons and atmospheric phenomena. Sometimes, though, something real is occurring. The Air Force's *Project Blue Book*, also, was not able to provide a rationale for 700 out of 12,600 cases of sightings between 1947 and 1969, when the project was abandoned.

In Appendix I to his book *UFO Exist!*,[33] Paris Flammonde talked about possible references to UFOs on prehistoric tablets as well as ancient religious and historical papyri, wall carvings and paintings. A number of 18th- and 19th-century astronomers reported unusual sightings. A "great airship" was reported in California and New York in 1896 and 1897. A number of UFO sightings was reported in the first half of the 20th century, including aerial ghost ships by fighter pilots in World War I and many sightings of "foo-fighters" by combat pilots in World War II.

The modern-day interest in UFOs stems from a 1947 occurrence when Idaho businessman Ken Arnold, while piloting a private plane over the Cascade Mountains, said he saw nine gleaming discs racing along at speeds of 1,000 miles an hour near Mount Rainier. He described these objects as moving "like saucers skipping across water." That started a deluge of sightings. Flammonde's Appendix I listed 18 pages of significant sightings between 1947 and 1975.

In an excellent article in the *Spiritual Counterfeits Project Journal*,[34] Christian researchers Mark Albrecht and Brooks Alexander agreed that UFOs exist. They said that it is the firm conclusion of scores of scientists and experts worldwide that 20% to 30% of the sightings cannot be explained through natural occurrences. "There are, by conservative estimate," Albrecht and Alexander continue, "over 2,000 cases of human encounters with landed UFOs and their occupants, and some 700 instances where physical evidence has been left behind. They have been tracked on radar at incredible speeds, fired on by jet fighters and antiaircraft missiles with no effect. They give off powerful electromagnetic charges, often causing the breakdown of engines and electrical circuitry; they evoke strange and fearful reactions in animals and frequently cause profound psychological disturbances in humans."[35]

Yet, in spite of these assertions, no incontrovertible evidence exists. There is no UFO anyplace that one can go to see. There are no parts extant that scientists agree without question come from a UFO. There are no indisputable photographs or movies. "Unverified sightings and contacts and a few fuzzy photos have fallen far short of the hard data scientists demand," Chandler observed.[36] He quoted Martin Gardner, a writer for the *Skeptical Inquirer*, as saying 40 years have gone by "without finding a single nut or bolt from a flying saucer."[37]

This is a key question. Are flying saucers nuts-and-bolts flying machines? If so, why don't we have conclusive evidence by this time that they exist? We have satellites flying around so sophisticated that they can identify very small objects. We have radar all over the place. Why can't we get indisputable proof of the UFOs?

Let's use common sense. Are UFOs flying machines made here on earth? The answer is clearly no. The two most technologically advanced societies are the United States and the Soviet Union. These two countries lead the way in air and space travel. Yet neither technology is in any way close to making a super-fast flying saucer that can hover and turn at right angles.

So, do UFOs come from another planet? This brings up a problem. If there is another planet supporting life as we know it, it is very, very far away. On February 24-25, 1977, the National Aeronautics and Space Administration (NASA) conducted a symposium on the subject of extraterrestrial intelligence at the prestigious Ames Research Center, Mountain View, Calif. One of the speakers, Bernard Oliver, chief of research for Hewlett-Packard, talked of the technological difficulties we would have to overcome if we were ever to contact another civilization or be contacted by one. Mark Albrecht summarized Oliver's conclusions: "He pointed out that the nearest star, Alpha Centauri, which is four light years away, represents an 80,000-year round trip from earth with our present technology. Beyond that, it is unlikely that any star within 100 light years distance is stable enough to support bio-chemical evolution."[38]

Where does that leave us? UFOs are not built on earth. It is extremely unlikely because of the vast distances involved that they come from another planet. So, what are they?

Let us pause here to note that it is possible, from a Christian viewpoint, that there are human beings living on remote planets. It is also possible that there are intelligent, created beings existing in other dimensions. This is not likely, but it is possible. What must be held by Christians is that there is only one God and that all other intelligent beings have been created by God. Protestant theologian Thomas C. Oden has written:

> If one takes seriously the physics of black holes and
> the expected disappearance of time and space—

and the potential re-creation of time and space—
one might hypothesize many different creations.
These speculations need not be viewed as a fundamental challenge to Hebraic-Christian faith in God
as Creator. Some physicists present probability
evidence that there could be a great many created
orders besides the one that we know. But one
could reasonably speculate that whatever creation
God created, it is likely that God would become
known to that world.

Suppose there is another world, entirely unknown
to and unknowable by us. Why would it not be
reasonable to hypothesize, on the basis of our own
salvation-history memory, that the same God who
has become self-revealed as a loving Parent in this
world would also become revealed as loving Parent in that world?[39]

This is certainly fascinating speculation, but it remains
speculation. In any case, it is not likely that UFOs come from
another planet or another dimension as ambassadors with a
revelation of the same Creator God who has been revealed to
us. There is nothing in the UFO phenomena that leads to the
belief in the one, true God. There is much in the UFO phenomena, on the other hand, that contradicts the ideas of God
as revealed in the Bible and Christian tradition.

Famed UFO researcher Allen Hynek came to ascribe a
"paraphysical nature" to some UFO experiences. Hynek
"believed in living forces that were not of this earth, but not
from other planets as such either,"[40] reported Clifford Wilson
in *The Alien Agenda.*

"Many UFO incidents appear to be contemporary versions of what was recorded long ago in mythology, religious
scripture, and spiritual traditions as encounters with angels,
demons, and the various inhabitants of other planes of existence," asserted John White in *New Realities.* "These meta-
terrestrial beings materialize into our space-time from other

levels of reality—traditionally called 'heaven and hell' in the Judeo-Christian worldview, but modernly understood as hyperspatial dimensions or supersensible space-time frameworks with a wide range of beings native to them, just as ours has creatures ranging from viruses to whales."[41]

Albrecht and Alexander adduced similar conclusions from other secular UFO researchers. Lynn Catoe, a senior bibliographer for the Library of Congress, reviewed some 1,600 articles and books for the annotated bibliography on UFO phenomena and commented in her introduction: "Many of the UFO reports now being published in the popular press recount alleged incidents that are strikingly similar to demonic possession and psychic phenomena which have long been known to theologians and parapsychologists."[42] An article in the reputable *Flying Saucer Review* reports: "Without citing scores of cases here, it is possible to realize that the features listed above as pertaining to demons crop up again and again in UFO reports."[43] John Keel, a self-described agnostic, suggested that UFO activity may be "actually a staggering cosmic put-on; a joke perpetrated by invisible entities who have always delighted in frightening, confusing and misleading the human race."[44]

Christian researchers generally agree with their secular counterparts that hard-core UFO phenomena are spiritual or psychic in nature. Some Christians see demonic influences. Here's how Bob Larson summarized the situation.

> The descriptions given of UFO occupants usually include grotesque features and oddly shaped structures. They may have enlarged heads, slits for eyes, ethereal forms, and antennae sticking out of their skulls. Most accounts are of beings which bear a distinct resemblance to the "familiar spirits" described in classical spiritualism.
>
> When UFO visitors speak, their message brings neither solace nor information in conformity with God's word. They talk of cosmic awareness and

transcendence to higher spiritual planes. Their discourses never glorify Christ as God and Creator. Instead, contactees are told to prepare for an age of peace that will be ushered in by these unidentified aliens. UFO occupants also encourage participation in a variety of psychic practices: astral projection, psychokinesis, automatic handwriting, clairvoyance, and levitation. Sin, judgment, and the redemptive work of Christ are never mentioned. Their words, their actions, and their appearances betray the concealed satanic origin of these beings.[45]

John Weldon, a Christian, has seen the diabolical purpose behind UFO phenomena as being "to deliberately move significant portions of an entire culture, or world, into acceptance of or involvement in the occult, and a collective alteration in worldview. This is preparatory for and necessary to the events surrounding the rise of the anti-Christ."[46]

Perhaps Weldon was being too alarmist. UFO literature does not encourage widespread depravity and evil, but it does not lead one to be a better Christian, either. It is something a Christian should approach with a great deal of caution.

Shirley MacLaine

In some ways, Shirley MacLaine is the current high priestess of the New Age movement. She has not contributed anything really new to the movement, but she is its popularizer *par excellence*. New Age writer Jon Klimo observed: "Critics and fans alike concur that MacLaine has done more than any other single person in recent times to soften the ground for people to believe and participate in things they once avoided for fear of being thought 'flaky.' "[47] Christian writer James W. Sire claimed that MacLaine herself realized this. She speculated that the reason she had this position was that she did not use her powers in a previous incarnation. Now she must atone for her failure. She wrote:

"Perhaps this was why I had created a role for myself this time around whereby I would be at the forefront of the New Age spiritual movement, heralding *the* giant truth that one individual is his or her own best teacher, and that no other idol or false image should be worshiped or adored because the God we are all seeking lies inside one's self, not outside."[48]

The way she appeared driven to promote New Age concepts reinforced this statement and made a quotation of hers in *Time* seem like false modesty. At the conclusion of the December 7, 1987, cover story, she was quoted as saying: "I'm not the leader of this movement. I'm not the high priestess of New Age concepts. I'm just a human being trying to find some answers about what we're doing here, where we came from and where we're going."[49]

MacLaine liked to talk about life being like a movie you are making for yourself by yourself. "Truth as an objective reality doesn't exist. There's nothing like making a movie to bring home that point, because you can make the truth anything you want it to be."[50]

By 1989, she had written five extremely popular autobiographies with total sales of over eight million copies. The last three were New Age. *Out on a Limb* (Bantam Books, 1983) talked about an intense love affair with a prominent politician and described her close relationship with her friend, David, who led her to explore the mysteries of karma, reincarnation and higher selves in the new metaphysical world. *Dancing in the Light* (Bantam Books, 1985) featured further metaphysical musings.

It's All in the Playing (Bantam Books, 1987) talked about the filming of her television miniseries based on her previous book, *Out on a Limb*. Here's really where fantasy and reality got pretty mixed up. Philosophically, she claimed we are all gods who can create our own reality, and she created a television program starring herself to tell us this. *"It's All in the Playing* is the story of playing God, in which the self— Shirley MacLaine's, that is—acts as the playwright, producer, star and audience in the New Age theater of the absurd," was the way Doug Groothuis began a review of the book in *Christian Research Journal*. "MacLaine's last three books and her countless media appearances," Groothuis continued, "have amounted to a massive endorsement for trance-channeling (mediumship), yoga, reincarnation, past-life regression, psychic abilities, UFO contacts, occult literature and more. And people are buying the message. The nationwide B. Dalton book chain reported that sales of the books on occult topics increased by 95% the week the *Out on a Limb* miniseries aired on ABC (in January, 1987)."[51]

Brooks Alexander was brutal in his review of *Dancing in the Light*. "I've just had one of the most disagreeable experiences of my life," he wrote. "I was not prepared for the incongruous combination of verbal froth and spiritual falsehood that characterizes *Dancing in the Light*. MacLaine treats her audience to a relentless patter of chatty celebrity gossip, interlarded with deep deception. Paying sustained attention to it is like sinking in a sea of poison syrup. I couldn't finish it."[52]

I also had a hard time forcing myself to read MacLaine. She was so chatteringly banal. She talked about very evil things in such a scatterbrained way. Her 1989 book, *Going Within: A Guide for Inner Transformation*,[53] was also lightweight and banal—but popular. Her 1989 videocassette, *Shirley MacLaine's Inner Workout*,[54] proved immediately popular upon its release. Her television miniseries, though relatively popular, was surprisingly lightweight and poorly made. People must have been pretty desperate to have made Shirley MacLaine the leading spokesperson for the New Age movement.

Christians have not been the only ones criticizing MacLaine. Secular critics have also not been that pleased with her. Science writer Martin Gardner called MacLaine's writing "kindergarten metaphysics" and described her miniseries as "pervasive, paranormal poppycock . . . its dialogue unbearably banal."[55] *New Age Journal* reviewer

Dennis Livingston ripped *It's All in the Playing* as "a plodding affair, rife with cliche-ridden characterizations, Day-Glo landscapes, and fortune-cookie wisdom. What MacLaine needs is less from the spirit guides, and more from a ghost writer."[56]

She makes money. Her books have grossed more than $40 million annually. Following the miniseries, she went on a 17-city nationwide tour conducting two-day seminars on "Connecting With the Higher Self." People paid $300 apiece to listen to her. Doug Groothuis estimated this tour earned her $3.8 million.[57]

What the people got for their $300 was New Age pantheism. F. LaGard Smith attended one of the seminars and recorded this conclusion that MacLaine gave to one of her visualization exercises: "Standing before you beneath the tree is the one you have come to seek. Let me introduce you to your Higher Self. Your Higher Self is the one to whom you have been praying. Your Higher Self is God!"[58]

Much of the book *Going Within* revolves around this nationwide tour. She said it was lots of fun. "People came bearing crystals, books, handmade presents, candy, carrot cake, even frankincense and myrrh,"[59] she said, apparently indicating that people were recognizing the divine in her. MacLaine threw away her prepared text and led the people in guided meditations and sharings. Sometimes the energy in the room, she claimed, was so intense that it could actually be seen. As she recounted events, the group's meditations affected circumstances around them. The music from a lively and distracting bar mitzvah next door abruptly ceased after they meditated and water from a break in a main in front of the hotel stopped flowing out in another instance. Unfortunately the water backed up and flooded the basement and knocked out an electrical transformer. "To me this was an example of the power of collective visualization," she wrote. "I was careful, after that, about how I used it."[60]

The book rambled on and on following the basic New Age menu—higher selves and crystals and chakras and meditating. She talked about going to Canada to meditate with the famous Crystal Skull. She extolled tantric sex. She observed the Brazilian channeler, Luis Antonio Gasparetto, as he allegedly became possessed by the spirits of three dead artists and simultaneously painted a Rembrandt with his feet, a Monet with his left hand and a Picasso with his right hand.

She observed Reverend Alex Orbito, a psychic healer from the Philippines, in action as he plunged his hands inside a friend of hers and then inside her own body. She talked about Orbito's hands "gently kneading the skin just below my navel. In about three seconds both his hands were inside my abdomen up to the wrists . . . . I felt no pain—only pressure. There was a great deal of sloshing as blood and guts were rocked from side to side . . . . He extracted more 'negative stress clots' and soon withdrew first his right hand, then his left."[61] The hole closed up and a little blood was wiped off and MacLaine was none the worse for the experience.

Some critics of psychic surgery have explained that the practitioner's hands do not actually penetrate the skin, but the strong pressure makes it seem that they do. The critics also allege that there is a lot of sleight-of-hand trickery in the phenomenon of psychic surgery.

Another chapter in *Going Within* was about Mauricio Panisset, a Brazilian occultist who glows in the dark. The light show MacLaine witnessed began after a period of chanting in a darkened room. "The entire room lit up with light coming out from the solar plexus of his body," MacLaine wrote. "I saw a jagged electrical charge emanate from the center of his torso and flash down his arms, through his hands, and out into the room! George Lucas would have been hard pressed to duplicate such an effect."[62]

The book involved very serious occultism. It was unadulterated New Ageism. There was no objective reality. Everything is created by the mind and can be changed by the mind. You can look to guidance from the superior entity dwelling inside you, like MacLaine's higher self. You are gods. There is no difference between good and evil. There is no death. There is reincarnation. Or, in the alleged higher self's own words from an earlier book, "The God energy is no judge of persons. In fact, there is no judgment involved with life. There is only experience from incarnation to incarnation until the soul realizes its perfection and that it is total love.... Until mankind realizes that there is, in truth, no good and there is, in truth, no evil, there will be no peace."[63]

"Having lost any clear notion of objective reality, Mac-Laine asserts that everything that happens to her is really a reflection of herself," Groothuis observed in his book review. "This is called solipsism. It reduces the universe, as G.K. Chesterton put it, to 'one enormously selfish person.' Shirley speaks much of love, but interpersonal love requires a real other person to be loved. If reality is merely a creation of myself, myself is all there is to love. All altruism then reduces to egoism!"[64]

This ideology can also be extremely cruel. Groothuis noted that, when MacLaine's daughter's acting teacher was burned beyond recognition in a head-on collision, MacLaine wondered: "Why did she choose to die that way?"

Chapter 5

Jeremy P. Tarcher,
Guide to New Age Living,
Volkswagen Ads, *New Age
Catalogue,* Intuitive Development,
Create Your Reality, Transitions,
Spirituality, Free Catalogue,
Electric Tarot

New Age Books, Periodicals

In this chapter, New Agers will have their say. I will quote some New Age enthusiasts talking about the movement from their own perspectives. I will also report on some New Age books and programs that may not have been mentioned elsewhere and I will give more examples of the New Age agenda discussed elsewhere in this book. This chapter is supposed to be a substitute for your visiting a New Age bookstore or attending a New Age fair or lecture.

I am not going to give the appropriate Christian teaching to refute every New Age position mentioned in this chapter. That would take far too long and would be too distracting. This book is written from a Christian perspective. Almost every major New Age idea and program mentioned in this chapter is diametrically opposed to basic Christianity and, of course, some New Age stuff is simply ridiculous. All the main New Age points are discussed and refuted in other chapters. Chapter Fifteen of this book repeats some of the basic Christian teachings on themes of importance to New Agers. For heaven's sake, don't be deceived by the opinions expressed in this chapter.

Jeremy P. Tarcher

Jeremy P. Tarcher is president of a Los Angeles publishing house bearing his name which publishes New Age books. He wrote an article in 1988,[1] contending that the New Age is based on a group of commonly held assumptions "about the place of humanity in the cosmos." These assumptions, he claimed, are a perennial philosophy underlying the tenets of traditional religion. He described this New Age worldview as having four key points.

* The everyday world and our personal consciousness is a manifestation of a larger, divine reality.

* Humans have a suppressed, or hidden, Higher Self that reflects, or is connected to, the divine element of the universe.

* This Higher Self can be awakened and take a central part in the everyday life of the individual.

* This awakening is the purpose or goal of human life.

This process of awakening, Tarcher said, is most commonly called "self-realization, enlightenment, or transformation." This is a profound experience. "Inevitably," he said, "this preliminary self-realization, this connection to new ideas and higher values, is accompanied by a massive shaking up of the individual's traditional perspectives." The new New Ager is ready to try anything. "The media have been accurate in reporting the interest of many New Agers in reincarnation, extraterrestrial contact, crystals, psychic phenomena, channeling, ... but it has totally ignored the core of New Age thought." By focusing on fringe activities instead of the efforts at personal and social transformation, Tarcher said, "the press has reported the carnival sideshow and not the acts in the big tent."

Guide to New Age Living

Florence Graves, editor and associate publisher of *The*

Guide to New Age Living,[2] bemoans in an editorial the propensity of the mass media to label as New Age "everything from 'healing' crystals to progressive business consultants." They seemed more interested in fads than substance. She said that some people are now shunning the term "New Age" because of this.

Graves defined the New Age as "an amorphous cultural transistion in the making (that) has no creed, no dogma, no leaders." She said the *New Age Journal* (parent publication of *The Guide*) was named after a London newspaper founded in the early 1900s, called *New Age.* It published such "forward-looking writers" as Ezra Pound and Upton Sinclair. "That's a tradition we are happy to embrace," Graves said.

"Our *New Age* is committed to bringing you the best of the creative thinking now being done in this diverse and provocative field. So if you want to explore alternative ways of living, if you want to redefine the boundaries of human potential and consciousness, we think you'll find this source book and our magazine useful tools."

The Guide has pages and pages of ads and resource listings grouped under such headings as health, peace groups, learning centers, books, music and video, travel and socially conscious investing.

Volkswagen Ads

As a public service, Volkswagen published a series of statements from "prominent figures in American culture" as part of their automobile ads. The statements were in the form of letters to people living 100 years from now. Guess what? Some were very New Agey.

Wayne W. Dyer, described as "one of our most popular philosophers," began by asking the people of 2088, "Have you evolved into a higher human being than those of us on earth in 1988?" He explained that in 1988 philosophers were awakening to the idea that "the development of a higher human being is a process involving the understanding that you see what you believe, rather than you believe what you see." Dyer expressed his hope that this subjectivist approach would lead to the development of a higher human being. He also hoped that wars and conflicts would have ceased and that all humanity would be working together harmonious-ly.[3]

In his letter to the people of 2088, Robert Jarvik, inventor of an artificial heart, expressed the hope that "someday humans will realize that we are a part of nature and not separate from it. We have no more basic rights than viruses, other than those that we create for ourselves through our intellect and our compassion." Extolling human creativity, he urged those in the future to "work on the hardest, most important problem to which your talents apply. And do it for yourself. Work for the feeling that you are alive and that you are part of it all."[4]

New Age Catalogue

To be informed on the New Age, you don't need to visit occult bookstores or New Age sections of conventional bookstores and spend hours taking copious notes on the wares offered for sale. The editors of *Body, Mind and Spirit* magazine did much of this work for us. Their book, *The New Age Catalogue*,[5] listed hundreds and hundreds of items, span-ning most of the New Age spectrum. The oversized book had 244 pages and many individual pages featured five or more items.

In his Introduction to the catalogue, Paul Zuromski, edi-tor and publisher of *Body, Mind and Spirit*, waxed eloquent about the age we live in.

> Basic metaphysics says that the Earth plane is a wonderfully instructive school. What we perceive in this reality is just illusion created by each one of us for the grand and important purpose of learn-ing.
>
> Spirit entities, the Bible, Nostradamus, Ruth Mont-gomery's spirit guides and virtually any other

New Age-conscious person you talk to says this
Earth plane is currently undergoing profound
changes . . . .

Assuming that we do create this plane of reality,
then it follows that we are also creating these
changes. We need to be aware of our role in creation, since the seeds of change are our individual
efforts. Consciousness is being raised. Awareness
is being heightened . . . .

The final choices are up to you, as they should be.[6]

I will resist the temptation to start talking about objective reality and God as Creator and the difference between
right and wrong. Also, where in the Bible does it predict that
the 20th century will see profound changes in the "Earth
plane"? As I said in the beginning of this chapter, much of
New Age thought is diametrically opposed to Christian
teaching.

Intuitive Development

The New Age Catalogue was divided into eight sections,
the first being "Intuitive Development." The first 10 pages—
remember, these were big catalogue pages—were devoted
to channeling. We considered this subject in Chapter Three.
Also mentioned was *A Course in Miracles*, which we will
discuss in Chapter Nine.

Other channeled works in the catalogue, not mentioned
in Chapter Three, included material from Ra, an "ancient
astronaut." Elwood Babbitt, "the medium from Massachu-
setts," had a number of audio tapes available. The catalogue
claimed that "for many years Babbitt has been channeling
entities like Mark Twain, Einstein, Wordsworth, Jesus
Christ and Vishnu." There were magazines devoted entirely
to channeling and many books of Ruth Montgomery were
featured. Her spirit guides communicate through automatic
writing.

Next in our exploration of "Intuitive Development," we

had seven pages on "Psychic Functioning." This included information on a psychic encyclopedia and a 103-year-old psychic-research society and 12 cassette tapes for $98.95 that included 33 guided meditations. "Jonathan Parker," the catalogue stated, "guides the listener from understanding your inner self to developing intuitive abilities, removing success blocks, aura reading, the nature of God, past and future lives, mental mastery and reaching levels of love and tranquillity and control in life."[7]

Up to page 16. We must press on. There were books on chakras and auras and crystals. The subsection on divination gave some tips "for sharpening your intuition." You were advised to keep a deck of Tarot cards readily accessible. "When the telephone rings, cut the cards and ask yourself, who is it and what is the message?" Numerology can also be utilized. "Notice the number of your parking stall. Keep it in mind as a clue to the theme of what you will experience after parking the car,"[8] *The Metaphysical Handbook* advised.

Next were books on astrology and horoscopes and more on numerology. "Numerologists believe that we are born at a certain date, hour and minute not merely by chance, but in order to learn important lessons and to perform specific tasks during our lifetimes and that the conditions and vibrations prevailing at the precise moment of our birth must be favorable if we are to fulfill our mission in life," claimed *The Numerology Workbook*. "Some also believe that the transmigration of souls and the possibility of reincarnation play an important role in their philosophy of life."[9]

There were books on Tarot cards, palmistry, graphology, dowsing, runes, *I-Ching* and ancient Egyptian magic.

Create Your Reality

The second section, "Create Your Reality," opened with books by Shirley MacLaine that we discussed in Chapter Four. Ten other books were mentioned in this subsection, "Transformational Journeys."

The journeys were very diverse. A syndicated columnist became a stenographer for spirit guides. A magician became a demonstrator of firewalking. Two physicians became aware of life. A woman shared her magic-induced dreams. The books were all breathlessly described as though these people had really discovered something important.

The subsection on "Self-Help" focused on a key element of New Age thinking—you are the creator. You can change your circumstances and your destiny. You are in charge. Sounds great, doesn't it? Here are some quotes.

> The body is the servant of the mind. It obeys the operations of the mind, whether they be deliberately chosen or automatically expressed. At the bidding of unhealthy thoughts the body sinks rapidly into disease and decay; at the command of glad and beautiful thoughts it becomes clothed with youthfulness and beauty.[10]

(Tell that to someone dying of cancer!)

> You should be able to manifest almost anything you are affirming within 21 days . . . . You should be able to feel the change. If the results aren't happening, it is only because you are affirming something else on a deeper, perhaps less conscious, level which is creating something contradictory to what you are affirming consciously.[11]

(If wishes were horses . . . .)

> Everyone has the potential to create one's own reality, so if you are not happy with the way it is, what mind has created, mind can change.[12]

(I'm dreaming of a condo by a golf course, but . . . .)

What is one way you can create your reality? Through meditation, of course. The catalogue featured a general guidebook on meditation and a book on how to meditate by counting your breathing. Another book had diagrams about how you should sit or lie to meditate. Some meditation centers were listed. Fabulous results were promised for those who listened to a cassette of *Astral Sounds*.

> Nearly all of the test participants reported entering into a natural deep rest where their body healed and was rejuvenated with additional energy and strength, where their stress, anxiety and worries disappeared while their physical pain was significantly reduced or vanished altogether. Some hallucinated beautifully, seeing colors, symbols, lights and faces pass before them as if in some magnificent and colorful parade. All test participants reported feeling better physically and emotionally after using the *Astral Sounds* tape cassette.[13]

Another way to create your reality is to utilize your dreams. "Properly used," Joan Windsor of Williamsburg, Vir., said, working with dreams "has the power to provide profitable business tips, comment on the body's physical condition, suggest treatment for its imbalances, enhance intuitive development, and teach us lessons in spirituality which inevitably culminate in soul evolvement."[14]

Then came astral projections and out-of-body experiences. The book *Astral Travel* described the practice as an improvement over Christianity.

> We will also teach you to travel into other realms— realms and realities beyond the known cosmos, realms impossible to reach without this training. You can bring back knowledge about the future and about other ways that will be of inestimable benefit to you in your present life.

> With the aid of the astral Little People (for little people really do exist) you will become able to find that proverbial pot of gold at the end of the rainbow. Age, upbringing, education—all totally irrelevant. Although we have found that it is slightly more difficult for a white Christian to accomplish

all that others can, this difficulty is so easily overcome by the institute's techniques as to be almost
nonexistent. If you devote a few of those Sundays
you would normally spend in church to the practice of these techniques, you will find that you can
accomplish just as much as any other citizen of the
world.[15]

(Does the extra work with the white Christian involve the
Christian giving up the faith? Who are these astral Little
People anyhow?)

"The thought forms of science and metaphysics are
merging into new theories of human potential," the editors
of the catalogue said in introducing a subsection on the
search for consciousness. "Science is discovering that our
reality is not objective and concrete but subjective and relevant to the perspective of the viewer. New Age metaphysical
literature is based on the premise that we create our own
reality."[16]

(But do the authors and publishers of these books expect
to be paid in hard-earned money or can we only *imagine* that
we are paying for the books, which they will then be happy
to forward to us?)

Many books were listed in this section on such subjects as
transpersonal dimensions in psychology, consciousness and
quantum physics, overcoming obstacles to human potential
and how to find a soulmate. There were books on rebirthing,
recharging the brain, flotation tanks, creativity and using
both sides of the brain. There was also a list of schools,
institutes and retreats.

Transitions

The third section of the catalogue was about life transitions such as birth and death. Cai Inderhill talked about birth
and death being similar because they both "involve a major
shift of energies into or out of a physical body."[17] There were
books on conscious conception, the life of an unborn child,
birthing and rebirthing. Then the section shifted to the other

end of the life cycle, to near-death experiences, death and reincarnation. (See Chapter Three.)

There were books in the catalogue on coping with the death of a loved one, euthanasia, reincarnation and the Tibetan tradition of death. We had books on "Walk-ins." What are "Walk-ins"? Ruth Montgomery tells us.

> The Guides, those mysterious pen-pals who communicate with me through automatic writing, describe Walk-ins as high-minded entities from the spirit plane who are permitted under certain circumstances to take over the unwanted bodies of other human beings . . . .
>
> The displaced Walk-out must be one who desperately wishes to depart, or who because of a clinical death or near-death experience is unable to keep his/her body alive. The Walk-in, coming directly from the spirit plane, is then able to re-energize the failing body, and because of high idealism and enthusiasm the personality of the "new" occupant often astounds friends and family members who had become accustomed to the discouraged, ineffectual mannerism of the body's original occupant.[18]

In her books, Montgomery identified the following as among the Walk-ins: Moses, Christ, Lincoln, Gandhi, Anwar Sadat and Dick Sutphen.

Spirituality

This catalogue treated Christianity as a second-rate religion at best. The section on spirituality opened by quoting the Dalai Lama. Then we had two pages, allegedly about Christianity. The first page mentioned three works, all dictated by spirit entities and all contrary to basic Christian teaching. These were books by Alice Bailey and Edgar Cayce and *A Course in Miracles*. The top of the second page listed three authentically Christian books on spirituality. The bottom of the page talked about *The Christ Book* by Christopher Hills. "In this book," the catalogue said, "Christopher Hills talks with his students about the true meanings of many of Christ's mysterious parables and miracles. Hills's perspective has a certain air of truth and relevance about it in light of present New Age philosophy and scientific documentation of paranormal experiences and yogic mastery."[19]

So much for traditional Christianity.

There were pages and pages in the catalogue on Hinduism, Zen Buddhism, Taoism, the *Kabbalah*, Sufism, yoga and spiritualism. "British spiritualism is roughly divided into two camps: those who accept the leadership of Jesus Christ and the majority who maintain that he was an ordinary mortal displaying mediumistic gifts,"[20] wrote Tony Ortzen, the editor of *Psychic News*, London.

There were books on Native American spirituality, women's spirituality and witchcraft. There was a notice that Our Lady of Enchantment Seminary of Wicca in Nashua, New Hampshire, offered a complete selection of courses in witchcraft, magic and the occult arts.[21] (See Chapter Eight.)

The New Age Catalogue also had sections on holistic health, herbology, massage and yoga. It also considered New Age lifestyles and planetary concerns. You name it, they had it.

Free Catalogue

If you were fortunate enough to live in the San Francisco Bay area, you didn't have to pay $15 for *The New Age Catalogue*. You could get a 127-page free catalogue entitled, *Common Ground: Resources for Personal Transformation*.[22] People with various New Age products and services bought descriptive ads in the publication. There were about eight ads per page. Here are selections from ads in the "Psychic Arts and Intuitive Sciences" section. (Italics have been added.)

> *Classes in faery tradition witchcraft* . . . meditation, purification, internal balancing, guided fantasy, energy work, the use of magical tools, operative magic, scrying, divine possession and ritual (p. 67).

Channeled healings ($65 an hour). Through light channeling, we raise the frequency of the body to rapidly burn off karma, release negativity, and transform raw emotional energy such as: fear into personal power, anger into creative self-expression, confusion into clarity of thought, and sadness into enthusiasm for life (p. 69).

Déjà Vu Hotline is a psychic referral service . . . . Among the types of readings available are: animal, astrology, aura, baby beings, birth, body weight, business, career, creativity, family, female, future, Kundalini, love life, male, money, numerology, nurses and health professionals, nutrition, palm, past life, pet, professional teachers, relationship, religious past lives, runes, spirit guides, Tarot, travel, voice, wedding, wellness, women over 40, women in the workplace (p. 69).

Since childhood I have had a *unique ability to time-travel,* journeying vividly into other lifetimes. As your guide, I can help you travel safely "between the worlds" into other lifetimes or shamanic states of consciousness (p. 71).

Humor relations consultant and intuitive counselor. I help you talk with your Higher Clown, the one who really knows what's going on and thinks it's funny. When you're centered in your sense of humor, you're in the position of greatest power and flexibility for making changes in your life (p. 71).

Medical astrology uses the horoscope for diagnosis and preventive medicine . . . . This includes diet, supplements, herbs, homeopathic remedies, flower essences, and crystals and gems as well as referrals for various types of body work and energy balancing (p. 73).

The Stellar Foundation was established to help individuals *attain a higher vibratory frequency* in their personal energy spheres . . . . Each session includes the transference of magnetic and spiritual energies into the electro-magnetic field interpenetrating and surrounding the physical body. The trance channeling of these higher light frequencies balance[s] the existing disturbances and initiate[s] the self-healing processes. Spiritual counseling follows each session (p. 76).

Communication with animals on all levels—physical, mental, emotional, spiritual—to help achieve a more ideal relationship, handle upsets and behavior problems and speed recovery from illness and injury (p. 77).

I hope you are having fun reading these ads. (In some ways, they are pretty pathetic.) Here are some more examples from the free catalogue, this time from the section on "Spiritual Practices."

The Aquarian Foundation is the most widely-based progressive New Age church worshipping Almighty God . . . . We have *Holy Communion seances* every Sunday afternoon at 3 p.m. Spiritual psychic readings demonstrated at all 11 a.m. public Sunday worship services (p. 101).

Mendocino Sufi camp . . . . *As we cosmically channel the exact color of our past life regression crystals,* there still exists a need to renew the basic love, harmony and beauty which initially inspired us (p. 104).

At the Union Temple of Isis, *we love and serve Mother Nature,* whom we recognize as the supreme power in the universe. Public services occur at solstice, equinox, cross-quarter and full moon points . . . . Dark moon circles for women only (p. 107).

Electric Tarot

We don't want to leave this chapter without mentioning a few more items of New Age nonsense. *The Llewellyn New Times* lets us in on how anybody can do Tarot divinations. Use the computer software of "The Electric Tarot." Press a key and the cards are shuffled. Press another key and a 10-card Celtic cross spread is laid out. An experienced Tarot reader, the ad told us, can read the cards. The tyro, however, needs only to press one key after another to get "an accurate, in-depth interpretation for each card." That's not all. By pressing another key, "the computer interprets all of the cards and synthesizes them in a complete, coherent, overall reading."[23] The program is supposed to be a big hit at psychic fairs.

The New Age Journal[24] also featured some unusual ads. There was a Guardian Angel doll and a videocassette of Mother Teresa and a taped recording to "turbocharge your brain." Another tape was designed to induce an altered state of consciousness and "intensify psychic performance." You could get hypnotized at home with videocassettes by Dick Sutphen.

Chapter  6

John Todd, Lord Maitreya,
Constance Cumbey,
Following Cumbey,
Dave Hunt, Marilyn Ferguson,
No Conspiracy

Conspiracy Theory

Some writers claim that the New Age movement is a monumental conspiracy. In some secret office someplace, someone with vast sums of money and a dedicated cadre of devotees is orchestrating the whole panoramic New Age movement. Is this true? We will start by talking about a pre-New Age conspiracy theory, one advocated by John Todd. It says something about how gullible Christians can be.

John Todd

In the September, 1978, *Spiritual Counterfeits Project Newsletter*,[1] David Fetcho and Brooks Alexander responded to a number of inquiries by writing an article on John Todd. Todd claimed to have been a "grand druid" of witchcraft and a member of the highest council of the "Illuminati" prior to his conversion to Christ in 1972. The "Illuminati" are allegedly a band of illuminated or enlightened persons, skilled in occult arts, who are trying to gain control over the world through the manipulation of political and fiscal events. (Whether or not they actually exist is another question.)

Fetcho and Alexander talked about a UPI story that appeared in June, 1978, with the headline: "Zionsville Baptists Prepare for Final War With Witches." It was about the effect of Todd's alarmist message on a Baptist church in Zionsville, Ind. According to the story, Todd had convinced the pastor and the congregation of the small church to lay in up to a year's supply of food because of a coming shutdown of all food delivery in the United States. He also urged them to arm themselves with guns in order to defend themselves during the coming witches' uprising.

"Both the fervor of Todd's oratory and his seeming command of minute esoteric data create the impression of a man who has truly been on the 'inside' of some vast conspiracy and has escaped to warn the unsuspecting world," Fetcho and Alexander commented. "Indeed, he claims to be disclosing *the* conspiracy which ties together all the disparate forms of evil in the world into one over-arching plan being worked out by an ultrasecret society of witches bent on taking over the world and ushering in the reign of Antichrist. In Todd's schema, virtually everything that happens of political, social, economic, or spiritual significance—even within the church—has been purposefully engineered by the Illuminati."[2]

The two cofounders of the Spiritual Counterfeits Project went on to list a number of criticisms of Todd and his message. Many of the allegations in Todd's talks were demonstrably untrue. For an alleged former high leader of witchcraft, Todd sometimes confused terminology and mishandled concepts that any witch should know. Todd often attacked other Christian leaders who were not as fundamentalist as he. He also painted a world picture in which Satan is in control, not God.

"Biblically speaking, there is no doubt that the Adversary is constructing a 'conspiracy' against God and humanity at many levels," Fetcho and Alexander wrote in conclusion. "However, to claim that this effort is centralized under the banner of any single group or movement is rash, to say the least. . . . It is common for recent converts to identify their previous guru as *the* Antichrist. It may well be that Todd is giving an account, accurate or embellished, of teaching he actually received through his involvement in some occult group. The real question is the extent to which that teaching corresponds to objective reality, and in this case it would seem to be questionable indeed."[3]

A few years later, a New Age conspiracy theory arose.

Lord Maitreya

Readers of the *Los Angeles Times* and 17 other newspapers worldwide were no doubt startled to read a full-page ad April 25, 1982, with this headline: "The world has had enough . . . of hunger, injustice, war. In answer to our call for help, as World Teacher for all humanity, THE CHRIST IS NOW HERE."

(OK, you got my attention; now whom are you talking about?) "Who Is the Christ?," a subhead asked. "Throughout history, humanity's evolution has been guided by a group of enlightened men, the Masters of Wisdom. They have remained largely in the remote desert and mountain places of earth, working mainly through their disciples who live openly in the world. The message of the Christ's reappearance has been given primarily by such a disciple trained for his task for over 20 years. At the center of the 'Spiritual Hierarchy' stands the World Teacher, *Lord Maitreya*, known by Christians as the *Christ*. And as Christians await the Second Coming, so the Jews await the *Messiah*, the Buddhists the *fifth Buddha*, the Moslims [sic] the *Imam Mahdi*, and the Hindus await *Krishna*. These are all names for one individual. His presence in the world guarantees there will be no third World War."[4]

Four organizations were listed as sponsors of the ad: Tara Center, North Hollywood, Calif.; Tara Center, New York; Tara Press, London; Information Center, Amsterdam. "Since July, 1977," the ad continued, "the Christ has been emerging as a spokesman for a group or community in a well-known modern country . . . . We will recognize him by his extraordinary spiritual potency, the universality of his viewpoint, and his love for all humanity . . . . He has not yet declared his true status, and his location is known to only a very few disciples. One of these has announced that soon the Christ will acknowledge his identity and *within the next two months* will speak to humanity through a worldwide television and radio broadcast. His message will be heard inwardly, telepathically, by all people in their own language. From that time, with his help, we will build a new world."

This was certainly an extraordinary claim. There has been one big problem, however. It's been many years since this ad appeared, but Lord Maitreya has yet to show up.

A week later, the Church by the Sea, Huntington Beach, Calif., and Media Spotlight took out another full-page ad in the *Los Angeles Times*. It ran under this headline: "Anti-Christ is now here and the world has had enough of false prophets! In answer to your need for truth, as Savior for all humanity, the true Christ has always been here."[5]

Shortly after the first ad appeared, a spokesman for Lord Maitreya stepped forward. He was Benjamin Creme, the founder of the Tara Center. A January, 1982, Tara Center newsletter identified him as a 58-year-old Scot, an artist by profession, who was interested in esoteric studies since his youth. The newsletter said that in 1959 he received a telepathic message from a member of the Spiritual Hierarchy giving him to understand that Christ was about to return and Creme would have a part in it. In 1975, the newsletter said, Creme was given the mission of announcing publicly the coming of Maitreya.

According to a 1982 *Media Spotlight Special Report*, Creme gave a press conference at the Ambassador Hotel in Los Angeles on May 14, 1982, about three weeks after the ad appeared. At that time, he revealed that Maitreya was living in the Indo-Pakistani community of London, though he did not give his name. He said Maitreya has been living in a totally indestructible body in the Himalayas for the past

3,000 years. In response to a question, Creme said that an assassin's bullet would not harm Maitreya. After he has made his appearance, Creme said, Maitreya will work with extremely high-level contacts and set up a new United Nations agency to deal with the problem of redistribution of resources. He will also take over governance of the Christian church by taking over the throne of St. Peter in Rome. The current pope will meekly step aside and assist him. At least that's what Creme said will happen.

In his writings, Creme has said that Maitreya took over the body of Jesus of Nazareth the last three years of his life and was the Christ. Creme has claimed that some Roman Catholic leaders have invited him to speak about Maitreya and have welcomed his message. He also indicated that Maitreya would introduce some sort of benign nuclear power that would answer the world's energy needs.

At his May 14 press conference, Creme said that Maitreya would make his appearance and address the assembled journalists in London in about a week. When Maitreya has declared himself as the Christ to the world, Creme said, "hundreds of thousands of spontaneous, apparently miraculous cures will take place."[6] Not only Maitreya, but also the 12 special disciples of Maitreya, will be able to raise the dead, make the lame walk and make the blind see.

This should prove very interesting! Where is this guy, Maitreya, anyhow?

Constance Cumbey

Though Lord Maitreya has yet to appear, the ads talking about him spurred Constance E. Cumbey to action. A Detroit trial lawyer and a member of a Baptist church, she suspended her law practice in June, 1982, to work full-time exposing the dangers of the New Age movement. In June, 1982, she gave a series of interviews to the Southwest Radio Church, Oklahoma City. Initially, these interviews were about Lord Maitreya and Benjamin Creme, but she expanded the subject to comment on Marilyn Ferguson's book,

The Aquarian Conspiracy, and on her own ideas on the world-wide New Age movement. These eight broadcasts were aired across the United States and later printed in booklet form. The Southwest Radio Church released a second series of interviews with her not long thereafter. That started Cumbey on a tireless series of speeches and interviews in churches and on radio and television. Her book, *The Hidden Dangers of the Rainbow,* appeared in 1983 and a second, *A Planned Deception,* appeared in 1985.[7]

The large-type introduction to her first book stated her basic thesis: "It is the contention of this writer that for the first time in history there is a viable movement—the New Age Movement—that truly meets all the scriptural require-ments for the anti-Christ and the political movement that will bring him on the world scene. It is further the position of the writer that this most likely is the great apostasy or 'falling away' spoken of by the Apostle Paul and that the anti-Christ's appearance could be a very real event in our imme-diate future."[8]

There was good news and bad news, from the Christian perspective, about Cumbey's crusade. The good news was that she was solidly on the side of the biblical Jesus Christ and she pointed out many problems and dangers connected with the rapidly growing New Age movement. The bad news was that she overstated the conspiracy elements in the New Age and that she was oversensitive to criticism from other Christians.

Two of the best critiques of Cumbey were a 1988 leaflet by Eric Pement (an updating of his 1983 article) and 1987 reviews of both her books by Elliot Miller.[9] Pement said that on February 11, 1983, he interviewed Cumbey by phone for one and a half hours and that he asked her if the New Age movement is "a conspiracy involving thousands of persons, all plotting to take over the world for the same person, intelligently acting in concert?" Her reply: "It is absolutely that!"[10]

According to Pement's analysis, Cumbey

... says the conspiracy is a network of all the cults, of political and humanitarian organizations, and of isolated groups. The movement's directives are literally called "the Plan," articulated by Alice Bailey in the 1930s; now they come from Lucis Trust in New York (custodian of Bailey's writings). The conspiracy allegedly follows Bailey "like a recipe." The Antichrist who is to come is Lord Maitreya, a deity venerated by certain Buddhists and occultists, whom Cumbey has suggested is now incarnate (via demon possession). When he is announced, all the world will have to undergo a Luciferic initiation and receive his mark. The vehicle which is coordinating the efforts to build the one-world government is Planetary Citizens (a New York-based corporation dedicated to creating a new global society).[11]

She declared that Planetary Citizens had established a timetable for taking over the world on June 21, 1983. Cumbey also claimed that the same sinister forces that orchestrated the rise of the Nazis were behind the New Age movement.

A modicum of common sense can show a perceptive Christian that Cumbey's basic thesis is false. The New Age movement is definitely not well organized. Almost every leading figure is a thorough individualist. Nobody is following orders. Everybody is doing his or her own thing. Even people who believe in Ascended Masters or the Spiritual Hierarchy have differing ideas about who these entities are and who their favorite earthly disciples are. The New Age movement is very freewheeling; it is not highly structured. These observations can be easily documented; Cumbey's allegations cannot. Furthermore, in actual fact, the Lucis Trust and Alice Bailey's writings have had very little influence in the highly energized New Age movement.

"For the New Age movement to be coldly orchestrating major developments on every level of society and capable of an imminent world takeover, it would have to be almost omnipotent and omnipresent!," Miller wrote in his book review. "In short, we would no longer be talking about a *movement* but a conspiracy in the most subversive and menacing senses of the word."[12]

This menacing conspiracy was exactly what Cumbey feared. If you really believe in this conspiracy, then persons who do not share your beliefs—including otherwise respected Christian writers—are also part of the conspiracy. They have sold out to the Antichrist. New Age writers who talk about a loosely knit movement are obviously trying to deceive the person who "knows" there is a conspiracy. Cumbey could trust no one except persons who accepted her conspiracy theory.

Pement also challenged some other allegations Cumbey made.

*Cumbey has difficulty identifying true New Age groups. In spite of her contention, it is hard to identify such cults as The Way International, the Children of God and the Unification Church as New Age. They are pseudo-Christian cults, but not New Age.

* New Age spokesman David Spangler, a board member of Planetary Citizens, has written that we must take a Luciferic initiation if we wish to enter the New Age.[13] "It is not true," Pement observed, "that this single statement can be logically extended to cover all New Age writers, and that it is in fact an overriding New Age goal. Though Spangler's definition of a 'Luciferic initiation' is 100 percent anti-Christian, it has nothing to do with taking a mark on one's hand, or a formal ceremony of Satan worship, as Cumbey suggested."[14]

* It is true that Alice Bailey (or her familiar spirit) wrote that the United Nations might use nuclear weapons to punish "aggressive action" by political or religious groups "such as the Church of Rome."[15] That does not mean that any individual or group today is seriously considering this or has the nuclear weapons to carry it out.

*It is also technically not possible to project a holographic laser light show off a satellite to fake the return of Christ as Cumbey fears.

Cumbey also had a tendency to attack as New Age any Christian writer who used such New Age buzzwords as "global village," "holistic" or "paradigm." Her fiercest wrath was reserved for any Christian apologist who happened to disagree with her conspiracy theory. She has repeatedly and unfairly attacked Walter Martin and the Christian Research Institute, for example. They have prepared a five-page response to her charges.[16]

According to a Religious News Service report at the end of 1988, Cumbey had returned to the practice of law. According to *Christianity Today*, she was still available for radio interviews and speaking engagements on the New Age movement.[17]

Following Cumbey

In 1988, a 32-page booklet was published that was warmly received by many segments of the charismatic renewal because the author was a popular charismatic writer, M. Basilea Schlink, a West German Lutheran nun. Unfortunately, her book was based almost entirely on Constance Cumbey's work and was therefore seriously flawed. It is hard to say whether the booklet did more harm than good.

Schlink stated in the beginning who her principal source was. "The spectrum of the New Age Movement is so vast that only the most essential points can be highlighted here," Schlink wrote. "A good source of information about the background and dangers of the New Age Movement is Constance Cumbey's book, *The Hidden Dangers of the Rainbow*, to which I shall mainly refer."[18] Eleven of 13 notes in Schlink's booklet were from Cumbey's book.

Another writer continuing to spread Cumbey's alarmist message is Texe Marrs, a retired U.S. Air Force officer turned Christian apologist. Marrs's book, *Dark Secrets of the New Age*, was "a less controversial but nonetheless almost exact reproduction of Cumbey's original thesis,"[19] according to a review of Cumbey's books by Elliot Miller.

"In the pages of this revealing new book, the secret 'plan' of the New Age movement is exposed for the first time in startling detail," proclaimed the back cover of *Dark Secrets of the New Age.* "Basing the book on an in-depth investigation of the movement, author Texe Marrs includes over 600 actual quotes from New Age leaders which unveil their 'plan' for establishing a New Age messiah to lead a one-world religion and a global government. As part of the 'plan,' the movement intends to wage a total spiritual war against Christian believers. Their ultimate goal? To eliminate every vestige of Christianity."[20]

Marrs was no less melodramatic in his presentation. "What I discovered staggers the imagination," he wrote in the preface to *Dark Secrets.* "The New Age movement has undeniably taken on the definite form of a religion, complete with an agreed-upon body of doctrine, printed scripture, a pattern of worship and ritual, a functioning group of ministers and lay leaders, and an effective outreach program carried out by an active core of proselytizing believers." This New Age religion has been developed according to a New Age plan which was "designed by none other than the master of deceit, Satan himself," Marrs said, adding that the first priority for those involved in carrying out the plan was "the subversion and conquest of Christianity."[21]

He didn't think Christians would give much resistance. "The plan of the New Age is to take over every Christian church and every Jewish temple [sic] in the world and to turn these great and small architectural structures into centers for the New Age world religion. This is an absolute fact," Marrs stated boldly. "New Age leaders are convinced that they will vanquish and destroy the Christian churches of America and the West *without so much as a whisper of protest* from the tens of millions of Christians in those churches."[22] As usual, he failed to produce any sort of reasonable documentation or argumentation to back up these melodramatic assertions.

Marrs continued to let his imagination run riot in his book, *Mystery Mark of the New Age: Satan's Design for World Domination.* "Satan intends to give his mark to every man, woman, and child on the face of the planet Earth," Marrs warned. "If you take his mark, he will own your own mind, your body, your spirit. He will be your father. And there will be no escape, no way out. You *will* be damned."[23]

In his 287-page book, Marrs never really said what this mark would be. It may be one of the symbols like a pentagram or a twisted cross that occultists use. Whatever it will be, Marrs expected it to be introduced with lots of flair. "The mass initiation ceremonies will be full of pageantry and pomp. They will undoubtedly be colorful sound-and-light spectaculars, rivaling the most gaudy of today's satanic rock concerts. Demonic tongues will be in evidence as the crowds work themselves into feverish ecstasy. Satanic symbols will be prominently displayed on the altar and walls, and celebrants will be expected to visualize and focus all their mental energies on these symbols."[24] Marrs speculated that human sacrifices may be offered at this time.

Marrs also speculated that between 1.5 billion and 2.5 billion men, women and children will be killed—most of these, presumably, Christians.[25] "The New Age teaches that the removal and physical destruction of all Christians will be a *holy act.* This is carefully and elaborately explained in a key New Age bible called The Keys of Enoch."[26] Marrs explained that this book was first published in 1978 by a group calling itself the Academy of Future Science. (In all the books and articles I have read on the New Age, I never found another reference to the book or the organization.)

From promotional materials I received in 1989, Marrs and his wife, Wanda, are cofounders of the Association to Rescue Kids, Living Truth Ministries and Living Truth Publishers, all of Austin, Texas. They are continuing to crank out sensationalist materials, including:

* *Ravaged by the New Age: Satan's Plan to Destroy Our Kids,* a book which is touted as unmasking "in startling detail the

shocking plan of New Age leaders to bring our children into bondage."

* Three other books: *Mega Forces: Signs and Wonders of the Coming Chaos, Texe Marrs's Book of New Age Cults and Religions* and Wanda Marrs's *New Age Lies to Women.*

* A two-hour videocassette and two audiocassettes—all on the New Age.

I do not find Marrs to be credible. I do not believe that he has adduced any real evidence of a conspiracy. Many of his quotations are obviously taken out of context. Many of the New Agers he cites are obscure and not influential. Furthermore, there is no evidence that New Agers have any sort of an armed force to carry out their designs. Their ideas are very dangerous, but they are not seeking to gain their ends through physical force. I think Marrs was primarily out to make a buck off the illogical fears of some Christians.

Other writers, however, also believe in the New Age conspiracy theory. Russell Chandler reported that Elissa Lindsey McClain, a former New Ager turned fundamentalist Christian, spoke of a "world 'plan' by New Age 'Wise Persons'" as being "practically identical to Adolph [sic] Hitler's SS Occult Bureau in Germany on which Nazism was founded."[27] She attributed this information to Constance Cumbey, who wrote the introduction to her book, *Rest From the Quest,* and to Dave Hunt, who laid out his conspiracy theories in *The Seduction of Christianity, Beyond Seduction* and *Peace, Prosperity and the Coming Holocaust* as well as other books.

"The trouble with these books, from a journalistic perspective," wrote Chandler, "is that the research, while extensive, lacks support from incontrovertible evidence. Facts are mishandled, claims are undocumented, conclusions are biased, and logic is flawed at vital connection points. That is not to say that all—or even nearly all—of the assertions are untrue. But they are often tied to unprovable assumptions as well as careless inferences."[28]

Dave Hunt

Dave Hunt has promoted an apocalyptic view of the New Age movement. "In the following pages, whenever we use the term 'New Age' we are referring to the 'great delusion' that the Bible warns will sweep the world in the 'last days' and cause humanity to worship the Antichrist," Hunt said in a book he wrote with T.A. McMahon, *The Seduction of Christianity*. "We are also warned in Scripture that many people who call themselves Christians will succumb to this deception and that a great apostasy will occur prior to the return of Jesus Christ; the delusion will sweep through the professing church as well as secular society."[29]

Later on in the same book, Hunt and McMahon stated: "There can be little doubt that we are in the midst of an unprecedented revival of sorcery worldwide that is deeply affecting not only every level and sector of modern society, but the church as well. Known as the New Age, holistic, human potential, or consciousness movements, at its heart is what anthropologists now call shamanism, which is simply the old occultism made to sound native, natural, Earth, and thus wholesome.... The same delusion that is preparing the world for the Antichrist is now seducing Christianity itself."[30]

What is this sorcery that is seducing Christianity? Hunt and McMahon defined it this way: "In the following pages, when we use that word [sorcery] our intended meaning will be: any attempt to manipulate reality—internal, external, past, present, or future—by various mind-over-matter techniques that run the gamut from alchemy and astrology to positive/possibility teaching."[31] This is a very broad definition.

Hunt continued his end-time warnings in the book he wrote as a sequel to *The Seduction of Christianity*, called *Beyond Seduction*. "The 'New Age' shamanism that secular society has embraced—especially its Hindu and Buddhist forms—is also powerfully seducing the church," Hunt charged. "Since the publication of *Seduction*, the apostasy which the book warned about and the popular delusions sweeping the church have not abated."[32]

In two earlier works, Hunt also promoted his conspiracy theory. In 1980, Marilyn Ferguson had come out with the very popular pro-New Age book, *The Aquarian Conspiracy*. In 1981, Hunt commented on her book: "Such a 'conspiracy' does indeed exist. The humans involved are sincere when they call it 'spontaneous and leaderless.' But it is actually a deliberate, carefully engineered program that is directed by a mastermind. The conspirators are not humans, but demons."[33] (This is somewhat ambiguous. Of course, Satan has a diabolical master plan, but are there any human agents working together in a worldwide conspiracy? That is the question we are considering in this chapter.)

A 1983 book by Hunt came up with a financial and political twist to the conspiracy theory. He claimed there existed

> . . . a conspiracy among top political leaders in Washington to betray America's national interests. These men, all members or former members of the Trilateral Commission and/or Council on Foreign Relations, are said to be working hand in glove with certain highly placed communist leaders in an international conspiracy to bring about a world government. Stretching from Washington to London, Paris, Bonn, Moscow and Tokyo, this mysterious web of intrigue is alleged to include the wealthiest families in the world. Names like Krupp, Rothschild and Rockefeller are mentioned along with the allegation that international bankers financed the Russian revolution 65 years ago and have been backing both sides in every war since then.[34]

For anyone who reads financial and political journals, Hunt's allegations are simply unbelievable.

"Dave Hunt . . . overreacts to the dangers of New Age, in

my opinion," Russell Chandler observed. "He uses a mile-wide brush to paint into the same corner everyone who even faintly entertains notions compatible with New Age thinking."[35] Book-reviewers Bob and Gretchen Passantino were not favorably impressed by *The Seduction of Christianity*. They wrote: "After careful study and review, we must conclude that Hunt and McMahon have failed to prove their larger case biblically, theologically, logically, and factually."[36] Hunt made some good points at times, but he was clearly wrong much too often.

Marilyn Ferguson

In some ways, Marilyn Ferguson's 1980 book, *The Aquarian Conspiracy*,[37] launched the current New Age movement. She did not start anything new, she simply pulled all the various strings together and described them in a book that became very popular. Then people were just becoming aware of the New Age. She used the term "conspiracy" not in the sense of a cabal conceived in a darkened room, but in the sense of a worldwide enlightenment happening in many fields of knowledge simultaneously.

In the 1970s, as Ferguson described the situation in the Introduction to her book, she began to become aware of a movement that was spreading "with almost dizzying speed, but it has no name and eludes description." Within recent history, the movement "has infected medicine, education, social science, hard science, even government with its implications. It is characterized by fluid organizations reluctant to create hierarchical structures, averse to dogma." While thinking about the movement in the next few months, Ferguson continued, "it suddenly struck me that in their sharing of strategies, their linkage, and their recognition of each other by subtle signals, the participants were not merely cooperating with one another. They were in collusion. 'It'—this movement—was a conspiracy!"[38] She said she chose the name "Aquarian" to describe the conspiracy to make it seem benevolent.

Ferguson called this spontaneous and widespread conspiracy a "paradigm shift," a term she said was introduced by Thomas Kuhn in his 1962 book, *The Structure of Scientific Revolutions*. A paradigm is a framework of thought (from the Greek *paradigma*, "pattern"), Ferguson explained. A paradigm shift involves a distinctly new way of thinking about old problems. These new ideas are invariably resisted for a time, but then take hold.[39]

Ferguson's book demonstrated much of what is attractive about the New Age movement. She was positive, optimistic, self-assured. Good people, spontaneously working together, would make this planet a much better place to live in. The Christian reader had to delve a bit to recognize the harmful philosophy and theology underlying all this optimism.

"The Aquarian Conspiracy is significant not because it puts forth any really new or original ideas, but because it consolidates those sentiments into a sort of manifesto that the New Agers can rally around," Mark Albrecht concluded in his review of the book. "From a theological perspective, it represents the same old gnostic speculations with their monistic bedrock, dressed up in New Age and psycho-scientific terminology. It rejects God as the personal, transcendent Lord of creation and erects the falsely deified self in his place."[40]

No Conspiracy

It seems very, very clear that the New Age phenomenon is not a conspiracy in the usual sense of the word. No human being or tightly knit group of human beings is pulling the strings. The New Age is simply happening. The New Agers, by and large, are too independent and too undisciplined to be following an overall plan.

Furthermore, those writers who claim there is a conspiracy have given us no proof. Of course, they can't give us proof. If there really is a successful conspiracy, nobody but the conspirators themselves will know about it. "It's easy to believe in conspiracy," an article in *The New Age Rage* began.

Time and time again warnings are sounded about totally evil conspirators who are manipulating the destinies of countries and empires. One of these cabals is alleged to be the Illuminati, the illuminated or enlightened ones. The modern Order of the Illuminati was founded in 1776 by Adam Weishaupt, a Bavarian professor of canon law at Ingolstadt University. The anarchist activism of the order was uncovered by accident (or Providence) when an Illuminati courier was struck and killed by lightning. The order was supressed in 1785.[41]

As conspiracy theories continue to roll on, the Illuminati are resurrected time and time again. Certain groups are often accused of being the diabolical conspirators: Catholics, Jews, Masons, international bankers. Some Protestant bookstores are still carrying comic books that claim the Vatican has a huge computer with the names of all Protestants in it and will use this information to do them in. Anyone with a little knowledge of the Vatican's good relations with Protestants as well as its slow acceptance of modern communication methods will realize how absurd this accusation is. Still, some people believe it.

"Conspiracy theories are believable, but not verifiable," *The New Age Rage* article concluded. The conspiracy concept "will limit our understanding of Scripture, producing a picture that humanizes the 'mystery of iniquity' and distracts our understanding from the real focus of the biblical prophecies. As a result, the issues are politicized, and the net effect is to divide Christians against one another on the basis of an essentially political standard of judgment."[42]

Douglas Groothuis has described the conspiracy theory as being an excuse for inactivity among Christians. The bad guys are so powerful that nothing can be done to thwart their machinations. Also, it is inevitable that evil will happen, so efforts at achieving peace and justice are fruitless. "Scenarios of doom replace visions of hope,"[43] Groothuis commented.

Christians should have hope. Groothuis has characterized the New Age as carrying the seeds of its own self-destruction. It is so diverse and loosely structured organizationally that it is hard to see how it can continue to spread its influence for a long period. New Agers also have a tendency to overstate their numbers and influence and "one cannot always trust their own reports of success," Groothuis noted. He went on to analyze this self-promotion.

In an article in *The Wall Street Journal*, Anthony Downs notes the tendency of three New Age-oriented books—*Megatrends* by John Naisbitt, *The Third Wave* by Alvin Toffler and *The Aquarian Conspiracy* by Marilyn Ferguson—to "mega-hype the pseudo-facts" through several methods. These "exagger-books" often made their case by these methods:

> **Proof by assertion.** Simplified generalizations replace factual arguments.
>
> **Proof by anecdote or global gossip-gathering.** A few examples of a supposedly sweeping phenomenon are cited from around the world without probing their statistical significance.
>
> **Hyper-extended novelty or "exagger-trend."** A barely noticeable development is prophesied to "dominate society at some unspecified later date."
>
> **Pseudo-data.** The display of distorted statistics. If John Naisbitt says that something happens in "as many as 80%" of the cases, this could mean anything from 1% to 80%.
>
> **Presumptive but plausible interrelatedness.** Positing an underlying, growing current of societal change at the expense of more detailed and careful analysis. Talk of "quantum leaps" and "paradigm shifts" may sometimes be more of a result of wishful thinking than sound social research.[44]

Russell Chandler also questioned the staying power of New Agers. He quoted sociologist-author Robert Bellah as saying in an interview: "They are not able to form strong groups; they're just too evanescent."[45] Chandler also quoted as being "sound advice" a 1985 statement by the Southern Baptist Convention:

> Be particularly careful that you are not inclined toward a kind of uninformed hysteria characterized by oversimplification and indiscriminate fear that you are threatened by conspiracies of all sorts. While New Age thinking and New Age-oriented activities are serious and dangerous, do not allow their presence and influence to drive you to indiscriminate distrust of fellow Christians and blanket disenchantment with authentic Christian institutions.[46]

Eric Pement also urged common sense and trust in the power of God. "There is no need to be put on the defensive, afraid of computerized banking, international food programs, or universal price code (UPC) symbols. The sin of the end times described in Revelation will not be in how we mark our food packages but in our willful allegiance to and worship of a system and a man in active rebellion against the Lord Jesus Christ," wrote Pement. "If we must have a conspiracy theory, then let us be part of it—an invading fifth column, working toward the final overthrow of the kingdom of darkness. Our words and actions should therefore spring not from the paranoia of the times, but from the forthright love and boldness of God."[47]

Part 2

New Age—
Where Is It?

In this section we'll consider the impact New Age thinking has already had in our society—in new cults, in mainline religions, in education, in politics, in scientific work, in the health fields, in business and in entertainment. By the end of this section, you will be able to see more clearly the New Age influences in the world around you.

Chapter 7

Transcendental
Meditation,
Silva Mind Control,
Scientology, Eckankar,
Elizabeth Clare Prophet,
est

Cults

This is a book on the New Age movement. Why are we talking about cults?

The cults that arose in the 1960s and 1970s in North America are the immediate predecessors of the New Age movement of the 1980s. In some ways, the New Age movement of the 1980s is the cultic movement of the 1970s without the latter's strict discipline and lifestyle. Some of the leading New Age teachers—in the human-potential and personnel-training fields, for example—were formerly members of the cults. We need to have an understanding of the cults to understand some key implications of the New Age movement. (We will not be talking about all the popular cults of the 1960s and 1970s for two reasons. Some are simply carbon copies of cults we do talk about—just different gurus. Some are basically heretical Christian sects and beyond the scope of this work.)

What is a cult?

"A cult is a perversion, a distortion of biblical Christianity and, as such, rejects the historic teachings of the Christian church," wrote Josh McDowell and Don Stewart. "All cults ultimately deny the fact that Jesus Christ is God the Son, second Person of the Holy Trinity, and mankind's only hope."[1]

"A cult is a religious group that has a prophet-founder called of God to give a special message not found in the Bible itself, often apocalyptic in nature and often set forth in inspired writings," commented Ruth A. Tucker. "The style of leadership is authoritarian and there is frequently an exclusivistic outlook, supported by a legalistic lifestyle and persecution mentality."[2]

Bob Larson noted that there are four things which most cults have in common:

1. a centralized authority which tightly structures both philosophy and lifestyle;

2. a "we" versus "they" complex, pitting the supposed superior insights of the group against a hostile outside culture;

3. a commitment for each member to intensively proselytize the unconverted; and

4. an entrenched isolationism that divorces the devotee from the realities of the world at large.[3]

Transcendental Meditation

Transcendental Meditation was developed through a calculated marketing strategy by the Maharishi Mahesh Yogi. He came to the United States in 1959 to promote Hinduism, and started the Spiritual Regeneration Movement. (Note the religious title.) It flopped. Hinduism was not popular. He came back a few years later, disguising his religion as a nonreligious relaxation technique. He called his new organizations the International Meditation Society and the American Foundation for the Science of Creative Intelligence. Thinking it nonreligious, gullible Americans were enthusiastic. An estimated one million persons have been initiated into TM.[4] The intiation fees are on a sliding scale, less for college students, for example. The average fee was probably about $100. That means the Maharishi has grossed to date about $100 million for his efforts. That's what creative marketing can do.

The Transcendental Meditation TM Book: How to Enjoy the Rest of Your Life was published in 1975 by TM people and used by TM people to promote TM. It started off by proclaiming in a headline: "The TM program does *not* involve religious beliefs." The text went on to say: "It's absurd to assume that just because the TM technique comes from India it must be some Hindu practice . . . . The TM program does not involve any religious belief or practice—Hindu or otherwise . . . . A scientist's personal religious beliefs have no bearing on the validity of his contributions to science."[5]

This is a lie. TM is a form of Hinduism. The TM proponents also tried to deceive Christians into accepting TM by having letters from a Catholic priest and a Lutheran minister prominently displayed in *The Transcendental Meditation TM Book*. I called both these men and both said they had not given TM authorities permission to reprint their letters and both said they had asked the TM people to stop using the letters.

By unabashedly lying about the basic nature of TM, the Maharishi and his followers were able to dupe hundreds of thousands of Americans into worshipping Hindu gods and practicing Hinduism. When the TM proponents tried to get the taxpayers to support TM in the public schools, however, they ran into problems.

On February 25, 1976, concerned parents and others sued "Maharishi Mahesh Yogi et al." in the United States District Court, Newark, N.J. The plaintiffs contended that the teaching of TM and the Science of Creative Intelligence in five New Jersey public high schools violated the Establishment Clause of the First Amendment. They asked the court to rule that both the textbook used to teach the course and the *puja* ceremony essential to the students' initiation into the practice of TM were religious in nature.[6]

On December 12, 1977, Judge H. Curtis Meanor ruled:

> That the Science of Creative Intelligence/Tran-
> scendental Meditation and the teaching thereof,
> the concepts of the field of pure creative intelli-
> gence, creative intelligence and bliss-conscious-
> ness, the textbook entitled *Science of Creative Intel-
> ligence for Secondary Education—First Year Course—
> Dawn of the First Year of the Age of Enlightenment,*
> and the puja ceremony, are all religious in nature
> within the context of the Establishment Clause of
> the First Amendment of the United States Con-
> stitution, and the teaching thereof in the New
> Jersey public schools is therefore unconstitutional.[7]

Judge Meanor decided the case by summary judgment—
in effect saying the case was so crystal clear that it did not
need to go to a jury. The court opinion described how each
high-school student, before receiving the personal mantra
(sound to meditate on), was made to participate in an initiation ceremony. The student was required to bring a clean
white handkerchief, a few flowers and three or four pieces of
fruit to the ceremony. These gifts were to be placed on a table
covered with a white cloth. Also on the table were a candle
and incense and a picture of the Guru Dev, the Maharishi's
teacher who had died more than 20 years before. The student
was required to remove his or her shoes and kneel or sit or
stand reverently while the TM instructor chanted a Sanskrit
puja (prayer).

The TM people, who submitted more than 1,500 pages of
testimony, said that the ceremony was only intended to
honor the Guru Dev and the other dead Hindu teachers who
had passed on the teachings that the Maharishi was promul-
gating. The TM people said the ceremony was not religious
because they did not consider it religious. The judge disagreed.

The judicial opinion quoted in full the English translation
of the Sanskrit *puja* that is chanted during each initiation

ceremony. The opinion notes that the *puja* calls for 19 offerings of gifts to the Guru Dev and 22 bows to the Guru Dev.
In commenting on the *puja*, Judge Meanor said that the Guru
Dev "is portrayed as a personification of a divine being or
essence." In confirmation of this opinion, the judge quoted
from the *puja*: "To the glory of the Lord [i.e., Guru Dev] I
bow down again and again, at whose door the whole galaxy
of gods pray (sic) for perfection day and night."[8]

Though it was not referred to in the court's opinion, the
plaintiffs also submitted testimony about the mantra. "The
mantra is a secret Sanskrit word which the teacher gives to
the meditator at the time of the initiation ceremony," Gregory J. Randolph, a former TM instructor, said in an affidavit submitted to the court. "It is the word or sound which is
the object or vehicle of meditation in TM. We were taught to
give the definite and deliberate impression to the general
public and to individuals we initiated that there are a very
large number of mantras and that each meditator receives a
mantra which is individually chosen for him and is uniquely
suited to his personality. In actual fact, however, each teacher
has a list of 16 mantras which are then assigned to meditators
on the basis of age classification."[9] Some Hindus believe that
chanting a mantra will put the person in contact with a
particular god whose sound the mantra embodies. Other
confidential TM literature indicates that there now are 24
mantras in use.

TM works, at least sometimes. Reports of demonic possession or obsession as a result of TM have surfaced. "I have
watched Hindu worshippers by the scores chanting for
hours before idols during a special puja season, and I have
literally felt the supernatural presence of the gods they were
invoking,"[10] reported Douglas Shah. "One night I awoke
with a sense of fear and apprehension, because a spirit was
putting pressure all over my body and head in an attempt to
enter and take possession of my body," stated former TM
instructor Vail Hamilton. "I commanded it to leave and
resisted it until it left." She also said that, as she continued to

practice TM, she began "to experience other supernatural sensations—ESP and clairvoyance, telepathy, and the beginnings of astral travel."[11]

In their book, *Occult Shock and Psychic Forces*, Clifford A. Wilson and John Weldon contended that the existence of demons is quite adequately proven from both biblical and occult sources. They said that psychic researchers such as Elmer Green of the Menninger Foundation have said that the evidence of thousands of years of demonic experience is not to be taken lightly. In noting the very real dangers from demons, Wilson and Weldon continued, Green "warns that psychic exploration can bring one 'to the attention of indigenous beings,' some of whom are 'malicious, cruel, and cunning.' They can obsess and even possess people by disrupting the nervous system and controlling the brain."[12]

In a chapter entitled, "Transcendental Meditation Is Occult, Not Christian," Wilson and Weldon continued: "TM does have its cases of spirit contact. In Hinduism, the departed master often reappears to the favored disciple to guide him psychically." They said they "suspect (this) is true for Maharishi," since two of his books are said to have come as blessings from the Guru Dev.[13]

Silva Mind Control

Silva Mind Control is similar to TM in that it also claims to be nonreligious while it really is geared to putting the initiate under the control of demonic spirits. Silva Mind Control was developed by a Texan, Jose Silva, the owner of a mail-order electronics business who was interested in hypnosis and parapsychology. The 40-hour beginning course consists of a series of lectures and exercises in self-hypnosis and altered states of consciousness. The individual practices such things as imagining being inside a metal cube or inside the body of a pet. There are also mental practices about imagining a person whose name is presented and then imagining that person's illness and imagining a cure for the illness.

At the conclusion of the program, the individual is asked to allow two demonic spirits to come into him or her and influence his or her judgments. These demonic spirits are called "counselors" by Silva. They are so controversial that in Silva's book, *The Silva Mind Control Method*, he did not describe in detail the final sessions of the course in which the demonic spirits are introduced, though he teased the reader with some accounts of the activity of these demonic spirits. On pages 93-94, Silva talked about one student whose demonic counselors took the forms of William Shakespeare and Sophia Loren. When they weren't giving advice, they were making passionate love—in the student's imagination. On pages 99-100, Silva told of another mind-control initiate having a dialogue with his spirit guides to find a lost manuscript. On page 107, a mind-control instructor psychically saw a demonic spirit in the form of the fictional character, Othello, try to enter one student and be rejected and then enter another student.[14]

Sid Roth, a Jew involved in the occult and Silva Mind Control, told about his conversion to Christianity in the book, *Something for Nothing*.[15] He talked about a conversation with a fellow mind-control student. He asked the other student to ask his spirit guide what Roth would be doing a year from then. The spirit guide, always very polite before, began to curse and use vulgar language and refused to answer the question. In less than a year, Roth had given up the occult and become a Christian.[16]

Among the critics of Silva Mind Control have been Dr. and Mrs. Elmer Green, biofeedback researchers at the Menninger Foundation, Topeka, Kan. The Greens have contended that Silva Mind Control's semihypnotic procedures invoke states which are similar to a trance condition. In such a condition people are open to "possession by spirits."[17] For the Greens, John P. Newport said, the counselors or invisible psychic advisors "may serve as masks for evil spiritual forces. These forces may later attempt to control the student's mental, emotional and physical behavior."[18] Newport added that the Greens' criticisms were similar to that of Dr. Shafica Karagulla, a California neuropsychiatrist, who warned that "unwise tampering with psychic forces can lead to possession by evil spirits."[19]

Newport, a professor of religious studies at Rice University, said Silva's philosophy is a mixture of deism and pantheism. Referring to the writings of Harry McKnight, a chief instructor of Silva Mind Control, Newport described some of its principal teachings as being: "Man is fundamentally good .... You can reach Christ-awareness, illumination, and enlightenment for yourself through the Silva method. Doing it yourself is the only way."[20]

Silva has gone out of his way to encourage priests and nuns to take the course. Some priests and nuns have been involved in promoting the program.

Scientology

As we have seen, one of the principal strategies of some of the modern cults is to get you to open yourself up to obsession or possession by demonic spirits. Another common theme is that you are gods. You have only to claim your godlike heritage.

In 1949, L. Ron Hubbard told a meeting of science-fiction writers: "Writing for a penny a word is ridiculous. If a man really wanted to make a million dollars, the best way would be to start his own religion."[21] The next year he did. His book, *Dianetics: The Modern Science of Mental Health,* was published in 1950, supposedly after a "lifetime of research," and the "religion" of Scientology was launched. *Freedom,* a Scientology publication, once stated that Hubbard spent 35 years in research before the final formulation of *Dianetics.* Actually, he was only 39 when *Dianetics* was published.[22] He died January 24, 1986, at the age of 74. For the previous six years, he had not appeared publicly, possibly to avoid a series of civil lawsuits by former Scientology church members against himself and the church. More than eight million copies of *Dianetics* have been published.

According to Bob Larson, *Dianetics* originally was intended as Hubbard's psychotherapeutic answer to the techniques of modern psychiatry, but strong opposition from the medical community prompted him "to formalize his theories into a religion and thus seek tax-exempt status and freedom from governmental interference for some of his organizations."[23]

Scientology has a unique concept of reality and a very confusing vocabulary to express this concept. This is the way Larson explained its basic teachings:

> Mankind is descended from a race of uncreated, omnipotent gods called *thetans*, who gave up their powers to enter the Material-Energy-Space-Time (MEST) world of Earth. Gradually, they evolved upward by reincarnation to become humans who could not remember their deified state. Scientologists are encouraged to awaken their dormant thetan potential by removing all mental blocks called *engrams*. By doing so they can realize their true personhood, achieving total power and control over MEST.[24]

Recapturing your thetanhood, however, will cost you money—lots of money. Larson reported that some former Scientology members paid more than $30,000 in an effort to clear themselves of engrams. Some of the techniques Scientology initiates paid for included:

Bull-baiting. The initiate stares at the instructor while the instructor hurls verbal abuse about the beginner's physical appearance, abuse often grossly sexual in nature, trying to make him or her flinch or react.

Dear Alice. Lines from *Alice in Wonderland* are recited while the initiate responds with a "thank you."

E-Meter. The E-Meter, which costs $125 or more, is used as a lie detector in a counseling session. The E-Meter is a simply made galvanometer which measures the resistance to electric current by recording galvanic skin responses. The initiate holds a tin can in each hand which is wired to the meter. The instructor asks various questions which may cause the needle to jump.[25]

As the student progresses through the various stages of Scientology, contact with demonic spirits is indicated when the initiate begins allegedly to interact with the thetan in the initiate's distant background. Occultic practices such as astral projection (out-of-body experience) are also encouraged.[26]

Scientologists have been very belligerent in responding to criticism. Some members have lost criminal and civil cases for harassment, intimidation and defamation of critics. With the death of Hubbard and after some serious legal setbacks, however, Scientologists seem to have become less contentious.

Scientology has been very influential in the murky world of contemporary cults. Brooks Alexander has linked a number of human-potential groups to Scientology—Silva Mind Control, *est*, Lifespring and Mind Dynamics. "Hubbard realized that in a largely secularized culture, ultimate human concerns could be addressed in a 'scientific' and 'therapeutic' way, rather than from a traditional religious standpoint," Alexander explained. "Hubbard made the first systematic attempt to unite the search for self with the search for ultimate reality, and to present it in a Western technological package."[27]

Eckankar

Another combination of occultic practices and contact with demonic forces is the cult Eckankar. In September, 1979, the Spiritual Counterfeits Project published a 55-page journal on Eckankar. Among other things, the SCP report documented the unabashed plagiarism of Eckankar's founder, Paul Twitchell. Selections from Twitchell's writings of the 1950s and 1960s were printed beside nearly identical passages from the writings of 1930s occultist Julian Johnson.[28]

Twitchell, a journalist and occultist who once served as a

staff member of the Church of Scientology, formed the first public Eckankar group in 1965. He claimed that his teaching came from his contact with two "Eck Masters" or demigods, Sudar Singh in India and Rebazar Tarzs in the Himalayas. However, no documented proof exists that Twitchell ever visited either place or that either man actually existed. (Twitchell and his widow had difficulty getting some basic facts straight. His death certificate stated he was born in 1922. His marriage license said he was born in 1912. Other official records stated he was born in 1908—probably the true date.)

According to Twitchell's account, the two Eck Masters from the East designated Twitchell to be the 971st living Eck Master, a *mahanta,* living manifestation of God. Twitchell said that such a demigod is "above the laws of man . . . omnipotent and omniscient." The Eck Master's purpose in life is to lead the souls of men to the heaven where God, known as Sugmad, dwells.[29] According to Bob Larson, Twitchell taught that life flows from Sugmad in the form of a cosmic sound current called Eck. (Eck is also often used as an abbreviation for Eckankar.) "Twitchell taught a variety of occult exercises by which the Eck student could tune into this ethereal sound of God. Foremost among these phenomena is an out-of-the-body experience Twitchell originally called 'bilocation,' and later changed to 'soul-travel,' which he declared is 'the secret path to God.' "[30] This soul-travel is the occultic experience usually referred to as astral projection.

This omnipotent and omniscient demigod, Twitchell, died suddenly of a heart attack in a Cincinnati hotel room on September 17, 1971. Darwin Gross took over as the living Eck Master #972. The mystical "rod of power" was allegedly transferred to him in the spirit world since Twitchell died too suddenly for an orderly transfer of leadership. Changes since then, according to Russell Chandler, have included a membership drop of "soul travelers" from an estimated 50,000 to 20,000 and the moving of world headquarters from Las Vegas to Menlo Park, Calif., then to Minneapolis. In

1981, Harold Klemp became living Eck Master #973.[31]

In preparing their journal on Eckankar, the Spiritual Counterfeits Project writers said they made special efforts to line up an interview with Gross and, as a last resort, offered to let him prepare a 1,000-word statement for the journal that would be unedited. One day Gross and two associates showed up at the SCP offices in Berkeley and demanded to see a copy of the journal manuscript. They left after a half hour of fruitless discussion. Eckankar representatives repeatedly refused to set up an interview with Gross unless the SCP handed over the journal manuscript. "Eckankar claimed that we might try to 'trap' Gross into 'out of context' remarks," the SCP editors reported. "We countered that since Mr. Gross is allegedly omniscient, the risk of entrapment would, in fact, be largely assumed by the SCP."[32]

> In the final analysis, the spiritual experiences generated in Eckankar seem to be a combination of cultivated and amplified imagination, classical ASCs (altered states of consciousness) such as yogis achieve in deep meditation, psychically induced phenomena, direct spirit implants of visual and sensual experiences, and temporary demonic possession. Paul Gayeski, a former Eckist from Portland, Ore., told the SCP that witchcraft and black magic are an integral part of the inner realities of Eckankar."[33]

Elizabeth Clare Prophet

In November, 1978, Elizabeth Clare Prophet gave a talk at the University of California, Berkeley. Advertisements proclaimed that she was "stumping for the coming revolution in higher consciousness." Members of the Spiritual Counterfeits Project handed out leaflets that gave a Christian critique of Prophet, also known as Guru Ma. SCP researcher Mark Albrecht wrote a review of her performance.

After a technically sophisticated sound and slide

show which attempted to integrate all forms of
spiritual expression into an all-embracing monis-
tic-mystical system of eclectic occultism, Guru Ma
emerged onto the spotlighted stage. Her long
harangue on the oneness of all things was delivered in a carefully cultivated, computer-like mono-
tone which was apparently intended to approxi-
mate a "spirit dictation." . . . Prophet led the
spellbound crowd through a meditation in which
each person was instructed to visualize the chest
cavity as being full of light. This, she explained, is
your own private *Holy of Holies*, where you enter in
and bow down to your own Trinity that lives
within you and is synonymous with your real
self.[34]

Each individual, Albrecht pointed out, was encouraged
to worship himself or herself as the Trinity.

Prophet was born Elizabeth Clare Wulf on April 8, 1940,
in Jersey City, N.J. "She claims that at an early age she
experienced visitations from the ascended master El Morya
and also began recalling her former lives," Robert Burrows
wrote. "The writings of the I AM movement did much to
shape her spiritual outlook, and she eagerly sought contact
with St. Germain, the ascended master so prominent in I AM
literature."[35] In 1961, she met Mark Prophet and, despite a
21-year age difference, they were married.

Mark Prophet was born December 24, 1918, in Chippewa
Falls, Wis. At the age of 18, he allegedly began to receive
revelations from the ascended master El Morya, who, in
1958, instructed Prophet to found the Summit Lighthouse in
Washington, D.C. Mark died of a stroke in 1973, but supposedly continued to communicate with the movement as the
ascended master Lanello. Mrs. Prophet married Randall
King shortly after her first husband's death. They were
divorced in 1977. She has since married Ed Francis. In 1976,
the name of the organization was changed to the Church
Universal and Triumphant (CUT). In 1986, CUT's headquar-

ters was moved from California to a 12,000-acre ranch in Montana's Paradise Valley, near Yellowstone National Park.

According to an August 28, 1989, *Time* article, the 1,000 CUT followers in Montana were preparing for nuclear attack in two months. (By the time you read this, you will know if Guru Ma's prediction was correct.) The CUT staff members were arming themselves to repel a communist invasion. Others from the 30,000 CUT members worldwide were converging on the sparsely populated region as they prepared to survive Armageddon in CUT bomb shelters.[36]

CUT's teachings are rooted in theosophy and the I AM movement. From theosophy they adopted belief in a body of all-knowing masters in the spirit realm known as the Brotherhood of the Great White Lodge and belief that the present time is the beginning of the Aquarian Age in humanity's spiritual development. The ascended masters of CUT literature are deceased persons of great spirituality who have joined other immortals of the Great White Brotherhood. The I AM movement of Guy and Edna Ballard, which flourished in the 1930s, was indebted to Baird T. Spalding's five-volume *Life and Teachings of the Masters of the Far East.* In particular, wrote Burrows, CUT "adopted Spalding's notion of the I AM Presence—the idea that the fundamental reality of humanity is deity and that the primary task of humankind is to realize and cultivate its divinity."[37]

According to Burrows, Mark Prophet claimed a long line of previous incarnations, including an Atlantian priest, the Pharaoh Ikhnaton, the Old Testament figure Lot, and Origen of Alexandria among others. Elizabeth Clare Prophet also claimed an illustrious lineage: Martha, the sister of Lazarus in New Testament times; Guinevere, the first lady of King Arthur's court; and a lady in ancient Egypt.

CUT teaching is eclectic. Literature promoting an ascended master retreat stated:

> Whether you are a follower of Jesus Christ or Mary the Mother, Moses or Mohammed, Gautama Buddha, Confucius, Lao Tzu, Zoroaster, or the Zen

masters, the gurus of the East or the saints of the West, you will find that your relationship to your own teacher is enhanced by the ascended master retreat experience and gains a meaningful soul dimension in the teachings of the Great White Brotherhood. This, then, is a true encounter with the Brotherhood of enlightened ones whose mastery of life has enabled them to transcend the cycles of time and space and whose footsteps before us lead to our own soul's acceleration on the path of the ascension.[38]

For CUT, explained Burrows, "Jesus is not the unique incarnation of God but an ordinary man who fully realized the innate divinity common to us all. Jesus is important to CUT as a symbol of the God realization that humanity in general is expected to seek and attain. The divine dimension in humankind is called 'the Christ,' 'Christ Self,' or 'Christ Consciousness.' "[39]

CUT *chelas* (disciples) are believed to be on a spiritual pilgrimage through many reincarnations from a lower self to a higher self, a journey toward realizing their own divinity. "Chelas are assisted in their pilgrimages by a variety of occult/mystical practices," wrote Larson. "Foremost among these is the use of 'decrees,' the mantra-like chanting of incantations. A favorite is, 'I am that I am,' an affirmation of self-deity which ensures ascension. Devotees also seek to cleanse their *karma* by being surrounded by the 'Violet Consuming Flame,' a sacred fire said to be made available by the spiritual merit of St. Germain (an ascended master)."[40]

est

Werner Erhard was born in 1935 in Philadelphia and named John Paul Rosenberg. In 1959, when he was 24, he left his wife, Pat, and four children, then took off west with a girlfriend, Ellen, later to become his second wife. They had three children. Eventually, he repaired his relationship with his first wife. He changed his name and sold used cars and encyclopedias. Walter Martin reports that Erhard "was later convicted by the State of California for using lies and trickery to persuade prospective customers"[41] in the encyclopedia business.

Erhard got involved in Scientology, Mind Dynamics, Silva Mind Control, Zen Buddhism, hypnosis, Subud, yoga, psycho-cybernetics, Gestalt, encounter therapy, transpersonal psychology and other intellectual and spiritual diversions. He claimed he got enlightenment one day while driving on the freeway. Later he summarized this insight by saying: "What is, is; and what was, was; and what isn't, isn't."[42]

At another time, Erhard explained the insight this way: "I realized I was not my emotions or thoughts, my ideas, my intellect, my perception, [nor] my beliefs, what I did or accomplished or achieved. I wasn't what I had done right or wrong . . . . I was simply the space, the creator, the source of all that stuff. I experienced Self as Self in a direct and unmediated way."[43]

According to an article by Carol Giambalvo and Robert Burrows, Erhard did not consider this enlightenment experience to be religious. "But the experience he had," they explained, "gave him the ultimate answer to ultimate questions, and his interpretation of it is drawn from the world's monistic religious traditions."[44]

This experience led Erhard to start *est* (spelled in lower-case letters) in 1971. The abbreviation *est* stands for Erhard Seminars Training and it is also the Latin word for "it is." The purpose of the training is to get the same insight Erhard had on the freeway. This insight, to put it another way, is that "the self *is* our experience, and the self is all there is to life," explained Stanley Dokupil and Brooks Alexander. They quoted Erhard as saying: "When I get in touch with my self and you get in touch with your self, we will see the same self. Self is all there is. I mean that's it."[45]

Est's understanding of the self "is no different from that of Vedanta (Hindu monism)," Dokupil and Alexander stated.

"Vedanta teaches that the self, and indeed the entire outward appearance of the world (*maya* or illusion), is only the one, impersonal, unchanging reality of Brahman."[46]

Incredibly, *est* courses proved very popular even though they were about as pleasant as a stay in a prisoner of war camp. Trainees, who paid about $400 for the experience, were subjected to harassment and verbal abuse for 60 hours on two weekends. They were not allowed bathroom privileges or snacks except for the breaks every four hours. They were not allowed to talk to one another. If they did speak out, they had to do so to the whole group through a microphone. They were often ridiculed and subjected to profanity and vulgarity. "Obscenity is one of the most pervasive features of the training," reported a Cornerstone Press leaflet. "In it, the participant is assaulted with gross, lewd words, specifically aimed at him, shouted at full volume."[47]

Persons undergoing psychiatric counseling must have release forms from the therapist. "A number of people without any previous history of mental illness have been hospitalized in emergency psychiatric episodes following the *est* training,"[48] Cornerstone Press reported. The 60 hours are taken up with lengthy philosophical lectures using new and difficult terminology, audience sharings and confessions, and guided fantasies or visualizations.

The punchline at the end goes something like this: "Enlightenment is knowing you are a machine, accepting what is. It's all a cosmic joke. That's it. There's nothing to get. Get it? Enlightenment is saying 'yes' to what is, taking what you get. What is, is."[49] Mark Brewer, writing for *Psychology Today*, called the *est* program brainwashing. He reported an *est* trainer as saying: "We're gonna throw away your whole belief system . . . . We're gonna tear you down and put you back together."[50]

In the early 1980s, as enrollment in *est* programs dropped sharply, the resilient Erhard diversified. He resurrected the *est* program in a toned-down format and called it the Forum. He started Transformational Technologies for management consultants and personnel trainers. (See Chapter 12.) He launched the Hunger Project, an incredible program to feed the world without food—you just meditate and the problems disappear. The *Spiritual Counterfeits Project Journal* in 1988 listed 26 programs, organizations and enterprises in Werner Erhard's expanding empire.[51]

Chapter 8

Cosmic Riders,
Satanism,
Satanic Murders,
Satanic Child Abuse,
Witchcraft,
Goddess Worship, Animism

More Cults

As we continue to consider the cults, the scene gets darker. Unspeakably depraved acts abound in some satanic cults and some Eastern communes. The New Age, though often relatively harmless, can lead to these same depravities because the underlying philosophy is the same.

Cosmic Riders

Of all the books I read as background for this book, none was more engrossing than Tal Brooke's *Riders of the Cosmic Circuit: Rajneesh, Sai Baba, Muktananda . . . Gods of the New Age.*[1] Brooke was writing from the inside. Before his miraculous conversion to Christ, for two years he was a top aide to Sai Baba, India's most influential guru. He did a lot of first-hand research at Rajneesh's ashram in India and was also well acquainted with Swami Muktananda. These three are spiritual leaders whom Brooke calls Riders of the Cosmic Circuit. They are members of "possibly the most exclusive, powerful, and secretive of inner-circles in existence." To become a rider, one has to "offer with total abandon one's soul on the altar of oblivion. The goal is an explosion of super-consciousness beyond the point of no return. What emerges from this transformation is an Enlightened Master who claims to be nothing less than god using a physical body as a medium."[2]

In an article in the *Spiritual Counterfeits Project Newsletter*,[3] Brooke told how his personal spiritual journey began. He got a Ouija board at the age of 10 and became interested in UFOs and ESP in his teens. He did the drug scene. After graduating from the University of Virginia, he went ashram-hopping in India, checking out various gurus for three months until he chose Sai Baba. "Practically every Indian I met swore to his authenticity, claiming that he was Lord Krishna and Christ reborn,"[4] Brooke said.

Sai Baba, who had some five million Indian devotees, was a miracle-worker. Brooke first saw him in 1969. Sai Baba regularly told persons secrets of their past lives and materialized a grey healing powder and pieces of rock sugar apparently out of thin air. On special occasions, he would pull phallic-shaped stones out of his mouth which he had purportedly created in his body. He took illnesses from other people on himself and then cured himself. He materialized special rings and enameled plates as gifts. One time in India, he gave a follower a computer card from a San Francisco bank that was dated that day. The fastest jet could not have flown it there. (Brooke, who was an eyewitness to many of these "miracles," takes them at face value. Nowhere does he hint that Sai Baba was using slight of hand tricks.)[5]

As a boy, Sai Baba exhibited psychic powers and was also able to materialize items like pieces of rock sugar and sweets not available in the remote area of India where he grew up. When he was 13, "the big transformation took place—the child hit the power line," Brooke recounted. "The cosmic personality took over with such force that his family did not recognize the former child."[6] On March 8, 1940, Baba screamed and collapsed. He was unconscious for several days. When he revived, "his family was shocked," Brooke said. "They could not recognize the new resident living within the body, for there was a complete transformation of personality."[7] His body became stiff at times and he became clairvoyant. Then he announced that he was Sai Baba and the people were to worship him. When someone asked the boy for supernatural proof, he took some jasmine flowers and threw them into the air. They hit the ground spelling out in Telugu the name, Sai Baba.

Muktananda, one of the other gurus, experienced his moment of enlightenment in the summer of 1947. Brooke described the experience, using Muktananda's own words. The process started through the catalytic power of the master guru, Nityananda. A ray of light seemed to come from the guru through Muktananda's body. Unusual and painful things happened to his body. He felt he was dying. "My fear increased every second. I heard hordes of people screaming frightfully, as if it were the end of the world," Muktananda recounted. "I looked and saw the sugar-cane field on fire through the window. Then I saw strange creatures from six to 50 feet tall, neither demons nor demigods, but human in form, dancing naked, their mouths gaping open."[8]

He sat paralyzed in a lotus position while a ball of light entered his body. He began to shake violently at times. Hindu gods possessed him. He had visions. "Sometimes my body would writhe and twist like a snake's while a hissing sound would come from inside me," Muktananda stated. "Sometimes my neck moved so violently that it made loud cracking sounds and I became frightened .... Sometimes my neck would roll my head around so vigorously that it would bend right below my shoulders so that I could see my back."[9] Finally came the explosion of enlightenment with the experiences of the Blue Pearl and the Blue Light of Consciousness.

All in all, this seems clearly a classic, detailed account of demon possession. In 1982, Muktananda had a severe heart attack and died.

For Rajneesh, enlightenment came in March, 1953, when he was 21. It took seven days. "That [final] night another reality opened its door, another dimension became available," he wrote. "It was nameless. But it was there—so opaque, so transparent, and yet so solid one could have touched it. It was almost suffocating me in that room . . . . For the first time I was not alone, for the first time I was no more an individual, for the first time the drop had come and fallen into the ocean. Now the whole ocean was mine, I was the ocean. There was no limitation. A tremendous power arose as if I could do anything whatsoever."[10]

In early 1981, Brooke and some friends went to Poona to investigate Rajneesh at the request of officials from various European countries. Brooke had become a Christian by this time and had written a book on Sai Baba. The officials were worried because many Europeans were joining Rajneesh and simply vanishing. Brooke's investigations turned up unbelievable depravity. Families were broken up on entering. Sterilization was almost always mandatory. Sexual promiscuity was encouraged and even mandated. Encounter sessions included rapes and beatings. Brooke talked to a woman who had been thrown off a cliff and left for dead. There were indications, though no actual proof, of ritual murder and sexual relations with corpses. Rajneesh participated in much of the depravity.

Brooke saw the whole thing as satanic. "Curiously," he said, "when the heavy-hitting gurus, the riders, emerged from the explosion (enlightenment experience), close associates and family usually used the term 'possession' in describing the change that they saw." But this was not your run-of-the-mill demonic possession. There is a "super-class whose possession is different—it is a perfect possession and the consciousness within the possessed is many levels beyond the standard possessor-demons," Brooke wrote. "What are they? Antichrists, claiming to be God!"[11]

The powers of evil can do extraordinary things, Brooke reflected. He began to realize that the riders were "a new class of creatures—superhumanly energized figures proclaiming to be God in human form, yet in a state of perfect possession. Not ordinary demonic possession, but perfect. The original human inhabitant now fully obliterated out of the body, blow-torched as it were. The new resident consciousness not your standard comic-book demon, but a massive, baleful intelligence that is ageless, that has witnessed cosmic creation, that is extremely powerful and extremely evil."[12]

On May 30, 1981, without advance notice, Rajneesh left his ashram in Poona and flew to the United States. His followers in India, many of whom had turned over substantial fortunes to him, were abandoned. Rajneesh moved to central Oregon where he set up another ashram on a 64,000-acre spread. The project collapsed in four years. Rajneesh was deported. Several top aides were arrested and jailed. After being booted out of 21 countries following his deportation from the U.S., Rajneesh returned to Poona where, in 1988, he was once again giving discourses to about 10,000 followers.[13]

Time's issue of January 16, 1989, reported that Rajneesh no longer wanted to be called bhagwan (God) because he said his body "was host to the ascetic soul of Gautama Buddha. Days later," *Time* continued, "Rajneesh kicked out Gautama, who he said disapproved of his Jacuzzi." His newest announced identity is "Zorba the Buddha," a pleasure-loving divinity.[14]

Brooke ended his book with a lengthy conversation he had in 1983 with Eckart Flother, a former top Rajneesh aide. Before his involvement with Rajneesh, Flother had been the senior editor of *German Business Week* magazine and did not have a religious background. He described to Brooke his miraculous conversion to Christ.

> All of a sudden in the left-hand corner of my hotel room I saw a bigger than man-sized, brilliant light. The sheer power, sheer presence was awesome. Rajneesh could not hold a candle to this. I felt instinctively that it was Jesus Christ . . . .
>
> All of a sudden I heard a mighty voice saying to

me, "I want you to become my disciple." I was absolutely shaken to bits. I knew right away that this was Jesus calling me . . . .

I returned to the ashram and asked for an appointment with Rajneesh to talk to him . . . . When I first sat down, Rajneesh was sitting back comfortably in his chair. He was leaning back just looking at me. Then his face shifted. It became irritated, then startled . . . as I shared the visitation. Then when I mentioned that it was Jesus Christ, his face became terrified, he shuddered. His hands got stiff. He came rigid, and began to sit back deep in his chair as though repelled . . . .

At that point I was telling him these words: "And now Jesus Christ is my Master!" Rajneesh sat for a long time stunned, as though unable to talk. Finally he hissed in a very low voice, sardonically, "Enjoy it." That was it; from then on I was free of him.[15]

In their conversation, Flother and Brooke, two writers with a professional concern for accuracy, shared incredible stories of the manifestations of diabolical power. Flother told of a man who experienced a picture of Rajneesh come alive and come down to him, tear out his heart and eat it. One woman talked of a terrifying experience of the ghost of Rajneesh, as it were, raping her. Flother told of witnessing a huge force or supernatural being racing down the streets of Poona one night at about 120 miles an hour. They also talked about more mundane topics like rape and orgies and followers being forced to eat feces. They talked about people losing all hope and being suicidal. They talked of seeing corpses from the communes with an incredible fear in their dead eyes from having experienced something truly horrible at the moment of death.

"What is systematically destroyed by Rajneesh, Sai Baba,

the other Riders of the Cosmic Circuit?," Brooke asked in his concluding chapter. "The mind, the ego, the will which is surrendered, the conscience, the sense of good and evil. But this rite can only be made consummate by an ultimate ritual .... One is seduced by high-sounding pantheistic philosophy until then, then he bows at the dark altar of the demon god, he kills or he eats feces, or he surrenders to the energy of an orgy ... and his dissolution is in effect. Then it is only a matter of time till full possession takes place."[16]

This is the depravity to which dabbling in the New Age can lead.

Satanism

According to one poll, 94% of Americans believe in God, but only 34% believe in a personal devil.[17] C.S. Lewis, in the *Screwtape Letters*, commented on belief in the devil. "There are two equal and opposite errors into which our race can fall about the devils," he wrote in the book's preface. "One is to disbelieve in their existence. The other is to believe, and to feel an excessive and unhealthy interest in them. They themselves are equally pleased by both errors, and hail a materialist or a magician with the same delight."[18]

In Chapter 15, we will talk about Satan from a biblical and theological viewpoint. If you are a Christian and do not believe in the reality of the devil, read that part of Chapter 15 now. In this chapter, we will talk about satanism, the worship of the devil, but I think we also need to talk a bit about the reality of the devil. We might note in passing that the Bible definitely believes in Satan. Nineteen of the New Testament books speak of Satan.

An excellent book about dealing with the devil is *Resist the Devil: A Pastoral Guide to Deliverance Prayer* by Father Charles W. Harris, a Catholic priest. (The book is also cited in Chapters 14 and 15.) He quoted extensively from Scripture, the church Fathers and official Roman Catholic documents in talking about the reality of the devil and how to deal with him.

Jesus in his ministry clearly distinguished between healing and driving out devils, Harris asserted.[19] He adduced a
number of Scripture texts that clearly show this distinction.
For example, Luke 6:17-18 states: "A great multitude of
people ... came to hear him and to be healed of their diseases;
and those who were troubled with unclean spirits were
cured."

Harris found special significance in the wording of
Matthew 4:24: "They carried to him all those afflicted with
various diseases and racked with pain: the possessed, luna-
tics, the paralyzed. He cured them all."

> This passage mentions categories of ills—physical
> illness, mental illness, demon possession. This
> clearly indicates that people of the time recognized
> a difference between mental illness and posses-
> sion. They lived much closer to illness than we do:
> those who were ill stayed in the home until they
> died, as did those who were mentally or emotion-
> ally disturbed, unless these were violent. As a
> consequence, people were more familiar with
> various illnesses and their symptoms than we are.
> It is a bit naive to suggest that they could not
> distinguish physical illness, emotional illness and
> demonic activity.[20]

Harris carefully distinguished the different stages of
demonic influence.

> *Ordinary temptations* are thoughts and images the
> devil uses in attempting to turn Christians aside
> from doing God's will.

> Temptations may also be *acute infestations* or *ob-
> sessions*. They are compulsive in terms of strength,
> persistence and continuity. They may play upon a
> moral, spiritual or physical weakness, or a combi-
> nation of these, and the temptations of the devil are
> carefully orchestrated to produce maximum effect.

While temptations are experienced as external to the person, in *possession* the devil acts from within. In possession, the activity of the devil can be clearly distinguished from the personal activity of the individual and is, in fact, opposed to it. The evil spirit makes use of the person's body, speaking through his mouth and compelling his movements. The person's imagination and sentiments are often filled with the devil, sin and hell. He or she may be besieged by terrifying or impure visions, plunged into despair, convinced of damnation. While the devil directly affects sensation, imagination and feeling, his presence also influences intelligence and will, which become troubled, darkened, paralyzed, constrained.

Supernatural demonic possession occurs when a person knowingly and willingly puts himself in a situation that invites demonic possession.

Spiritual demonic possession takes place contrary to the person's will. There is no pact with the devil, either implicit or explicit. Generally, this may occur when the avenues of the conscious or subconscious mind are left unguarded. Thus, a child not yet aware of good and evil (see Mark 9:14-29) may be so invaded, particularly if the environment is steeped in sin or subject to the occult. Invasion by evil forces may also occur when a person is unconscious either through accident, illness or anesthesia. It may take place when a habit of sin has left a person careless with respect to temptation and occasions of sin. Mental, moral or emotional weakness may also afford opportunity for demonic manipulation. Demonic forces may enter a person through emotional excess: hate, suspicion, terror and various forms of perverted sex. Attack is not inevitable in these situations, but it is possible and may be the cause of problems which are apparent only later.

In *physical possession*, the demonic power possesses the person's body and uses it as an instrument. This may cause the person to manifest extraordinary strength, climb walls, or move through the air—situations as bizarre to others as they are frightening to the victim.

In *psychological possession*, the demonic power uses the victim's psychological faculties. Thus the person may speak or understand a language totally unknown to him and reveal things which are hidden, such as the existence of buried treasure or others' secret sins.[21]

There are a number of other good books on demonic influence and prayers of deliverance and exorcism. *Deliverance Prayer*, edited by Fathers Matthew and Dennis Linn,[22] contained a number of papers developed by the Catholic bishops' National Steering Committee of Diocesan Liaisons for the Charismatic Renewal. Other books about the deliverance ministry include *Deliverance from Evil Spirits: A Weapon for Spiritual Warfare* by Randy Cirner and Father Michael Scanlan; *Spiritual Warfare: Defeating Satan in the Christian Life* by Reverend Michael Harper; *A Manual for Spiritual Warfare* by Reverend Don Basham.[23] These books and Harris's book also have helpful bibliographies.

A different type of book was *Masks of Satan* by Christopher Nugent.[24] It talked about the demonic in history, including case studies of the Marquis de Sade, Friedrich Nietzsche, Aleister Crowley and Adolf Hitler and other leading Nazis.

An AP story described how a Chicago hospital has set up a special treatment program to wean teen-agers from satanism. "The kids who will be admitted will be here primarily because of their behavioral and emotional problems," explained Michael Weiss, an adolescent psychologist at Hart-grove Hospital. The treatment at the new Center for the Treatment of Ritualistic Deviance will seek to undermine satanism's underlying belief system, which hampers conventional treatment.

Satanism "gives them the promise of power and privilege beyond anything they ever imagined. Not only can they have everything they want, . . . but they can do so while totally indulging themselves in drugs, sex or any momentary pleasure," Weiss said. "We try to help them see how unrealistic the promises are. Our ultimate goal is to make them able to function in the world so they can have a reasonable and successful life for themselves and not harm anyone else."[25]

Satanic Murders

Grisly stories of satanic murders are unfortunately becoming rather common in the daily newspaper and on television. A heart-wrenching tale began unfolding April 11, 1989, in Matamoros, Mexico, when Mexican soldiers and police uncovered 12 mutilated bodies at the ranch of a bizarre drug-smuggling cult. Another body was dug up two days later and eventually a total of 15 murders was reported. The story was given wide front-page coverage. Matamoros is just across the border from Brownsville, Texas. Here's the way *Time* described what the police found on the scene.

> In and around a corral, they found several make-shift graves; the overpowering stench of decaying flesh led to digging that eventually uncovered the corpses of 13 males, one as young as 14. Several of the victims had been slashed with knives, others bludgeoned on the head. One had been hanged, another apparently set afire and at least two pumped with bullets. Some had been tortured with razor blades or had their hearts ripped out. Nearly all had been severely mutilated: ears,

nipples and testicles removed, the eyes gouged from one victim, the head missing from another.

[In a shack, police] found a squat iron kettle whose contents suggested that more than just a band of ruthless killers had been at work. Inside the pot, resting in dried blood, were a charred human brain and a roasted turtle. Other containers held a witch's brew of human hair, a goat's head and chicken parts.

. . . The Mexican police pieced together a horrific tale of a voodoo-practicing cult of drug smugglers who believed that orgies of human sacrifice would win satanic protection for its 2,000-lb.-a-week marijuana-running operation in the U.S.[26]

On May 6, 1989, while trapped by police in a Mexico City apartment, the cult's leader, Adolfo de Jesus Constanzo, 26, and his right-hand man, Martin Quintana Rodriguez, were killed with a machine gun by an associate, Alvaro de Leon Valdez, 22. Valdez told police the leader ordered him to kill the two men "because if I didn't it was going to go very badly for me in hell." Arrested after the incident along with Valdez and three other cult members was Sara Aldrete Villarreal, 24, the alleged "godmother" of the cult.

Among the victims was Mark Kilroy, 21, a University of Texas premedical student who was kidnapped while he was partying in Matamoros. He was killed with a machete and his legs were cut off. His brain and spine were removed, the latter to be made into a necklace.[27]

Here are some more stories of satanic murders.

*On December 8, 1987, the battered body of a 19-year-old youth and a cat carcass were found in a cistern in southwestern Missouri. He had been beaten to death by as many as 50 blows to the head. Four bloodied baseball bats were found nearby. Three 17-year-old youths were arrested and charged with first-degree murder. "They thought they somehow would be rewarded by Satan," a defense attorney said. "All three of these boys were deep into this heavy metal music."[28]

* On January 9, 1988, a 14-year-old eighth-grader at a Catholic school in New Jersey killed his mother and himself. He stabbed his mother at least two dozen times with his Boy Scout knife and killed himself by slashing his wrists and cutting his throat. "There were no indicators . . . that there were any problems with the boy at all," a county prosecutor said. About a month before, the boy began reading books on the occult and Satan worship. Investigators found a suicide note in which the boy indicated the murder and suicide were planned and influenced by his interest in the occult.[29]

* On October 25, 1988, Geraldo Rivera brought his controversial television program to prime time for a special show on Satan worship. Perhaps the grisliest episode was an interview with two women, each of whom said she had bred a child for ritual murder by satanists.

* In his book, *Satanism: The Seduction of America's Youth,* Bob Larson recounted an instance on his radio call-in show in which a teen-age girl told of two satanic cult murders she witessed. "They burned my girlfriend alive while I watched. She wasn't the only one they killed. Another friend of mine was forced to say 'Satan, I give my life to you now' as they pushed him over a cliff."[30]

* Many mass murderers in recent times, including Charles Manson and the southern California "Night Stalker," have been linked to satanism. Chicago Police Detective Robert Simandl, an expert on satanism, said many self-styled satanists have a scanty knowledge of satanism but use it to justify their bizarre crimes. In this category, he put Illinois murderer Robin Gecht, who mutilated prostitutes, killed them and afterward ritually ate parts of their bodies.[31]

In a 1988 interview, Simandl said teen-age crime growing out of devil worship was on the upswing nationwide. The crimes included thefts of chalices from churches, graverobbing and animal mutilation—all carried out to obtain elements needed for devil worship.[32] Speaking of satanism,

San Francisco Police Detective Sandi Gallant said in a 1988 interview that she received four calls a day from around the country about crimes with satanic or occult overtones. "Three years ago, nobody wanted to hear it, nobody believed it was real," she said. "Now I'm seeing them tuning into it, looking to see it is a reality and facing it head-on."[33] Researcher Ted Schwartz said in 1988 that he believed satanism existed in some form in every community. He had spent five years interviewing law-enforcement officers, former satanists and victims of satanic abuse.[34]

Satanic Child Abuse

Ritualistic child abuse is spreading, observers contend. Sandi Gallant said in 1988 she believed ritualistic abuse was occuring nationwide, although not on a widespread scale.[35] Robert Simandl said psychiatrists are beginning to take more seriously mental patients who tell of being kidnapped as children and forced into pornography or prostitution amid trappings of devil worship. He recounted a chilling account of a child subjected to satanic abuse in a day-care center. After she was sexually abused, the four-year-old girl was told to draw a picture of a bunny rabbit. A real rabbit was then brought into the room and killed in front of her. She was told that this would happen to her if she told her parents. The picture of the rabbit was sent home with the girl and the proud parents posted it on the refrigerator, not knowing that it was a daily reminder to the girl not to talk.[36]

The book, *Michelle Remembers*, tells of the abuse a five-year-old girl suffered at the hands of a group of satanists, including her mother. The girl was smeared with excrement and placed on a black altar amid lighted candles. More than once, she was put down in an opened grave and dead cats thrown in with her and the stone pulled back over the opening. Twice they tried to kill her. The girl was forced to participate in rituals that had to do with dead cats and human cadavers and dead babies. They tried to make the girl eat ashes that she was convinced were from a cadaver. In a satanic Easter Sunday ritual, horns were attached to her head and a tail to her spine and she was "birthed" through a statue of Lucifer. As an adult, the woman received help from a psychiatrist and Christian counselors.[37]

In 1988 in Roseburg, Ore., Edward J. Gallup, Sr., an elderly Nazarene minister, and his adult son, Edward Gallup, Jr., were convicted of molesting children in the family's three day-care centers. The children alleged that chanting, wearing of black robes and the burning of candles were part of the ritualistic abuse, according to prosecutor Bill Lasswell.[38]

The celebrated McMartin case of 1983 to 1990 catapulted ritualistic abuse to national attention with tales of drugs, bondage and animal sacrifice at a prestigious southern California preschool. In an 80-page report concerning specific charges of satanic child molestation brought against a day-care center, the California attorney general observed that the sheriff's deputies so doubted the accusations that they neglected to search for additional evidence. "This failure to substantiate the children's claims became more pronounced when allegations of satanic rituals and homicides emerged. The more bizarre the allegation—and the lack of evidence to support it—the more the children's credibility suffered," the report said.[39]

Bruce G. Frederickson wrote that, in another case, police tended to dismiss allegations of satanic rituals and cannibalism until a national pattern of abuse began to emerge. "Investigators reasoned that if children reported sexual matters of which they previously had no knowledge, and if identical reports were filed from children who were unacquainted with each other and separated by great distances, there must be at least *some* truth to the charges of ritualistic satanic abuse,"[40] Frederickson stated.

Some believe ritualistic abuse occurs on a large scale, and that a satanic conspiracy is not out of the question. "It's pandemic," commented Larry Jones, a Boise law-enforcement professional who has studied cult crimes. He said he believed some high-ranking satanists may have directed an

organized assault on youthful innocence, but admitted no
hard evidence existed.[41]

The number of children who are killed by child molest-
ers may be fairly high. "The number of missing children in
America is between 1.5 million and 1.8 million," the Spiritual
Counterfeits Project staff reported in 1989. "Many of these
are runaways who return home within 72 hours, but what
about the ones who don't? Each year between 2,500 and
5,000 *unidentified* children are found slain, and many are
thought to be the victims of child abductors."[42]

Some specialists have urged caution when talking about
satanic child abuse. "Some kids may be making it up, some
are confused, some may be manipulated into saying these
things," contended John Rabun, a Baptist minister and dep-
uty director of the National Center for Missing and Exploited
Children. "But some of it is undoubtedly true. I can't see
how in this day and age someone can say this is not going
on." Rabun and other observers said they believed that ritual
abuse has occurred only in a very small percentage of child
sexual-abuse cases, trailing far behind incest and conventional forms of day-care abuse.[43]

According to the *National & International Religion Report,*
a two-year investigation by the Committee for Scientific
Examination of Religion determined that satanic crime is
vastly exaggerated. Of the more than one million violent
crimes reported in the United States in the previous five
years, only about 60 were listed by police as involving
satanism.[44]

A cautionary note on reporting alarmist stories was
sounded at the annual meeting of the Religion Newswriters
Association in Las Vegas in June, 1989. J. Gordon Melton, a
researcher at the Institute for the Study of American Religion, Santa Barbara, Calif., and an authority on satanic
groups, said there is "no real evidence of an increase in
satanism in recent years." He said that most reports of ritual
mutilation of animals can be explained by the sharp teeth of
predators; stories of women abused and chosen as breeders

of children to be sacrificed in satanic rituals cannot be corroborated. Some law-enforcement agencies possess handbooks on dealing with satanic cults that have their roots in misinformation and hysteria, Melton suggested.[45]

In an excellent article in *Forward*, Craig S. Hawkins described seven types of satanists.

> 1. *Traditional satanists.* They have a complete disdain for things Christian and mock and desecrate rituals held sacred by the church. For instance, they might recite the Lord's prayer backwards or insert blasphemies in it. The communion cup is often filled with animal or human blood or with urine. Likewise, the host or communion wafer is profaned or substituted with certain detestable items. (These practices derive from the infamous Black Mass.) In extreme cases, animal or human sacrifices may be offered to add greater efficacy to the rite. Christianity's doctrines are also perverted. In essence, almost everything believed or done is a reversal or inversion of the Christian counterpart.
>
> 2. *Nontraditional satanists.* They are just as secretive as the traditional satanists, but much more eclectic in beliefs. They mock much in Christianity, but this is not the primary catalyst for the development of their dogma and rites. For instance, they may believe in innumerable reincarnations of earthly lives in which they will be able to fully indulge their carnal appetites, and not in the traditional Christian concepts of heaven and hell. They may also hold that God and Satan are approximately equal in power and ability. Animal or human sacrifices may not be parodies of Christian rites, but could stem from the belief that there is an invisible force (*mana*) that can be transmitted to the recipient through the consumption of blood or certain organs, such as the brain or heart. These

groups may also be heavily absorbed in sex and the taking of drugs, often in connection with religious and magical rites.

3. *Public satanists.* They are not "underground" or secretive concerning their existence. There are close to a dozen of these groups in America. Most, but not all, are greatly influenced by Gnosticism or Anton LaVey's writings. The most infamous public satanist organization is Anton LaVey's Satanic Church in America, founded in 1966. The Satanic Church's creed is based upon a denial and reversal of orthodox Christianity. What the Christian church calls the seven deadly sins—greed, pride, envy, anger, gluttony, lust, and sloth—LaVey says are to be fully indulged as they lead to physical, mental, or emotional gratification. LaVey's beliefs are a combination of Machiavellian social ethics, hedonism, and simple narcissism as the highest good. (On some college campuses, LaVey's *Satanic Bible* reportedly outsells *The Holy Bible.*)

4. *Youth gang satanists.* These groups are composed of young people (predominantly white males), ranging in ages from early teens to early twenties. The gangs cohere due to a commonality of satanism, often identifying with a particular genre of rock music (heavy metal, black metal), and not primarily, like traditional gangs, because of ethnical or territorial considerations. Many come from middle to upper-middle class families. Over 90 percent who get involved are "dabblers"; they are not true or serious satanists. Nevertheless, even granting that their nonchalant involvement with satanism is merely a phase of "normal" adolescent rebellion, the potential consequences to the individual's physical, emotional, and spiritual health, and to society at large are by no means in-

nocuous. Furthermore, a small percentage of these young people become religious satanists, adopting satanism's belief and value system as their own adult worldview.

5. *Fringe group satanists.* Their primary interests and activities are centered around one or more deviant, and in many cases illegal, activity. Satanism is only a secondary interest which forms a kind of backdrop for the primary pursuit. Deviant interests may include pedophilia (this type of satanist is the most likely to practice child abuse), group sex, sado-masochism, homosexuality, and taking drugs.

6. *Individual satanists.* They do not participate in a group context because they are not aware of any groups in their area or because they do not feel the need to get involved with one. Their initial interest in satanism was likely stimulated by any one, or combination, of the following sources: a) reading horror stories, occult literature, or specifically satanic material; b) seeing horror movies, especially those that romanticize the devil; c) listening to certain types of music with either subtle or blatant satanic lyrics and art work; d) through an acquaintance who is more or less familiar with some form of satanism. Their views and practices cover the spectrum of satanism.

7. *Psychotic individual satanists.* These are individual satanists who are seriously mentally deranged. It may be that some satanic serial killers have a minimal knowledge of satanism, and use it to express rage rather than religion. It is possible that some psychotic satanists were expelled from some satanic groups because their behavior was too volatile. The group may have feared being publicly discovered or linked to criminal activities.

From the Christian standpoint, it is highly probable that many of these deranged individuals are
demon possessed.[46]

Some satanists believe there is a monumental struggle
between Satan and God, but they differ on the outcome.
Some believe Satan will win and satanists will enjoy an
eternity of unbridled debauchery. Others believe, like Christians do, that God will win and Satan and all who have
followed him will suffer eternal torment. "Many satanists
actually know that they will suffer excruciating anguish
throughout eternity, but still persist in their choice to follow
the devil," Hawkins explained. "Satanists may hold this
seemingly incomprehensible position because of their seeth-
ing hatred and utter contempt for God and Christians. God
is viewed as a contemptible, weak-willed, spineless, maud-
lin chump, a cosmic bore and 'nerd' of infinite proportions.
Christianity is viewed as a nuisance and hindrance to living;
as a dreary, tedious and lifeless religion. Thus, some satanists reason, who could possibly want to spend eternity with
this kind of God?"[47]

Satanists, like persons involved in witchcraft, practice
magic. They believe magic works. They believe occultic
rituals cause real effects in the real world. The mysterious
force that is tapped into to cause these effects is deemed by
different satanists to be: a) latent psychic abilities; b) impersonal supernormal forces of nature as yet undiscovered
by modern science; or c) supernatural personal beings, demons.[48]

New Agers in general, of course, are a far friendlier
group than satanists, but what do New Agers think of Satan
and evil? Russell Chandler visited Marilyn Ferguson at her
home and asked her about this. "The real perversity we
have—the way we behave in a way that has evil consequences—it's because of the classical Luciferian attitude: we
want to be God," Ferguson said. "We don't understand our
boundaries . . . . It's a failure to understand our rightful
place."

Chandler countered, in the New Age aren't we all "God"?

"We *are* God, but not all of God," Ferguson responded. "People get overly carried away when they realize they create their reality . . . . There are other people out there and their needs and their realities have to interact with mine . . . . You can tap into this power, but you're not the sum total of it."[49]

Witchcraft

"Practitioners of New Age witchcraft are coming out of the broom closet," Russell Chandler noted wryly. "By late 1987, religion experts estimated there were perhaps 50,000 witches in the United States, although the figure could be higher since many still choose anonymity."[50] Contemporary witches, by and large, are not satanists. Witches are neo-pagans or worshippers of nature. They are practitioners of wicca or "the craft." "Practicing 'black' magic, sacrificing animals, casting evil spells, and engaging in voodoo rites and sex orgies are downplayed, and most witches deny that they believe in—much less worship—Satan,"[51] Chandler observed.

This may be true today, but it was not true of European witchcraft. Respected scholar Jeffrey Burton Russell stated: "European witchcraft is best viewed as a religious cult of the Devil, built on the foundations of low magic and folk traditions but formed and defined by the Christian society within which it operated. The action of Christianity on European witchcraft produced, among other characteristics, the sabbat, or witches' meeting, usually under the presidency of the Devil and entailing some form of reverence to the Devil coupled with a renunciation of Christ."[52] "Low" magic is defined as being practical and aimed at obtaining immediate effects, in contrast to "high" magic which seeks through occult knowledge to understand the universe.

Russell said that witches dealt with three kinds of evil spirits: minor demons, major demons and the devil himself. He said there were "at least five degrees of closeness in the relations that one might have with evil spirits: incantation, where they are called up and compelled to do one's bidding (this could be done with demons much more easily than with the Devil); an implicit pact with the spirits; an explicit pact promising something in return for their aid; sacrifice, homage or other reverence; and finally worship."[53] Given the Christian environment, "European witchcraft is best considered a form of heresy, for in order to worship the Christian Devil one must first be a Christian,"[54] Russell noted.

"Without denying that many of the traits ascribed to witchcraft are physically improbable or that many of the witches condemned were innocent, one is obliged to regard witchcraft as a reality,"[55] Russell concluded. Activities ascribed to witchcraft include sex orgies, rape, murder of children and cannibalism.[56]

In the Middle Ages and colonial times, 100,000 or more witches were estimated to have been executed by church and civil authorities. The small town of Salem, Mass., was seized by witchcraft hysteria in 1692. Though the town only boasted about 100 households, some 150 persons were arrested. Of these, 31 were tried and 20 were executed. Two others died in jail.[57]

Witches certainly have a better public image nowadays. Miriam Starhawk, a witch or proponent of wicca, has been teaching at an institute of spirituality at Holy Names College, Oakland, Calif. She is an associate of Matthew Fox. (See Chapter Nine.) Sociologist Ron Enroth reported that Harvard Divinity School has offered courses on neopaganism and hosted meetings of witches.[58]

The great majority of people who call themselves witches, according to Gordon Melton of the Institute for Study of American Religion at Santa Barbara, "follow the nature-oriented polytheistic worship of the Great Mother Goddess," whose names include Diana, Isis, Demeter, Hecate, Cybele or Demeter, as well as Gaia.[59] "There are goddess bookshops and jewelry stores," reported Chandler, and "pagan Alcoholics Anonymous meetings and performance theaters; witches' newspapers, computerized information networks, and professional societies. Even a witches' cemetery was dedicated near Los Angeles."[60] In addition to feminine goddess worshipers, Chandler explained, "neopagans" can include Celtic revivalist witches; creators of Greek, Egyptian, Norse and Druid revivals; and those who experiment with various forms of magic (or "magick"), sorcery, animism, divination and witchcraft.[61]

Starhawk sees witchcraft as a very personal religion. "The coven is a witch's support group, consciousness-raising group, psychic study center, clergy-training program, college of mysteries, surrogate clan, and religious congregation all rolled into one," she wrote in *The Spiral Dance*. "In a strong coven, the bond is, by tradition, 'closer than family': a sharing of spirits, emotions, imaginations . . . . The coven structure makes the organization of witchcraft very different from that of most other religions. The craft is not based on large, amorphous masses who are only superficially acquainted; nor is it based on individual gurus with their devotees and disciples. There is no hierarchical authority, no Dalai Lama, no Pope. The structure of witchcraft is cellular, based on small circles whose members share a deep commitment to each other and the craft."[62]

Goddess Worship

"In the occult tradition, women are regarded as evil," Colin Wilson stated unchivalrously. "In numerology, the female number 2, which represents gentleness, submissiveness, sweetness, is also the devil's number. The Hindu goddess Kali, the Divine Mother, is also the goddess of violence and destruction."[63] He explained this—rather lamely—by saying that women were not supposed to have good long-range vision.

Well, times they are a-changing! It's the male who gets blamed for everything now. According to *Green Politics: The Global Promise* by Fritjof Capra and Charlene Spretnak, only a female goddess from the East can deliver humanity from the authoritarianism of an oppressive patriarchal style of religion that has dominated in the West. There is a powerful strand of New Age philosophy that blames men for the evils of human history, including wars and the suppression of women.[64] Even Kali (see page 38) is a good goddess now. She is the Great Mother who encourages personal awareness. A feminist spiritual movement that developed in the 1970s, often referred to as "ecofeminism," viewed men "as brutalizing women through sexual violence and pornographic exploitation, and dominating them through a stern, overbearing, male 'sky-god,' "[65] Chandler reported. Neopaganism and the worship of nature became popular. Charlene Spretnak spoke about this at a conference on ecofeminism.

> We would not have been interested in "Yahweh with a skirt," a distant, detached, domineering godhead who happened to be female. What was cosmologically wholesome and healing was the discovery of the divine as immanent in and around us. What was intriguing was the sacred link of the goddess in her many guises with totemic animals and plants, sacred groves, womblike caves, the moon-rhythm blood of menses, the ecstatic dance—the experience of *knowing Gaia* [Earth], her voluptuous contours and fertile plains, her flowing waters that give life, her animals as teachers.[66]

Feminist spirituality has captivated many women dropouts from traditional Christianity, Chandler noted. Twelve of 17 former nuns who left their orders to embrace lesbianism now practice neopaganism, according to the book *Lesbian Nuns: Breaking Silence*. The book stated that these "New-Age nuns" are into "astrology, Goddess imagery, Tarot, dreamwork, I Ching, herbal healing, meditation, massage and body . . . and psychic work. We are creating communal rituals for solstices, equinoxes, and full moons."[67]

Some religious feminists go even further. They want to

bring back holy prostitutes as conduits of the sacred. In a speech at a Conference of Feminist Art and Culture at California State University, Long Beach, Deena Metzger talked on "Re-Vamping the World: On the Return of the Holy Prostitute." According to Robert J.L. Burrows, Metzger had more than simply temple attendants in mind. "She is advocating the role for *all* women as a means of resacralizing the body and regaining feminine spiritual power lost with the advent of patriarchical religion," he said. He quoted Metzger as saying: "The task is to accept . . . sexuality and erotic love as spiritual disciplines."[68]

Animism

James W. Sire has described the New Age worldview as having philosophical roots in naturalism, Eastern pantheistic monism and animism. He defined animism as "the general outlook on life that underlies primal or so-called pagan religions."[69] He lists six notions held in pagan religions that are reflected in New Age thought:

1. The natural universe is inhabited by countless spiritual beings, often conceived in a rough hierarchy, the top of which is the Sky God—vaguely like theism's God but without his interest in human beings;

2. Thus the universe has a personal dimension but not an infinite-personal Creator-God;

3. These spiritual beings range in temperament from vicious and nasty to comic and beneficent;

4. For people to get by in life the evil spirits must be placated and the good ones wooed by gifts and offerings, ceremonies and incantations;

5. Witch doctors, sorcerers and shamans, through long, arduous training, have learned to control the spirit world to some extent and ordinary people are much beholden to their power to cast out spir-

its of illness, drought and so forth;

6. Ultimately there is a unity to all of life; that is, the cosmos is a continuum of spirit and matter; "animals may be ancestors of men, people may change into animals, trees and stones may possess souls."[70]

The New Age movement, Sire continued, "reflects every aspect of animism, though often giving it a naturalistic twist—or demythologizing it by psychology."[71] This animistic viewpoint was popularized by the first three books of Carlos Castaneda: *The Teachings of Don Juan* (1968), *A Separate Reality* (1971) and *Journey to Ixtlan* (1972). While working for a doctorate in anthropology at the University of California at Los Angeles, Castaneda began studying the effect of psychedelic drugs in North American Indian culture and then apprenticed himself to Don Juan, a Yaqui sorcerer. "Having completed the initiation rites over several years," Sire observed, "Castaneda became a sorcerer whose alleged experience with various kinds of new realities and separate universes makes fascinating, sometimes frightening, reading."[72]

Another anthropologist, Michael Harner, wrote a book, *The Way of the Shaman: A Guide to Power and Healing*, that was, according to Brooks Alexander, a detailed description of shamanistic practices and "a tract of passionate advocacy." Harner became an active participant in shamanism while doing field study on the Conibo Indians of the Peruvian Amazon. Alexander saw the book as an effort to interest others in shamanism and to provide fatherly advice to "those of you who wish to become professional shamans."[73]

One of Harner's students, Jose Stevens, studied shamanism while pursuing a doctorate in psychology. Along with his wife, Lena S. Stevens, he wrote a book about his experiences: *Secrets of Shamanism: Tapping the Spirit Power Within You*. The book started with a woman, Shawna, tapping the spirit power within her to get financing for an anthropological trip to Peru. She beat on a drum given her by an old Apache Indian and called up falcon spirit. Falcon told her to "call Melanie." She did and Melanie came up with the money.[74] How did this work? The back cover explained: "Psychologist Jose Stevens and his wife Lena demonstrate how the ancient techniques of shamanism can be adapted to the needs and concerns of the modern world. Through a series of simple exercises, lessons, and rituals, they teach you to identify and communicate with your inner spiritual guides—and how to achieve professional success, psychological enlightenment, and personal fulfillment."

Chapter  9

Matthew Fox,
Cosmic Christ,
Enneagram,
Holy Order of MANS,
Potpourri,
Yoga Christianity,
A Course in Miracles

Religion _____

Why and how have New Age ideas become so popular among Christian believers? New Age teachings are so banal, so plastic, it seems that it would be almost impossible for a Christian to be taken in by them. Perhaps, after all, no prayerful Christian who has a good grounding in the faith is ever taken in by New Age ideas, but there are apparently many superficial Christians who are being fooled.

Another problem is that many Christians apparently have forgotten how to think. A sort of mold is growing over their minds. They no longer realize that, if the Apostles Creed and the Nicene Creed are true, then opinions which contradict these basic Christian teachings cannot be true.

A five-inch by four-inch ad in the *Indianapolis Star*, May 1, 1989, page A11, trumpeted: "The greatest discovery you'll every [sic] make . . . is the potential of your own mind!" The ad was placed by a Franciscan Catholic priest, Father Justin Belitz, for the Hermitage, a Catholic retreat house in Indianapolis. The ad was promoting training in the "Silva Method of Mind Development." As we saw in Chapter Seven, Silva

Mind Control is designed to put oneself under the influence of demonic spirits. Also, I always thought that a Christian would say that the "greatest discovery" a person could make is Jesus.

In his book, *Peace of Mind Through Possibility Thinking*, Reverend Robert H. Schuller equates monks gazing at a crucifix with Transcendental Meditation devotees chanting a mantra. He thinks they are equally effective means of combatting distractions in prayer. Schuller, a southern California pastor and popular television personality, states that TM "is not a religion nor is it necessarily anti-Christian."[1] (Remind me to send him a copy of this book with a suggestion that he read Chapter Seven.)

Cardinal Jozef Tomko, head of the Vatican's Congregation for the Evangelization of Peoples, criticized a theology professor at a Catholic university in Cincinnati for promoting views the cardinal said are helping to weaken the church's mission work. According to a Scripps Howard News Service report, Paul Knitter, professor at Xavier University, in two of his books "joins a number of other theologians who are beginning to closely examine the teachings of other religious figures such as Buddha and Mohammed and questioning whether Jesus Christ is the best and final revelation of God."[2]

In his speech at an international conference on mission work, Tomko said some missionaries are applying this theological thinking to their work in foreign countries in such a way that they concentrate on feeding the hungry and changing political systems instead of proclaiming the gospel. "There is the attitude that if we can't save them from hell, then why should we be there?," Knitter said in reply. "The cardinal wants to close the discussion and deny the question before we've had a chance to ask it."[3]

This is not New Age teaching, it's an example of a Christian not being sure that Christian truths are true. Feeding the hungry and obtaining clothing and shelter for the poor are important, but it is no less important for the Christian to share the good news that God has sent his only Son to redeem the world and give us eternal life and give us the Holy Spirit to be our comforter.

Matthew Fox

In 1988-89, Matthew Fox, a Catholic priest and proponent of what he terms "creation spirituality," took a year's sabbatical of silence at the request of the Vatican. After earning a doctorate in theology at the *Institut Catholique* in Paris, Fox, a member of the Dominican religious order, returned to the United States in 1970 and began developing his ideas on spirituality. In 1977 he founded his Institute in Culture and Creation Spirituality (ICCS), which was affiliated with Mundelein College in Chicago. In 1983, he moved the institute to Holy Names College, Oakland, Calif.

In 1988, a student at ICCS could earn a Master of Arts degree in spirituality in any of three tracks: Culture and Spirituality, Creation Spirituality and Geo-Justice, and Creation Spirituality and Psychology. Instructional staff included a masseuse, a Zen Buddhist, a martial-arts instructor, a yoga teacher, a "priestess of Oshun in the Yoruba Lucumi African tradition" and teachers from more traditional academic backgrounds. Instructor Buck Ghost Horse, a Native American spiritual teacher from the Lakota and Hunkpapa Nations, announced office consultations would be held out of doors unless it was raining. Starhawk (a.k.a. Miriam Simos) taught a course on creating rituals. A self-proclaimed witch, she is a follower of wicca, a matriarchal, native European, earth-based religion.

Fox also started a bimonthly magazine, *Creation*, which, a promotional brochure stated, "brings you new insights into our Western religious tradition through scripture, the creation mystics of the West, the wisdom of earth-centered native spiritualities and through the most creative contemporary thinkers in the fields of Green politics, bio-regionalism, humanistic psychology, social transformation, the new physics, and creation spirituality."

Response to a readership survey published in the July/ August, 1987, issue indicated that about half of *Creation's* readers were Roman Catholic and many of these were nuns. "This magazine helps me to integrate my many spiritual loves: the Catholic Church, native spirituality, Wicca," one respondent wrote.

"Human sexuality is meant to be experienced as mysticism," Fox wrote in an article in the May/June, 1987, *Creation*. "Creation spirituality challenges men and women to gratitude for their sexuality and for the unique person they are— woman, man, heterosexual, homosexual or bisexual—by gift of the Creator and the creative universe. Diversity is to be celebrated, not regretted." The article is illustrated by photos of a naked man which were taken by a nun.

In 1984, Fox ran into trouble with the Vatican, allegedly as the result of a complaint from members of Catholics United for the Faith. This conservative group complained about Fox's participation in a Seattle program sponsored by Catholic homosexuals. Cardinal Joseph Ratzinger, prefect of the Vatican's Congregation for the Doctrine of the Faith, in July, 1984, asked the master of the Dominicans, Father Damian Byrne in Rome, to have Fox's activities and three of his books examined—including the book, *Original Blessing*. Byrne turned the matter over to Fox's provincial superior in Chicago.

In May, 1985, a 20-page examination of Fox's works by three American Dominican theologians was forwarded to Byrne and then to Ratzinger. Nothing warranting "condemnation" was found, but the theologians judged that Fox should better integrate certain teachings on sin, the cross and asceticism into his thought.

This did not satisfy the Vatican and an exchange of letters between the Vatican and the Dominicans ensued. In May, 1988, Fox was ordered to take a sabbatical year and refrain from teaching and lecturing during this period. The sabbatical year began December 15, 1988. Fox did not take his silencing quietly.

On December 13, 1988, a full-page ad appeared in the *New York Times*, paid for by the California-based Friends of Creation Spirituality. In the ad, Fox accused the Catholic Church of "fundamentalist zeal." The ad portrayed Fox, liberation theologian Leonardo Boff, moral theologian Charles Curran and Seattle Archbishop Raymond Hunthausen as "victims of the Roman inquisition."

In a front-page article in the October 21, 1988, *National Catholic Reporter*, Fox indicated he told Byrne that his "work is just too pressing to be postponed until a neurotic papal regime dies out."

Cosmic Christ

Late in 1988, after he was ordered to take a sabbatical, Fox's new book, *The Coming of the Cosmic Christ*,[4] was released. Here are some quotes from the book and some brief comments.

> The Cosmic Christ and the living cosmology that the Cosmic Christ ushers into society and psyche have the power to launch an era of what I call deep ecumenism. Deep ecumenism is the movement that will unleash the wisdom of *all* world religions—Hinduism and Buddhism, Islam and Judaism, Taoism and Shintoism, Christianity in all its forms, and native religions and goddess religions throughout the world. This unleashing of wisdom holds the last hope for the survival of the planet we call home. For there is no such thing as a Lutheran sun and a Taoist moon and Jewish ocean and a Roman Catholic forest. When humanity learns this we will have learned a way out of our anthropocentric dilemma that is boring our young, killing our souls, trivializing our worship, and exterminating the planet. Universalism is a common characteristic to all the traditions of the Cosmic Christ in the Scriptures and in Western history.[5]

In fact, however, there are four basic views about God:
Atheism: no god at all.
Pantheism: there is no personal god; all is god.
Monotheism: there is one personal God; this is held by Christians, Jews and Muslims.
Polytheism: there are many gods.
These ideas are mutually exclusive. If monotheism is correct—if there is only one God—the other views are all wrong. It is logically impossible to mix all four ideas together into one cosmic stew.

> Today we can respond to the challenge deep ecumenism poses. Does the fact that the Christ became incarnate in Jesus exclude the Christ's becoming incarnate in others—Lao-tzu or Buddha or Moses or Sarah or Sojourner Truth or Gandhi or me or you? . . . One of the more surprising areas of deep ecumenism may well prove to be that between goddess religions and Christian mysticism.[6]

For Fox, evidently, the historical Jesus is not uniquely the Son of God.

> Where can men turn to recover their origins? To the sacredness of phallos . . . . The oldest of the world religions of today, Hinduism, which dates to 10,000-8,000 B.C., celebrated this hierophany of phallos. The god Shiva is creator and destroyer of things and is lord of the dance. Shiva's symbol is the lingam or phallos. Shiva speaks: "I am not distinct from the phallos. The phallos is identical with me. It draws my faithful to me and therefore must be worshipped." . . . This is Cosmic Christ language. The word of God who is present intimately in all things is also present intimately in the reproductive and sexual powers of the male and female.[7]

You may want to reread what I wrote about Shiva in Chapter Two.

Persons of color will invariably find that their ancestors were deeply imbued with a living cosmology before the white colonists arrived bearing a religion that, at that time in history, had lost practically all contact with the Cosmic Christ. The power of native religions to regenerate Christianity and to reconnect the old religion with the prophetic Good News of the Gospels has yet to be tapped.[8]

Is divine revelation not good enough for Fox? Does Christianity have to be regenerated by native religions—which are pantheistic, polytheistic and steeped in the occult?

Today in Boston—so Irish and Italian and Roman Catholic—I encounter the best of the Second Vatican Council Catholics who have left their church and attend Unitarian or Quaker services because they feel so deeply unrepresented by the current Catholic hierarchy of that city.[9]

Fox evidently thinks it's an improvement to abandon the doctrine of the Trinity to become a Unitarian.

The name "Christ" means "the anointed one." All of us are anointed ones. We are all royal persons, creative, godly, divine, persons of beauty and of grace. We are all Cosmic Christs, "other Christs."[10]

This sounds very like the fundamental New Age tenet: "We are all gods!"

Perhaps it is time to back huge moving vans up to our seminaries, load up the immense theological paraphernalia that has accumulated around the theme of the historical Jesus, and channel religion's resources in another direction—the quest for the Cosmic Christ.[11]

I always thought the key element in Christianity was that God became human in history in Jesus.

The *National Catholic Reporter* noted that Fox was very popular in some Protestant churches, especially the United Church of Christ (UCC). The 700-member Community Congregational Church (UCC), Tiburon, Calif., studied *The Coming of the Cosmic Christ*. This congregation offered services with Tibetan bells, Buddhist chants and various forms of meditation. Reverend Frank Evans, the pastor, said his congregation was "considered way ahead"[12] of other UCC churches in its eclectic use of spiritual disciplines often associated with the New Age movement.

A book reviewer in the moderately conservative publication *National Catholic Register*, on the other hand, called Fox "certainly an outright heretic." The reviewer, Peter Kreeft, a philosophy professor at Boston College, however, also found in *The Coming of the Cosmic Christ* "much genuine wisdom, intuition, awe and beauty." Kreeft added: "Fox is certainly not a Catholic. He's a pagan child who never grew up."[13]

Enneagram

Out of nowhere, the enneagram burst onto the Christian scene and became very popular with publishers and retreat houses. The enneagram is a circular diagram on which personality types numbered one through nine are symbolically represented at nine equidistant points on the circumference. The numbers are then connected by arrows in significant patterns which point the way to health (integration) or to neurosis (disintegration). Each human personality is said to fall into one of these nine types.

The personality types and the animals symbolizing them are:

1. Perfectionist/reformer, terrier
2. Helper, cat
3. Status-seeker, peacock
4. Artist, basset hound
5. Thinker, fox

6. Loyalist, rabbit
7. Fun-loving/generalist, monkey
8. Powerful, rhinoceros
9. Peacemaker, elephant.

In an article in *New Heaven/New Earth*,[14] Dorothy Ranaghan raised a number of criticisms of enneagrams. To begin with, she had problems with its origin in contemporary Sufism. (Sufism is a mystical offshoot of Islam.) "There is much in the zeal, devotion and asceticism of Sufis that is admirable," she wrote. "Yet, in contrast to the contemplation and the yearning for holiness of the Muslim mystics of former ages, contemporary Sufism, which claims over 40 million adherents, has become a mix of pantheism, magic and rationalism with a belief in telepathy, teleportation, foreknowledge, transmigration of souls and a denial of a personal God."[15]

Ranaghan also had problems with some of the terminology which seemed Christian, but was not. "Redemption," for example, does not mean, among Sufis, the saving action of God in our lives, but "return from ignorance." The very worst thing, according to Sufi doctrine, is "not sin, but ignorance." "All Gnosticism flows from this premise,"[16] Ranaghan observed.

The goal of Sufism is to make a person whole and the enneagram chart seeks to enable healthy integration of the personality as the path to redemption. "Jesus can and does heal and restore sight to the blind and hope to those who are cast down," Ranaghan wrote, "but brokenness in mind or body is not necessarily an obstacle to holiness. Furthermore, even the most authentic, self-discovered, psychologically healthy, integrated and whole person on earth can go to hell."[17]

In her book *A Closer Look at the Enneagram*, Ranaghan said the man primarily responsible for transmitting the enneagram into the West was George Ivanovitch Gurdjieff, an Armenian occultist who lived in Russia from 1877 to 1947.

He also had a great influence on the contemporary New Age movement. Gurdjieff's writings, Ranaghan noted, are "filled with descriptions of planetary influences, astral bodies, clairvoyant and telepathic experiments, and with explanations of the true significance of occult interests such as *kundalini* and the Tarot."[18] For Gurdjieff, the enneagram had secret powers not particularly allied to personality typology. "The enneagram is a universal symbol," Gurdjieff believed. "All knowledge can be included in the enneagram and with the help of the enneagram it can be interpreted."[19]

The enneagram seems very faddish. It seems to be the *in* thing. Proponents seem so excited because they claim it comes from the wisdom of the ancient Sufis, but they are hard-pressed to mention any book from the Sufis that is generally accepted as a work of great wisdom. (Sufis are known for having spawned the whirling dervishes, who spin themselves into an altered state of consciousness.) The enneagram symbol is often portrayed in promotional materials as something magical and mystical in itself. Authors assure us that there are only nine personality types. "The term 'enneagram' is derived from the Greek word 'enneas,' meaning nine," a 1985 book stated. "According to the enneagram system, there are nine, and only nine, types of human personality."[20]

I have personally challenged a number of enneagram proponents about there being *only* nine personality types possible. Everyone I talked to backed off. Some mentioned that the complete enneagram system itself allows for flexibility in assigning personality traits to people. A 1987 book agreed with this: "While the nine personality types of the enneagram form discrete categories, you should not think of them as iron-clad entities. You will find that the enneagram is open-ended and extraordinarily fluid, like human beings themselves."[21]

Furthermore, Christian proponents of the enneagram are sometimes forced to encourage Christians to bend their Christian standards to deal with their problems. "Progress in the enneagram seems to be movement from one sin type to another sin type," Ranaghan wrote. "Persons who are 2s (the 'nervous breakdowns' in the world) need, according to Sister Mary Helen Kelley, to 'come to conscious selfishness' for redemption. Sister Barbara Metz states that 'to come to wholeness . . . the 6 (the loyalist) needs to walk into the darkness of deviance and disobedience.' "[22]

Holy Order of MANS

The Holy Order of MANS (HOM), an organization with cultic and New Age overtones, purportedly moved from being a cult to becoming Christian. According to Bob Larson's *Book of Cults* (using research from the Spiritual Counterfeits Project), HOM previously denied that Christ was the only Savior and defined him as an infusion of "radiant energy." HOM endorsed meditation techniques designed "to reach the higher beings and your own inner being." HOM also promoted involvement in Tarot cards, astrology, psychic power, *Kabbalah* and parapsychology.[23]

"The main thrust of the order is an appeal to achieve a higher consciousness," Larson wrote. "This exalted state is to be achieved by attaining the same 'Christ consciousness' as Jesus, who was merely a god-realized man. Members will then be prepared to enter the New Age of man's spiritual understanding."[24]

Then, allegedly, things changed. According to a report in the *Christian Research Journal*, the Holy Order of MANS changed its name to Christ the Savior Brotherhood and joined the Eastern Orthodox Church. "However," the journal explained, "the leader of the Greek Orthodox Archdiocese of Queens, New York (Vasiloupolis jurisdiction), with which the HOM was granted affiliation, is not a member of the Standing Committee of Orthodox Bishops of America, which oversees most United States groups in the Orthodox tradition."[25]

The new organization had embraced orthodox Christianity, asserted Andrew Rossi, director general of the sect and successor to the late Earl Blighton, who claimed he founded the sect after receiving a "divine revelation." According to the *Christian Research Journal*, Rossi said his order repudiated all occult beliefs and affirmed biblical orthodoxy, including the belief in the Trinity, salvation through faith in Jesus Christ alone, and the Nicene Creed.

"We had a lot of New Age elements in the brotherhood," Rossi said. "What they (the Spiritual Counterfeits Project) were critical of, they had a right to be. We began to purge ourselves of New Age elements and by 1979 we started going the other direction .... The mysticism got out of hand. We were searching for experiences and found that it would lead us astray without sound doctrine."[26]

Rossi said in 1988 that the group, headquartered in Forestville, Calif., then had about 1,000 members in the U.S.

At this writing, I am not convinced that the leopard has changed its spots so easily. I would not recommend that any Christian join the Christ the Savior Brotherhood until much more probing investigation by competent Christians has been done.

Potpourri

Here's a potpourri of more instances of New Age thinking creeping into Christianity.

The Transcendental Meditation TM Book, published in 1975 by TM people, included letters from a Catholic priest and a Lutheran minister advocating TM. As I mentioned earlier, I called both these men and both said they had not given TM permission to reprint their letters and both said they had asked the TM authorities to stop using the letter. This was just one instance of TM using deceptive promotion which, nevertheless, turned out to be quite effective. Many professing Christians took the TM initiation.

As we saw when we considered Matthew Fox's book, Christians are being encouraged to disavow the historical Jesus for a cosmic Christ. New Ager David Spangler understands Christ to be a cosmic spirit who utilized Jesus' body.

"Any old Christ will not do, not if we need to show that we have something better than the mainstream Christian traditions. It must be a cosmic Christ, a universal Christ, a New Age Christ," Spangler wrote. The Christ is not so much a religious figure, "but rather a cosmic principle, a spiritual presence whose quality infuses and appears in various ways in all the religions and philosophies that uplift humanity and seek unity with spirit."[27]

The group of satanic drug-smugglers that killed 15 people near Matamoros, Mexico (see Chapter Eight), was also linked to Santeria, a mixture of Catholicism and an ancient African religion brought to the New World (mostly to the Caribbean) between the 16th and the 19th centuries by slaves from the West African Yoruba tribe. "Essentially," William M. Alnor wrote, "Santeria is a polytheistic, occultic religion that [deifies] certain Catholic saints along with Yoruban gods. A central cleansing ritual of Santerians is bloodletting through animal sacrifice, mostly of goats and chickens." "*Santeria*" means "worship of the saints" in Spanish. It teaches that, although the universe was created by the one supreme God, the care of the world has been entrusted to many smaller gods, called *orishas*.

"As Santeria grew in the New World, certain Catholic saints were identified with orishas," Alnor continued. "Experts say the main reason slaves did this was to protect their African religion while appearing to be Catholic converts." Santeria has 75 million to 100 million followers worldwide.[28]

The book *God Calling* was among the top five bestselling Christian books listed in the April, 1988, *Christian Retailing*. According to a lengthy book review by Edmond C. Gruss in the *Christian Research Journal*, this book should not be called "Christian."[29] First published in the mid-1930s, *God Calling* has long been stocked by many Christian bookstores where it has been a perpetual bestseller. The basic problem, according to Gruss, is that the book was written through automatic writing, a form of spirit channeling. The dictator of the message claimed to be Jesus and claimed that this book was much better than the Bible. Gruss pointed out many other passages that contradict biblical teaching.

According to *Forward*, the Chinook Learning Community in the State of Washington, a New Age group similar to and in close fellowship with Scotland's New Age Findhorn community, received an annual $3,000 grant from the North Puget Sound Presbytery of the United Presbyterian Church.[30]

Russell Chandler talked about a popular New York minister, Reverend Eric Butterworth of the Unity Church, who preached about self-help through spiritual awareness. His message was simple: "We alone have the power within us to solve our problems, relieve our anxieties and pain, heal our illnesses, improve our golf game or get a promotion."[31] We can presume this means that God is not important.

Chandler also talked about the popular Jewish psychotherapist Ira Progoff and his "Intensive Journaling" seminars. About 35% of them are held under Catholic auspices, including sessions in monasteries and retreat centers. Another 35% of the 400 that he and his corps of 125 leaders conducted around the country each year were sponsored by other religious groups and churches. Based on prayer, meditation and writing exercises (journaling), Progoff's intensive seminars involved getting in touch with "a quality of wisdom that is in us but beyond us . . . an expression of touching a depth level where we sense truths that are larger than personal in their significance." Participants were told to meditate on a self-chosen "mantra crystal," a short phrase intended to create a "pendulum rhythm" and to express "the crystallized essence of your life and experience."[32]

Prolific Catholic author Louis M. Savary in his 1973 book, *Passages: A Guide for Pilgrims of the Mind*, written with Marianne S. Andersen, gave an uninhibited endorsement of altered states of consciousness.[33] He suggested no hint of the dangers of psychological damage or obsession by demonic spirits from these practices. His 1988 book, *Kything: The Art of Spiritual Presence,*[34] written with Patricia H. Berne, talked about a practice that really sounds weird. Kything allegedly puts one's life energy in union with the life energy existing in other people and in plants and animals. By joining with others in the practice, one can hope to "raise the level of human consciousness and to transform the mental and spiritual climate of the planet."[35] In case you weren't able to pick up easily the New Age connection, the authors quoted favorably such New Age figures and institutions as Marilyn Ferguson and the Lucis Trust.

Another book, *Bio-Spirituality: Focusing as a Way to Grow*, written by two Catholic priests, Father Peter A. Campbell and Father Edwin M. McMahon, propounded a very eclectic concept of meditation. "At a deeper level . . . focusing becomes a form of spiritual meditation that helps people find their own form of self-transcendence," the authors wrote in the Foreword. "Meditation has taken many forms in world religions: from wordless, imageless centering of Zen Buddhism and Christian Zen, the metaphysical mantras of the Orient and the popular 'Jesus Prayer' which developed within Eastern Orthodox Christianity, to the mandalas of Tibet, the icons of Orthodoxy, and the Ignatian contemplations on the mysteries of Jesus' life in Western Christianity. Each form draws a person to a transcendent cosmic truth beyond ordinary life while yet within it."[36] The reader was left with the distinct impression that one religion is as good as another.

The August, 1989, newsletter of the Wanderer Forum Foundation talked about a Midwest order of Catholic religious sisters that had become enthusiastic about the New Age. Following indoctrination from New Agers Beverly Galyean and Jean Houston, the sisters were treating their students in Indiana, Missouri and Ohio with so-called mind-expanding exercises such as "meditating on their peaceful center," rhythmic breathing, visualization, "mental journeys" with "guided imagery" and "painting with love."[37]

One of the sisters, in April, 1988, travelled at community

expense on a spiritual pilgrimage to India, "where she wandered alone from ashram to ashram," the newsletter reported. "Her letters back (home) told how she greeted one guru by kneeling before him and touching her forehead to the floor 'to give him reverence as a God-realized being.' " On her return home two months later, she and several companions founded an ashram in Wisconsin called The Christine Center for Meditation. It was dedicated to "a unitive planetary spirituality." It offered hermitages or lodge rooms to guests who come for retreats, spiritual development seminars and body energetics work, yoga, psychocalisthenics, reflexology, acupressure, Tarot, astrology and transpersonal psychology. For Mass, retreatants had to go to the nearest parish church.[38]

A book that was really weird from a Catholic perspective was *Fatima Prophecy: A Psychic Channels the Controversial Prophecy of Fatima for the New Age* by Ray Stanford.[39] Many Catholics believe that the Blessed Virgin Mary appeared to three children in Fatima, Portugal, in 1917 and asked them to pray and perform penance to save sinners from hell. Stanford went on from there to give pages of channeled messages allegedly following up on this. The messages predicted dire consequences for the world because of sin. He also claimed to have witnessed the landing of a UFO and to have experienced the music of the spheres. Since Catholic Fatima devotees are usually very conservative spiritually, I wonder what they think of Stanford's book—if they ever come across it.

A Presbyterian pastor in Endwell, N.Y., Reverend Barry H. Downing, said that UFOs are real and that recognizing their existence could do much to strengthen faith and renew confidence in biblical accounts. He described as UFO-caused phenomena the parting of the Red Sea and the leading of the Israelites out of Egypt by a pillar of cloud by day and a pillar of fire by night. According to an Associated Press story by George Cornell, other UFO-related biblical events were: "The fire-like phenomenon on Mount Sinai in which Moses

received the Ten Commandments, the Prophet Elijah taken
to heaven in a fiery chariot, the star of Bethlehem, the en-
gulfing light of Jesus' transfiguration, his being 'lifted up' at
his ascension and the blinding visitation of Paul en route to
Damascus."[40]

According to an article in the *National Catholic Reporter*,
the 1989 Gifford Lectures in Edinburgh, Scotland, were
delivered by a Catholic priest who said he was also a practicing Hindu and Buddhist. Father Raimundo Panikkar, a
retired professor from the University of California at Santa
Barbara, also considered himself a secularist. The theme of
the Gifford presentations was the trinitarian nature of the
universe.[41]

Yoga Christianity

An excellent article in the international Catholic magazine
30 Days talked about the commingling of Eastern meditational and Roman Catholic spiritual practices. Gianni Valente's lead article in the September, 1989, issue was entitled:
"Deep Prayer: Deep Void." A subhead read: "Nuns who
pray in the lotus position, friars who recite their mantras in
their cells, courses in Zen in parishes and convents: Oriental
prayer techniques are ever more common in the church.
Journey through the world of yoga Christianity."[42]

In the lengthy article, Valente recounted instance after
instance of Catholic monks, priests and nuns adopting Eastern meditational practices. This was said to be happening all
over the world. "The spread of practices originating in Buddhism and Hinduism is not only quantitative but also quali-
tative," Valente wrote. "Congregations of religious women
propose yoga sessions as annual retreats; in many parishes
Zen is the basis of many catechism classes; monks practice
transcendental meditation as their private prayer in their
cells. In short, it is precisely the experts in Christian spirituality who often seem most interested in Eastern meditation."[43]

Valente reported that in the seven religious bookstores

near the Vatican regularly frequented by priests and members of religious orders in search of pastoral updating, the manuals of Christian yoga and instruction books on deep prayer "sell about the same number of copies as the classics of Christian spirituality."[44]

Some Roman Catholic bishops are encouraging the acceptance of Eastern religious practices. At a plenary assembly in November, 1978, the Asian bishops emphasized that "Asia has much to offer to authentic Christian spirituality: a type of prayer that develops the human person in his body-mind-spirit unity; traditions of asceticism and renunciation; techniques of contemplation found in the ancient Oriental religions, like Zen and yoga."[45]

Another article in *30 Days* talked about a new Japanese movement, *Mahikari,* which is becoming popular in Europe. It has roots in Shintoism, Buddhism and Christianity. It defines itself as the "union of pantheism, monotheism and polytheism." Among its teachings is a doctrine of reincarnation and an ancient Japanese tradition according to which Jesus Christ was not crucified (his brother is said to have sacrificed himself in his place) but died at 118 years of age in Herai, Japan, where he is buried. A key technique is a gesture called *okiyome* in which the initiate transmits a healing "Light of Truth." Some priests in Belgium and elsewhere were active in the movement.[46]

Theologian Castellano Cervera has cautiously supported the new trend of introducing Eastern religious techniques to Christianity. "The peculiarity of Christian prayer must be kept in mind. Christian prayer is a personal response to God, who invites us to communion with him, while in the Eastern religions one easily slides into self-deification or into pantheization in the relationship between the human and the divine," Cervera said. "Christian prayer must be Christological and Christocentric. Once these premises have been laid down, Eastern spirituality teaches us three very important values: a return to interiority, the recovery of the bodily dimension in prayer, and the emphasis on the function of the spiritual guide. Certain techniques are neither Christian nor anti-Christian. They are simply anthropological condition-ings."[47]

Another theologian, Francois Dermine, was considera-bly more negative about Eastern inroads.

> It is difficult for there to be compatibility between these techniques and the Christian faith. To en-trust one's salvation to a technique is profoundly anti-Christian . . . . With these techniques there is the danger of wanting to win one's own salvation through conquest. Further, in the entire phenome-non there is a background which I would define as gnostic, present in Eastern cultures in the past. . . . Man is seen as a spark of the divine which does not know itself and must return to the consciousness as a part of the all. Yoga and Zen can furnish a method to the new gnostic reductions of Christian-ity.[48]

The *30 Days* article included extensive quotes from an-other theologian, French Bishop Albert Marie de Monleon.

> In many Christians who practice these techniques, one often notes that there is a progressive transfor-mation from the techniques used as a preparation or help for prayer to the techniques as a substitute for prayer. The method quickly becomes the con-tent, the technique the central concern.
>
> In chapels, changed into "prayer rooms" or "med-itation rooms," a symbolism of the void, an initia-tion into the absent, replaces the Christian sacra-ments. One "meditates" in places which are not inhabited. In the long run, these attitudes, these ceremonies, these places emptied of the Presence end up shaping an entire way of behaving, a men-tality and interior life which has nothing to do with the center of the Christian life, which is commun-

ion with God by means of his grace.

In the recourse to techniques and practices, there is
a latent Pelagianism, so common to many Western
Christians. This consists in the secret conviction
that, by paying a certain price for it, one can receive
grace; that man, that is, possesses the necessary
resources in and of himself to climb the different
steps of the spiritual life. But the divine life is given
to us, and it is given gratuitously.

In reality, the meditation methods, proposed as a
higher knowledge, as a realization of oneself, as an
escape from the suffering and evil of this world,
are nothing more than contemporary forms of
gnosticism.

Synthesizing in the extreme, one could say that in
the Eastern mysticisms a spiritual experience or
mental state is sought, while in Christian mysticism the most important thing is an encounter with
Someone.[49]

A Course in Miracles

A counterfeit Christianity was being built up around *A
Course in Miracles*, a three-volume work allegedly dictated
by Jesus Christ. The navy-blue volumes encompassed 1,188
pages and some half-million words. It was reportedly dictated clairaudiently between 1965 and 1972 to the late Columbia University psychologist Helen Schucman, a self-
professing atheist at the time. As of 1987, more than 160,000
of the three-volume sets had been sold for a price that
increased from $25 to $40 per set after it was first published
in 1975.[50]

"The worldview of *A Course in Miracles* is a mixture of
metaphysical and gnostic elements," Dean C. Halverson
wrote. "The *Course* is metaphysical because it portrays God
as an abstract and impersonal oneness of Mind. It is gnostic
because the reality of the physical creation is denied. God,

according to the *Course*, had nothing to do with creating the physical world. It is an illusory projection of the ego, created to escape the judgment that the ego believed God was about to bring against it."[51]

"My salvation comes from me. Nothing outside of me can hold me back. Within me is the world's salvation and my own." Thus spake *A Course in Miracles Workbook*, page 119.

Kenneth Wapnick, who established a foundation to promote the course, candidly admitted in an interview that the course "is not compatible with biblical Christianity, traditional Christianity."[52] He pointed out that the course teaches that God did not create the world, that we are all equally Christ and that Jesus did not suffer and die for our sins. Jesus, in fact, could not suffer because suffering is not of the body; it is of the mind and comes from guilt.

Another pseudo-Christian "Bible" is *The Urantia Book*. It was channeled through automatic writing by anonymous individuals in the 1930s. Its 2,100 pages, said Elliot Miller, detailed "a vast aggregate of ascending universes and evolving beings, and [it] purports to disclose previously unknown information about the histories of the Earth (Urantia) and Jesus."[53]

The 196 channeled documents were studied by a group of 36 persons for 20 years and then they were published as *The Urantia Book* in 1955. One of the presidents of the Urantia Foundation was Meredith Sprunger, an ordained minister in the United Church of Christ. The convoluted teachings of *The Urantia Book* boiled down to basic Gnosticism.[54]

Chapter 10

Education,
Federal Funds Used,
Catholics,
Values Clarification,
Global Education,
One World,
Hunger Project, Science

Education,
Politics, Science ——

New Age ideas are seeping in everywhere—in education, in politics, in science and in just about any field you can think of.

Education

Russell Chandler mentioned a number of New Age inroads in the field of education.

> * Children's book buyer Tim Campbell of Austin, Texas, says he goes out of his way to find New Age books "that tell kids you *can* take control of your life." Most of these are books for first to third graders. Besides an ongoing fascination with Eastern spirituality, Campbell sees a resurgence of interest in Native American literature (p. 153).[1]

> * Harriette Davis, a trance therapist teacher in North Hollywood, Calif., conducts Rainbow Bridge workshops for parents and children who may have "trouble integrating on this Earth plane." The

classes include "past life regresson" and "psychic awareness" (p. 154).

* Citrus Community College in Azusa, Calif., gives credit for self-hypnosis classes and parapsychology courses that teach about ESP, telepathy, clairvoyance, how to see and interpret auras, how to recognize out-of-body experience, and how to harness the secrets of spoon-bending through psychokinesis (p. 156).

* Sexual counseling derived from Tantric and Taoist practices is offered at the California Institute of Integral Studies in San Francisco through a class designed to meet the human sexuality requirement for the California psychology license. The school is accredited by the Western Association of Schools and Colleges and grants a Ph.D. in psychology and a master's degree in anthropology, philosophy, and religion (p. 156).

* Other alternative-style universities in the San Francisco Bay Area alone include the Rosebridge Graduate School of Integrative Psychology (the Ph.D. combines "western psychology with the wisdom of the body, mind and spirit of the East"); Antioch University (its M.A. in somatic psychology and education covers "bioenergetics, primal therapy, gestalt, various forms of Reichian therapy and a host of lesser known modalities"); and John F. Kennedy University (offering master's programs in psychology, holistic health, the arts and consciousness) (p. 156).[2]

The winter, 1988, *Eagle Forum*[3] had several articles on New Age workshops held as part of a September 17 Learning Fair sponsored by the Women's Center at Red Rocks Community College, Lakewood, Colo. The center received both state and federal funds. The newspaper reprinted an article on the subject by Terry Mattingly, religion writer for the *Rocky Mountain News*. There were classes and workshops on crystal-gazing, channeling, witchcraft, past lives, magic, hypnosis and spiritual healing.

All the workshop presenters were "practitioners of New Age skills and religion," wrote *Eagle Forum* reporter Samantha Smith, "although for fear of public scorn, organizers denied advocating any particular religion or cult. Carol Cram, representing the Women's Center, stated that none of the presenters consider what they do to be religious."[4]

Johanna Michaelsen wrote about the occult entering a kindergarten program in southern California. The children were given a piece of thick orange wool string with a loop tied in one end like a head. A mimeographed letter accompanied the string, stating that a "ghost is attached to the orange string." The children were informed that the ghost "will sleep in the air beside you all the day." One mother confiscated the string and put it in the garage until she could figure out what to do with it.

The next day the child's sister was in the garage, unaware of the string. "Suddenly she was frightened by the sense of a threatening presence around her," Michaelsen recounted. "She heard the sounds of a cat hissing in a corner and something like a chatty doll mumbling incoherently at her. Later that night they threw the ghost string into the garbage pail and prayed to bind and remove the entity. They were never bothered by the presence again."[5]

New Agers are sneaky. They are adept at disguising their religious views and practices as nonreligious psychological approaches. New Age activist Dick Sutphen talks about this.

> One of the biggest advantages we have as New Agers is, once the occult, metaphysical and New Age terminology is removed, we have concepts and techniques that are very acceptable to the general public. So we can change the names and demonstrate the power. In so doing, we open the

door to millions who normally would not be receptive.[6]

New Age educators Jack Canfield and Paula Klimek advised fellow New Agers to introduce Eastern meditation techniques into the public classroom by calling it "centering." "Many educators proudly wearing the label of 'progressive' greet with open arms New Age practices as all the rage, while pushing away 'old age' traditions as outmoded relics,"[7] Douglas Groothuis sadly observed.

Federal Funds Used

Federal funds paid for three New Age programs in Los Angeles public schools. The so-called confluent education programs developed by Beverly Galyean took a holistic approach using thinking, sensing, feeling and intuition.

According to an article by Frances Adeney, Galyean's system of confluent education "relies heavily on meditation techniques as well as a forthright proclamation of Hindu and occult beliefs. Children meditate daily. They are taught to visualize a light within them which contains all knowledge and all love, and to which they turn for insights and power. First graders are introduced to spirit guides."[8]

Adeney summarized Galyean's belief system in three points:

> 1. In essence we are not individuals but part of the universal consciousness, God or spirit, which has manifested itself in the material world. At its base, this universal consciousness is love.

> 2. Because each person is part of the universal consciousness which is love, each child contains all the wisdom and love of the universe.

> 3. Each person creates his or her own reality by choosing what to perceive and how to perceive it. As we teach children to focus on positive thoughts and feelings of love, their reality will become that. This is an assumption that the physical world is an

illusion, that what we perceive is in our minds . . . .
The reality of evil is thus denied.[9]

"In a pluralistic society we cannot ask the public schools to teach children about Jesus Christ," Adeney wrote in conclusion. "On the other hand, we do not want to see advances in education wedded to untrue religious concepts and practices."[10]

Chandler noted that a similarly New Age-oriented program, Project GOAL (Guidance Opportunities for Affective Learning), was developed with federal and state funds to help handicapped students in 54 school districts.[11]

Catholics

Catholic writer Helen Hull Hitchcock attended the 1985 convention of the National Catholic Education Association (St. Louis, April 8-11) and was distressed to find the New Age promoted in official NCEA publications, keynote talks, workshops and exhibit booths. In a lengthy article in *Fidelity* magazine, she said that pervading the convention was the theme that society (including religion) must be restructured "to conform to a 'global model' which will insure peace and justice and perfect harmony in the New Age toward which humanity is inevitably 'evolving.' "[12]

According to Hitchcock, the speakers who dominated the 1985 NCEA convention were out to destroy the Catholic Church. These speakers' view of Catholicism was one "which none of the great saints of history would recognize. For some of these leaders the Catholic Church, through its school system, is primarily a worldwide institution which can be used to effect certain social and political goals, destroying its religious mission in the process."[13]

Jean Houston gave one of the major addresses March 29, 1989, at the NCEA 86th Convention in Chicago. As the director of the Foundation for Mind Research, Pomona, New York, she was described by Bob Larson as being "well-positioned to promote New Age teachings within influential circles." She "encourages the study of ancient Mystery

School religions. The 10 books she has written deal with self-induced states of altered consciousness, self-healing, and the development of psychic forces as part of what she calls sacred psychology, which involves past lives regression, including man's evolutionary past as an animal."[14]

Values Clarification

"Values clarification" is a very popular program in public and private schools that fits in extremely well with the New Age agenda. While the New Age tells us to create our own reality, values clarification tells us to create our own morality.

"Formulated in the mid 1960s by social scientists Louis E. Baths, Merrill Harman, Sidney B. Simon, and others, values clarification plays a pivotal role in both humanistic and transpersonal education," wrote Elliot Miller. "Holding that values emerge from within and therefore should not be imposed from without (a view compatible both with basic humanism and the transpersonal 'Inner Wisdom' concept), it attempts to help students discover and clarify their *own* values."[15]

The basic assumption of values clarification is that there are no objective norms, no objective values. Everything is subjective. (This is not New Age, strictly speaking, but there are so many striking parallels between the extreme subjectivism of values clarification and the New Age that I think some comments are warranted.)

"If parents object to their children using pot or engaging in premarital sex," an article in the *Wall Street Journal* noted, "the theory behind values clarification makes it appropriate for the child to respond, 'But that's just *your* value judgment. Don't force it on me.' "[16]

"The only thing prohibited by the values clarification method is a recognition of and respect for the objective, universal and absolute moral law of God," wrote Douglas Groothuis. "Immature, subjective impulses can be 'clarified,' thus obscuring objective verities."[17]

The book *Child Abuse in the Classroom* contained a number of complaints about values clarification courses. The book, edited by Phyllis Schlafly, consisted of excerpts from testimony before officials of the United States Department of Education in seven hearings at various sites in the nation in March, 1984. Archie Brooks, speaking of the situation in Lincoln County, Ore., told of children being embarrassed by being put on the spot concerning personal religious beliefs. Others were hassled by students after being compelled to share personal feelings about the death of a parent or the pending divorce of parents. Another child reported: "Daddy spanks me and sometimes pulls down my pants to spank me." Daddy was then taken to the police station.[18]

In her testimony, Flora Rettig of Center Line, Mich., blamed the suicide of her 22-year-old son, Joe, on the values clarification course in school. Rettig charged that the course encouraged Joe not to talk with his parents about his problems with drugs and the occult. Consequently, his parents were not able to help him. Rettig also blamed the suicide of a 22-year-old neighbor on the values clarification course.[19]

In the April,1989, *Journal of the American Family Association*, W.R. Coulson, one of the early proponents of value-free education, said he owed parents an apology. "Youthful experimentation with sex, alcohol, marijuana and a variety of other drugs—whatever's popular at the time—has been shown to follow affective, value-free education quite predictably; we now know that after these classes, students become more prone to give into temptation than if they'd never been enrolled," Coulson wrote. He pointed out that a leading tobacco company is contributing substantially to the support of several values-free educational programs.[20]

Global Education

Global education ideas have been spreading in American public education and they are rightfully raising concerns among Christians. We are not talking about improved geography or history or world economics courses. As Douglas

Groothuis described it, global education is "a method of teaching the humanities and social sciences that often either advocates or assumes a New Age ideology of relativism, religious syncretism and one-worldism."[21] Groothuis noted that global education has received the support of such influential organizations as the National Association of Elementary School Principals, the American Association of School Administrators, the American Federation of Teachers, the Council of Chief State School Officers, the National Association of State Boards of Education, the National Education Association, the Parent-Teachers Association, and the National School Board Association.[22]

One good example of global education was a course for educators at Western Washington University, "Foundations of Education," taught by Philip Vander Velde and using his book *The Global Mandate*, along with *The Turning Point* by philosopher/physicist Fritjof Capra. According to Groothuis, the course taught that the world is facing extinction and needs a new spirituality which turns out to be—surprise! surprise!—Eastern mysticism. Vander Velde hailed the "universal or cosmic mind" embedded in the "All" and Capra dispensed with "Christian theism in favor of an impersonal monistic and evolutionary perspective," Groothuis noted. "Monotheism, Capra pronounces, will destroy us; monism will deliver us."[23]

Groothuis outlined five key points of global education.

1. *A desire to politicize children.* The aim of global educators is not detached geographical, historical, political, or philosophical study, but conversion—and conversion at an early age.

2. *A very liberal or pacifistic internationalism stressing disarmament as the only approach to conflict.* The peace-through-strength perspective—held by a high percentage of taxpayers—is seldom, if ever, represented as a plausible option.

3. *Ethical relativism.* Values clarification programs are advocated as well as a "nonjudgmental" approach to studying other cultures. The curriculum guide *Perspectives* tells us that, while we provincial Westerners "tend to see the world in terms of competing interests, . . . in Eastern philosophy . . . conflict and paradox (represented by yin and yang) are part of harmonic unity." It then suggests that "the roots of our attraction to conflict" come from the "Western tradition and religious values." It urges teachers to "explore with the students the good guy/bad guy dichotomy that pervades our Western mythology and our texts, or the God and devil imagery that is part of the Christian ethic."[24]

4. *Moral equivalence.* The idea that "all nations are morally equal" tends to flow from point three. Yet oftentimes the thesis is revised to mean "all nations are morally equal but the United States is less morally equal than others." This is suggested by the scant attention usually paid in global education to America's unique form of civil government, its history and positive achievements of political liberty and economic opportunity. Likewise, an objective treatment of Soviet injustices worldwide—such as Stalin's elimination of millions of dissenters and Soviet global imperialism which includes invasions into Hungary, Czechoslovakia and Afghanistan—is often conspicuously absent.

5. *One-world government.* Cooperation must replace any military or economic competition as we realize that "we are all one" and need to become "more one" through dissolving national sovereignties. Although many non-New Agers stump for world government for a variety of reasons, the idea has particular appeal to New Age monists who stress the oneness of all things. For them, if all

is one metaphysically, all should become one po-
litically. What is largely lacking from global educational materials is an awareness of the fact that
real evil exists and may need to be resisted by military force.[25]

One World

The New Age has a broad agenda, Chandler noted,
which "advances ecology (nature and God are merged);
androgyny (because all is one, male-female distinctions are
irrelevant); world peace and nuclear disarmament (including rapprochement and possible political unification between the United States and the Soviet Union); and natural
foods and healing processes." Chandler listed other New
Age goals as being "to overcome world hunger; humanize
technology; dismantle much of corporate America and replace it with 'alternative' economic units such as small
industrial and agricultural collectives; foster collective living styles; and organize global politics."[26]

National boundaries become irrelevant in one-worldism. "The New Age agenda calls for an emerging global
civilization and one-world government, including 'planetary taxation' and the United Nations as the sole central
governing agency," Chandler continued. "It would also
create an eclectic 'world religion' that closely resembles
Eastern religious systems rather than Western monotheistic
faiths."[27]

Christians are rightly concerned about peace and justice
and racial harmony and ecology and the elimination of
worldwide poverty and hunger. Also, Christians should be
willing to work with all persons of all faiths to achieve these
worthwhile goals. Still, Christians must be prudent and realize that New Agers are basically out to destroy the Christian faith.

"Just as New Age (occult) spirituality is repugnant to,
and incompatible with, Christian faith, so orthodox Christianity is repugnant to, and incompatible with, the kind of

global society New Agers are working toward," wrote Elliot Miller. "In the New Age, there would be no comfortable (more likely no *tolerable*) place for true Christianity. Christian dogmatism could easily be viewed (in fact, already is) as antievolutionary: a threat to the global unity necessary for racial survival."[28]

In other words, Christians say there is a Creator God who laid down rules of conduct for his creatures. Humans are not gods. In fact, humans are basically weak with tendencies toward evil behavior. They need redemption and God's grace to live good and meaningful lives. All these things are in direct conflict with basic New Age beliefs.

The United States was founded on Judeo-Christian insights and principles. For this reason, an occurrence like the Pentagon Meditation Club seems somewhat disturbing. An article in *Meditation* described a Friday morning meeting in the Pentagon which began with chants of "*om.*" The speaker said:

> We image our world leaders coming together—all influential leaders, spiritual leaders, religious leaders at all levels, joining together, resolving issues, resolving conflicts, learning to communicate with one another. We're conscious of the divine light radiating from within our being, the light of life shining out into the courtyard, into this building, filling it with the light of life, touching everyone we meet, everyone who isn't here .... We expand the vision to include the entire nation, then expand it to include every part of the world, particularly military installations scattered around the world.[29]

Peace is wonderful. Communication between leaders is very desirable. Resolution of conflicts is eminently worthwhile. A Christian cannot object to the goals of this meditation session. The problem is that this "divine light" they called upon was not the one true God. It was the impersonal god of pantheism and this "god" cannot save anyone.

Paul McGuire said the Pentagon Meditation Club was founded by scientist Ed Winchester. He applied his theories of creative intelligence to the Pentagon management systems and evolved the practice from Transcendental Meditation. The purpose of the Pentagon Meditation Club was to launch a Spiritual Defensive Initiative (SDI) or "peace shield of energy and light all over the planet."[30]

Hunger Project

One example of the absurdities that New Age thinking has led to was a charity rip-off, the Hunger Project. Founded in 1977 by Werner Erhard of *est* fame (see Chapter Seven), the project later separated from *est*, though Hunger Project staffers were pressured to take the *est* course.[31]

How would the Hunger Project feed the hungry of the world? Would it buy food and send it to areas where people are starving? Send experts out to help poor people grow better crops and obtain better supplies of water? Support laboratory work to develop hardier strains of grain? No, the people of the Hunger Project would do none of these things.

In this blatant rip-off, gullible people paid $30 (at one time sent directly to the *est* organization) to learn a few facts about hunger and then sit around and think about the problem. According to the New Age theory of reality, if enough people sit at home in their easy chairs thinking about hunger, starvation will be magically eliminated.

According to Bob Larson, the Hunger Project's Canadian division spent 56% of revenues on salaries, benefits and telephone calls.[32] An article by Carol Giambalvo (a former Hunger Project briefing leader) and Robert Burrows reported that the project "has taken in close to $40 million. Of that figure, only about $1 million has been given in grants. Even those grants are not, in most cases, given to agencies doing the work of development or relief."[33]

Science

Pantheism and Eastern mysticism have entered the scientific world. (A physicist friend of mine has asked me not to dignify the monistic ramblings of some contemporary physicists by calling them "science," but that's a different story.)

Here's the way Fritjof Capra, a physicist at the University of California, Berkeley, and a New Age author, described the situation.

> As Eastern thought has begun to interest a signifi- cant number of people, and meditation is no longer viewed with ridicule or suspicion, mysticism is being taken seriously even within the scientific community. An increasing number of scientists are aware that mystical thought provides a consis- tent and relevant philosophical background to the theories of contemporary science, a conception of the world in which the scientific discoveries of men and women can be in perfect harmony with their spiritual aims and religious beliefs.[34]

"Specifically," as Elliot Miller explained, "scientists like Capra have been popularizing the idea that such 20th-cen- tury developments in physics as quantum and relativity theories offer scientific backing to the beliefs of ancient mystical traditions. Many further argue that monistic and mystical perspectives are necessary to *understand* these re- cent discoveries, and to make further progress in the new frontiers of science."[35]

Scientists, by and large, however, are not jumping onto the New Age bandwagon. Scientists have traditionally be- lieved in objective reality, in a physical universe that existed long before anybody was around to observe it. Eastern mystics would have us believe on the one hand that every- thing is illusion and on the other hand that we create reality with our own minds.

Capra's credibility as a scientist can come under question when he candidly admits that his new insights into science came, not as the result of laboratory experiments or careful reasoning, but as the result of a mystical experience helped, in part, by the use of psychedelic herbs. In his book *The Tao of Physics*, Capra told of his visionary experience, which amounts to a religious conversion.

> Five years ago, I had a beautiful experience which set me on a road that has led to the writing of this book. I was sitting by the ocean one late summer afternoon, watching the waves rolling in and feeling the rhythm of my breathing, when I suddenly became aware of my whole environment as being engaged in a gigantic cosmic dance . . . . As I sat on that beach, . . . I "saw" cascades of energy coming down from outer space, in which particles were created and destroyed in rhythmic pulses; I "saw" the atoms of the elements and those of my body participating in this cosmic dance of energy, I felt its rhythm and "heard" its sound, and at that moment I *knew* that this was the Dance of Shiva, the Lord of Dancers worshipped by the Hindus.[36]

This is science? "In the face of such an account," Mark Albrecht and Brooks Alexander commented, "it becomes clear that Dr. Capra is not reasoning from premise to conclusion. He is not proposing a theory but announcing a revelation."[37] A revelation, in fact, it may be. In another part of *The Tao of Physics*, Capra indicated that he thought some sort of spirit guide was dictating his writing.[38]

"Although the act of observation does affect the universe, as quantum physics says," Dean C. Halverson commented, "the universe does not depend on our observation for its existence. Reality exhibits an objectivity because its existence depends on something other than us: God. A personal, transcendent God makes science possible. Through scientific techniques, we are able to discover laws in the universe—not because we mentally invent them, but because the Creator placed them there. They are a reflection of his coherence, not ours."[39]

Chapter 11

Health

This is a very complicated subject. The advances of modern traditional medicine are astonishing. Medical professionals are hard put to keep abreast of the latest developments. Now charging onto the scene are such elements of nontraditional medicine as therapeutic touch, acupuncture, biofeedback, holistic medicine, homeopathy, visualization and inner guides. Add to this both Christian and New Age religious healing practices and things can be very complicated indeed.

Traditional medical professionals frequently differ with one another about the merits or dangers of new discoveries. They have been very slow to accept nontraditional medical discoveries or approaches. Frequently, on the other hand, nontraditional medical journals or conferences seem to lack responsible self-criticism. Off-the-wall approaches are included cheek-by-jowl with reasonable techniques propounded by persons with sterling credentials. It is hard to make an accurate, unbiased assessment of this complex situation, but we will try to give some guidance to the Christian who wishes to look at healing practices today.

Imagery

Golf magazines say you can improve your swing without leaving your easy chair. All you do is imagine yourself swinging a golf club. Imagine every move you make and imagine the golf ball taking off down the fairway. That's a positive and certainly harmless use of imagination. Some modern imaging techniques, however, seem positively dangerous.

"Imagery is a self-healing technique that can lead to relief in 90 percent of the problems people bring to their primary care physicians," the editors of *New Age Journal* said in introducing an article entitled "The Healing Power of Imagery" by Martin L. Rossman, a San Francisco physician. "From minor ailments such as back pain, neck pain, palpitations, dizziness, and fatigue, to illnesses as serious as cancer, arthritis, and heart disease," the editors continued, "Rossman encourages patients to use imagery to address the emotional aspects of their illnesses, thereby helping the physical healing."[1]

Unfortunately, what Rossman means by imagery often includes putting oneself under the influence of demonic spirits. "We have much more information inside us than we commonly use," he rhapsodized. "An inner adviser is a symbolic representation of that inner wisdom and experience. Your inner adviser should be thought of as a friendly guide to these valuable unconscious stores—an inner ally who can help you understand yourself more deeply." He went on to talk of a number of patients and the particular spirits they conversed with. "Inner advisers often come as the classic 'wise old man' or 'wise old woman,' but they come in many other forms as well. Sometimes they come in the form of a person you know, a friend or relative who has fulfilled this function for you in real life. Advisers may also be animals or birds, plants, trees, or even natural forces like the wind or the ocean. Sometimes people will encounter religious figures like Jesus, Moses, or Buddha, while others will find an angel, fairy, or leprechaun."[2]

The occult has come to modern medicine. You do not "converse" with your golf swing. You only "converse" with entities that have a separate existence. Since these entities do not give glory to God and the real Jesus, we know that they are not angelic entities.

Writing in the New Age magazine, *New Realities*, C. Norman Shealy, a physician, said, "When I was in medical school (in the 1950s), I was taught that 85 percent of the people I would see later in my office would have 'psychosomatic illness'—what I now call 'stress diseases.'" He reports all his class time was spent on how to treat "the remaining 15 percent with acute, serious, life-threatening or terminal illness."[3] He said he was convinced even those 15 percent "usually are ill as the result of an attitude which has led them to choose unhealthy habits." (While psychosomatic illnesses do exist, much of our health depends on circumstances beyond our control.)

People must be educated to take responsibility for their health attitudes and health habits, Shealy said. He supported the holistic health approach and said contemporary medicine needs to change. "It is true that organized medicine has lobbied extensively against, and helped to prevent, alternative approaches from being used," he charged. "Acupuncture, homeopathy, chiropractic, herbal medicine, dietary therapy, and just plain common-sense health-promotion and disease-prevention educational programs are generally ignored or pooh-poohed by most traditional physicians."[4] Though a lot of what Shealy said should be taken seriously, he also advocated the New Age teaching that we create our own reality. We are healthy or sick because we want to be healthy or sick.

Marilyn Ferguson has been as enthusiastic about New Age advances in medicine as about any New Age development. "For all its reputed conservatism, Western medicine is undergoing an amazing revitalization," Ferguson wrote in

The Aquarian Conspiracy. "Patients and professionals alike are beginning to see beyond symptoms to the context of illness: stress, society, family, diet, season, emotions."[5] She noted that hospitals are developing more flexible policies and providing more humane environments for birth and death. She commented that medical schools are now trying to attract more creative, people-oriented students.

"No one realized how vulnerable the old medical model was," she said. "Within a few short years, without a shot having been fired, the concept of holistic health has been legitimized by federal and state programs, endorsed by politicians, urged and underwritten by insurance companies, co-opted in terminology (if not always in practice) by many physicians, and adopted by medical students."[6]

Nontraditional medical practices can be fine and beneficial, but New Age philosophy is wrong and not beneficial.

Holistic Medicine

Russell Chandler tackled the definition of holistic medicine by suggesting a difference between "wholistic" and "holistic." He quoted Jack Gordon, editor of *Training Magazine,* as saying: "If they bring in a motivational speaker who tells you how to accomplish anything you set your mind to, at work or in life, that's wholistic, with a 'w.' If they bring in an Apache medicine man and a live eagle, that's holistic."[7]

"Holistic medicine, to say the least," Chandler explained, "is a complex and controversial topic that includes a baffling grab bag of quasi-medical therapeutic techniques. But it is also an emerging force in medical practice, based on the concept that body, mind, and spirit are interconnected and that true health—being whole, from the Anglo-Saxon word *haelen*—results from the proper interaction and alignment of all three."[8]

The Association for Holistic Health, according to Elliot Miller, described the holistic approach as "person oriented rather than disease oriented," having "full vibrant health (positive wellness), not symptom amelioration," as its objective, and "primary prevention rather than crisis intervention"[9] as its focus. The American Holistic Medical Association has reported that 2%, or about 10,000, of all doctors in the United States practice some form of holistic medicine.[10]

Nontraditional medicine is undoubtedly doing a lot of good, but, for the Christian at least, it is also introducing a lot of problems. "Holistic thought and practice are so often interlaced with occultism that, in its search for alternative approaches to healing, an entire generation is in danger of being baptized in psychic power,"[11] Miller warned. He quoted a statement in *International Journal of Holistic Health and Medicine* as being of concern to Christians:

> The Eastern philosophy/spiritualism movement has also contributed to holistic health by its appreciation of a unifying invisible dynamic force within and around the human body that is called "Chi" by the Chinese, "Ki" by the Japanese, "prana" by the yogis and numerous other names by various cultures throughout the world. Unlike the word "spirit" in the West, the words for this energetic force in the East generally have a very practical meaning and have direct and specific influences upon health.[12]

"Historically, under various names such as those the author lists, the same force has always appeared in the context of spiritistic paganism," Miller warned. "Thus the Christian has every reason to consider it supernatural, demonic, and dangerous."[13]

Christian Healing

An extremely helpful article, "Evaluating Methods and Theories of Healing," appeared in the spring, 1987, issue of *Journal of Christian Healing*.[14] The article was written by Sheila Fabricant and Douglas Schoeninger. Fabricant works full-time in a healing ministry and Schoeninger is president of the Institute for Christian Healing and editor-in-chief of

Journal of Christian Healing. He is a deacon in the Presbyterian Church.

"In this paper we are initiating a dialogue about criteria for discerning the variety of healing methods, therapies, and philosophies we encounter," the article stated. "On the one hand, we want to be careful not to be seduced into promoting methods that undermine faith in Jesus Christ. On the other hand, we do not want to close ourselves to the truth and help for our clients available in a particular method, just because it has been designated 'evil' by certain Christian groups or because it has been developed within a non-Christian tradition or secular context."[15] The authors listed 10 general perspectives and assumptions "to acknowledge the underlying orientations that influence us."[16] (Here, these perspectives are greatly abbreviated and sometimes paraphrased.)

> 1. *A positive God-image provides a sound basis for discerning truth.* The image of a faithful, abiding God who endows us with freedom to explore creation and gives us the gifts of intuition and reason leaves us able to see truth. On the other hand, an image of a God who controls us through threats of abandonment operates to separate us from truth by keeping us fearful of making mistakes and hostile toward God.

> 2. *A basic question to keep asking in evaluating is whether it leads us toward or away from Jesus.* While certain methods may hold the danger of leading us to spiritualism (seeking power or knowledge from spiritual beings who are less than God), traditional medical methods may hold the danger of leading us into materialism. An example of materialism would be the assumption that taking a pill equals a cure.... Another facet of this question is whether use of a healing method (or the theory behind it) opposes or supports simple faith in the authority of Jesus to heal.

3. *Different perspectives may be based on differences in faith and/or personality development.* For example, a person who was converted to Christianity through the experience of God's presence in all creation will perceive openness to such presence as leading one closer to God. But one who was converted through an experience of deliverance from evil will be likely to perceive avoiding certain aspects of creation as leading one closer to God.

4. *The genuine pursuit of truth may require stretching our boundaries and expanding our vision beyond the logico-deductive method.*

5. *Authentic search for truth will ultimately deepen rather than destroy faith (trust) in God and God's relation with creation.* Truth is one, whether we search for it in a Bible-study class or a medical laboratory. When we are quick to condemn something as "demonic" or "occult," is it really our fear of going beyond familiar boundaries? Is our discernment of the demonic *sometimes* just our fear of the unknown?

6. *Refusing to integrate the unfamiliar risks the development of heresy.* Heresy is a distortion of a truth, or a partial truth treated as if it were the whole.

7. *God's love and goodness underlie the universe.* From a biological viewpoint, the fact of natural healing power in the body implies a basic goodness in the cells that constitute the human body. One criticism of nontraditional healing methods (e.g., those involving energy systems) is that they are used by a "New Age movement" that denies the reality of sin and our need for a Savior and deifies men and women. This can be a valid concern, but if it springs out of a fundamental distrust of creation, it can also blind us to the underlying value

and potential of a given method. The problem at issue here is the problem of evil, of the fall. Various Christian traditions deal with this problem differently. Some traditions take a more optimistic approach, emphasizing the fundamental goodness of creation and seeing Jesus' work as redeeming that which was flawed but never destroyed. Other traditions take a more pessimistic approach, emphasizing the radical depravity of creation brought about through the fall, and seeing Jesus' work as recreating something damaged beyond repair.

8. *A primary issue is not only whether a theory or practice is basically good, but also how we use it.* There are only two directions: toward God and away from God. Nothing is neutral as soon as it comes into relationship with a human will. Nature has a meaning in and of itself, but it has no destiny separate from ours. Thus at a certain point it becomes irrelevant to say that a method or created thing is basically good because it is "natural." As soon as a human being interacts with it, we need to ask whether that interaction leads the person (and the method or created thing) toward or away from fuller union with God. We can open ourselves to God's presence in each method, letting God work with us to discriminate and integrate, even as we rely on God to protect us from harm.

9. *God dwells within us as well as beyond us.*

10. *Personal experience.* (Fabricant talks about a personal experience of the benefits of being open to new ideas.)

The article by Fabricant and Schoeninger followed these 10 general perspectives and assumptions with 10 suggested criteria for discerning healing methods, theories and phi-

losophies. Before talking about these criteria, however, I
want to give some examples of nontraditional medicine that
a Christian may be called on to evaluate. Some seem very
good and positive and some are quite weird.

Rusty Knife

In the literature of the paranormal, one of the more
incredible stories is that of Arigo, a peasant surgeon in Brazil.
This well-documented story was recounted in *New Age
Medicine* by Paul C. Reisser, Teri K. Reisser and John Weldon.[17] (Russell Chandler mentioned another psychic healer
in Brazil, Edson Quieroz, who operates with a rusty knife
and no anesthesia.[18]) Arigo's story was told in detail in John
G. Fuller's biography, *Arigo: Surgeon of the Rusty Knife.*[19]

Arigo was an uneducated government clerk who lived in
the mountain village of Congohas do Campo, about 400
kilometers south of Rio de Janeiro. His name was Jose Pedro
de Frietas, but he was widely known as Arigo, a Portuguese
word roughly translated as "country bumpkin." He was
jovial, burly, rustic in appearance and a natural leader. In
August, 1963, two Americans—Henry K. (Andrija) Puharich, a physician, and Henry Belk, a businessman—visited
Arigo's clinic. With about 200 persons present, Arigo began
with a tirade against alcohol and tobacco. This was followed
by prayer. "He then entered a small cubicle, emerging
moments later a different man," the authors recount. "The
bumpkin suddenly behaved like a displaced Prussian general, speaking Portuguese with a thick German accent."[20] He
invited the Americans to watch his work closely. According
to Fuller's biography, this is what they saw.

> Suddenly and without ceremony, [Arigo] roughly
> took the first man in line—an elderly, well-dressed
> gentleman in an impeccable gray sharkskin suit,
> firmly grasped his shoulders, and held him against
> the wall, directly under the sign THINK OF JESUS
> .... Then, without a word, Arigo picked up a four-

inch stainless steel paring knife with a cobolawood handle, and literally plunged it into the man's left eye, under the lid and deep up into the eye socket.

In spite of his years of medical practice and experience, Puharich was shocked and stunned. He was even more so when Arigo began violently scraping the knife between the ocular globe and the inside of the lid, pressing up into the sinus area with uninhibited force. The man was wide awake, fully conscious, and showed no fear whatsoever. He did not move or flinch. A woman in the background screamed. Another fainted. Then Arigo levered the eye so that it extruded from the socket. The patient, still utterly calm, seemed bothered by only one thing: a fly that had landed on his cheek. At the moment his eye was literally tilted out of its socket, he calmly brushed the fly away from his cheek.

As he made these motions, Arigo hardly looked at his subject, and at one point turned away to address an assistant while his hand continued to scrape and plunge without letup. In another moment, he turned away from the patient completely, letting the knife dangle half out of the eye.

Then he turned abruptly to Puharich and asked him to place his finger on the eyelid, so that he could feel the point of the knife under the skin. By this time, Puharich was almost in a state of shock, but he did so, clearly feeling the point of the knife through the skin. Quickly, Puharich asked one of the interpreters to ask the patient what he felt. The patient spoke calmly and without excitement, merely stating that although he was well aware of the knife, he felt no pain or discomfort.[21]

Arigo treated some 200 patients that morning, spending

scarcely a minute with any one of them. Many received hastily scribbled prescriptions. "These contained unlikely concoctions of vitamins, common medications, and outdated or experimental drugs, often having no logical relation to the apparent illness," the authors reported. "A few patients received the eye socket treatment, while others watched as tumors or other growths were slashed painlessly from their bodies. What little bleeding occurred stopped quickly on Arigo's command. There was no trace of sterilization—Arigo usually wiped his instruments on his shirt—but there was never an infection. No one received an anesthetic, but no one felt any pain."[22]

During a career spanning two decades, Arigo treated more than a million patients, averaging 300 per day, without charge. "Peasants and political leaders alike (including former Brazilian President Juscelino Kubitschek) came for healing or brought loved ones, and scores of unusual cures were medically documented," the authors stated. "Extensive physiological tests (and films of his surgeries) conducted in Congohas do Campo by North American researchers under Puharich's direction failed to supply an explanation for Arigo's abilities."[23]

Arigo himself explained that his miraculous surgeries and prescriptions were actually the handiwork of Adolpho Fritz, a German physician who died in 1918. In the spirit world, Fritz gathered together a team of other spirits with medical expertise to assist him and then Fritz chose Arigo as his vehicle for operating. In 1971, Arigo died in an automobile acccident.

Cult researcher Kurt Koch believed Arigo's phenomena were authentic: "Let us be quite clear about this: Arigo's cures were not a trick or a swindle. They were real operations."[24]

Many of the psychic surgery phenomena have been proven to be tricks by sleight-of-hand artists, but some cures cannot be explained by natural means.

What should a Christian do? Clearly, a Christian should

avoid frauds and charlatans, but what about Arigo? Could a Christian with a cancerous tumor go to him to be cured?

Personally, I would not. I know God can cure me and I would trust in him and medical science. If, however, God allows me to die, at least I can come before the judgment seat of God with a clean conscience in this respect. I have not sought healing from demonic powers—for Arigo's preternatural power, in spite of some rambling prayers, clearly did not come from God.

Edgar Cayce

Edgar Cayce (pronounced as "Casey") was born on March 18, 1877, in Hopkinsville, Ky., and died on January 3, 1945, in Virginia Beach, Va. He never progressed beyond grade school in spite of an extraordinary psychic ability to commit school books to memory by simply sleeping with them under his head. As a young man, Cayce suffered from severe headaches and in 1900 he was found wandering in a daze. Rescued by a family friend, he regained consciousness, but he discovered he had lost his voice. On two occasions traveling hypnotists were able to cure Cayce's hoarseness, but he was only able to speak while in a hypnotic trance. Then, in a trance, he explained the problem as a partial paralysis and verbally commanded the circulation in the neck area to increase. It did and he was healed.

Working for several months with a hypnotist and then acquiring the ability to put himself under hypnosis, Cayce developed the ability to diagnose illnesses and prescribe cures. "In a typical session, he would recline on the nearest couch and enter a self-induced trance. The name and location of the patient would then be read to him, without any indication of symptoms. After a few minutes he would clear his throat and announce in a firm voice, 'Yes, we have the body.' Then he would begin the 'reading,' an explanation of the cause of the illness followed by a detailed prescription which might include a special diet, current or outdated medications, osteopathic manipulations, massage, electricity, castor oil packs, enemas or homeopathic remedies."[25]

Cayce left behind 14,249 stenographically recorded readings for 5,772 different people, totaling some 50,000 single-spaced, typewritten pages.[26] An estimated 16,000 readings were given during his lifetime, but most of the earliest were not preserved. Cayce never remembered the content of his readings, which usually included concepts and vocabulary extending far beyond the limits of his grade-school education. The treatment recommended was for the specific subject of the reading and would not be beneficial for other persons with similar illnesses. He rarely received payment for his services.

Besides the health content of his trance messages, Cayce also talked philosophy. He endorsed such cultic and New Age themes as monism, universal consciousness, reincarnation, karma and so forth.[27] In his trance state, he made a number of predictions: portions of Japan will slip into the ocean; the lost continent of Atlantis will rise from the ocean; communism will end in Russia; a tilt in the Earth's rotational axis will cause a reversal of climates.[28]

Cayce's readings are on file at the Cayce Foundation—the Association for Research and Enlightenment—in Virginia Beach, Va.

Nontraditional Healing

If I have broken a bone or need an operation or a prescription for a bad case of the flu, the personal theology or philosophy of the physician is irrelevant. Only the medical knowledge and skill of the physician are important when dealing with traditional medicine. The doctor is not attempting to tap into some source of psychic power or to contact demonic spirits.

Things are different in nontraditional medicine. The worldview, the philosophy, the theology of the physician are very relevant. The nontraditional physician may be contacting demonic spirits. The physician may believe that we are all gods and that we have an innate creative power that can be utilized. On the other hand, the nontraditional physician may merely be trying to tap into natural curative powers. The Christian must use discernment.

We will now consider some examples of nontraditional medicine.

Yoga. As we saw in Chapter Two, yoga means union of the soul with God. Through Hatha yoga, an altered state of consciousness is achieved through special physical exercises. The purpose of these exercises is spiritual enlightenment, not simply physical health.

"The goal of yoga is the same as Hinduism—Hindu god-realization, i.e., for the yoga devotee to realize that he is one with Brahman, the highest impersonal Hindu god," wrote Clifford A. Wilson and John Weldon. "The physical exercises of yoga are designed to prepare the body for the psychospiritual change vital to inculcating this idea into the consciousness and being of the person. Hence talk of separating yoga practice from theory is meaningless . . . . Those who do 'yoga exercises' alone run the risk of spiritual warfare entering their lives."[29]

H. Rieker, a yoga advocate, warned that "yoga is not a trifling jest if we consider that any misunderstanding in the practice of yoga can mean death or insanity" and that in Kundalini (Hatha) yoga, if the breath is "prematurely exhausted, there is immediate danger of death for the yogi."[30]

There are some yogis, Wilson and Weldon continued, who believe that the bizarre and fatal cases of spontaneous human combustion—people bursting into flames—are the result of malfunctioning Kundalini.[31]

Acupuncture. Here again we have the problem: can the technique be separated from the underlying philosophy? Here's how a Christian physician, Paul C. Reisser, described the situation.

In traditional Chinese medicine, the proper function of the body (not to mention the mind and spirit) hinges on the proper flow of "life energy," or Ch'i, through the body. Ch'i supposedly circulates through 12 pairs of invisible channels called meridians, most of which are identified with organs such as the liver and heart.

If the flow becomes sluggish or blocked, you might develop symptoms or overt disease. While the diagnosis is based partly on your history and general appearance, it depends most of all on the radial (wrist) pulses. With proper training (and much patience) the Chinese therapist can presumably assess all 12 meridians by feeling six positions at each wrist. If the flow of Ch'i needs to be improved, the therapist stimulates specific points on the skin, either by needling (acupuncture) or by applying finger pressure (acupressure).

Applied kinesiology (and some of its offshoots, such as behavioral kinesiology and Touch for Health) has as its belief that the strength or weakness of certain muscle groups reflects the status of your internal organs, nutrition, emotional well-being, and even your spirituality . . . .

The idea that Ch'i flows through your body in defined channels comes from Taoism, and it is now deeply tied, in contemporary New Age spirituality, to the belief that this universal energy is what Western religions have traditionally called God . . . .

Some Christian practitioners who use these New Age techniques argue that they are simply making use of a neutral phenomenon (as electricity is neutral). They say the fact that we don't understand why something works shouldn't automatically consign a practice to the realm of the occult . . . . This is, unfortunately, easier said than proven, especially when the concept is a basic precept of a religious system.[32]

Therapeutic Touch. We are not talking here about the benefits of a mother hugging a sick child after giving a dose of medicine or of a nurse holding a patient's hand while discussing treatment. We are not talking about Christians laying on hands while praying for healing. We are talking about a redistributing of the *prana* in the patient, using the Hindu concept of a universal energy that flows through the body.

Therapeutic Touch is a psychic healing procedure developed by New York University Nursing School Professor Dolores Krieger. After studying yoga, Hindu medicine and Chinese medicine, Krieger came to the conclusion that *prana*— the Hindu version of universal energy—is "at the base of the human energy transfer in the healing act." She wrote: "Conceive of the healer as an individual whose health gives him access to an overabundance of prana and whose strong sense of commitment and intention to help ill people gives him or her a certain control over the projection of this vital energy. The act of healing, then, would entail the channeling of this energy flow by the healer for the well-being of the sick individual."[33]

In a trancelike state, the healer moves his or her hands over or just above the patient's body, hovering where the healer senses "accumulated energy." Then the healer tries to transmit a feeling of well-being to the patient, channeling *prana* and redistributing the patient's energies.[34] "The practice of Therapeutic Touch is highly intuitive and subjective, having been aptly described as a healing meditation,"[35] Reisser *et al.* noted.

The first assumption of Therapeutic Touch is that "people are energy fields," observed Janet Quinn in an article in *New Realities.* "We are not saying that people have energy fields in addition to what they are. We are suggesting that the energy field is the fundamental unity of the living system, and that the physical is but one manifestation of that energy field." Quinn added that another assumption is that "when a person utilizes his or her intent to help or to heal another person, an energy transfer takes place between them, stimulating the subject towards greater wellness."[36]

Inner guides. The conjuring up of inner guides who talk to the individual and give advice is a very widespread nontraditional healing practice today. Earlier in this chapter, we talked about Martin L. Rossman, the San Francisco physician, with his "inner advisers." Russell Chandler talked of an osteopath, Irving Oyle, who, in his book *The Healing Mind,* described methods of helping his patients achieve an altered state of consciousness. In this state they "talk" with their "inner guides" to aid in diagnosing and treating a health-related problem.[37] Dr. and Mrs. Carl Simonton of Fort Worth employ holistic therapies in treating cancer patients. "Using relaxation, meditation, and visualization, the Simontons teach that a person's 'active imagination' can prod the body's immune systems into destroying even widespread malignancies,"[38] Chandler reported. The Simontons also teach ways to find one's inner guide through directed meditation. An apt pupil of theirs, Bernie S. Siegel, has written a bestselling book about holistic medicine, *Love, Medicine and Miracles.* Siegel is strongly committed to meditation and visualization and, as a result of the Simontons' training, he has his own inner guide. According to a book review by Paul C. Reisser, Siegel approached a Simonton seminar on guided meditation with considerable skepticism. He was surprised, however, "to meet George, 'a bearded, long-haired young man wearing an immaculate flowing white gown and a skullcap' whom he praised as 'my invaluable companion ever since his first appearance.' "[39]

What should a Christian think about these inner guides? The authors of *New Age Medicine* responded:

> The meditative techniques for procuring the services of a guide, as described by the Simontons and many others, are strikingly similar to the old occult practice of contacting a familiar spirit. Both inner guides and familiar spirits are often said to appear in the form of friendly animals or humans who

give advice and counsel upon request. At worst, this may begin to transform patients into spirit mediums. At best, it assumes that one's subconscious is an infallible fountain of wisdom, a naive and shaky presupposition for sorting out life's problems.[40]

Some even try to conjure up Jesus as a personal spirit guide. "If Christians falsely assume that their visualizations will invoke the real Jesus, they could be setting themselves up for deception,"[41] Douglas Groothuis warned.

Homeopathy. The practice—the name literally means "same disease"—is based on the principle that the best remedy for a disorder is a substance that causes the same symptoms in healthy persons. The medicines used are often greatly diluted, but are considered to work as sources of energy affecting the life force of man.[42]

Biofeedback. Biofeedback involves the use of special electronic equipment to gain some control of a body function which we normally cannot consciously regulate. It is often used in the management of headaches. Generally speaking, biofeedback is a part of traditional medicine and does not rely on pantheistic or occultic concepts. Usually, there is no problem with Christians using it.

The authors of *New Age Medicine* judged biofeedback to be a neutral technology which "can be used for good or ill depending on the philosophy of the trainer. It can relieve suffering, prove to be a costly waste of time, or serve as a thinly veiled mechanism to usher the unwary into altered states of consciousness. Anyone who considers using this technique as part of a pain management program should check carefully the credentials and orientation of the therapist."[43]

Groothuis pointed out that biofeedback's origin is related to the scientific study of yogis and Zen masters who could voluntarily—and without outside technology—control their automatic functions. He quoted holistic theorist Kenneth Pelletier as stating: "Self-healing by means of biofeedback inevitably involves the individual in a process of psychological development and may elicit profound experiences of altered states of consciousness . . . . The person may experience a unitive sensation in which he merges with the room, chairs, light, or therapist."[44]

I would like to repeat that, generally speaking, the Christian should feel free to seek medical help through biofeedback. There usually is nothing occultic or pantheistic about the procedure, which is quite common in Western medicine. However, as the quote from Pelletier indicates, some holistic health theorists see a New Age pantheistic result coming from some types of biofeedback. Pelletier is writing from a New Age position, not a traditional medical position.

Reflexology and iridology. Reflexology and iridology are two therapies with no basis in anatomy or physiology, according to physician Paul C. Reisser. Reflexology claims to treat ailing organs by massaging particular areas of the hand or foot. Iridology proposes that disease (past, present and future) in all parts of the body is reflected by spots on the iris, the colored center of the eye. One study at the University of California at San Diego, Reisser reported, showed that iridology was less able to identify patients with advanced kidney failure than random guessing.[45] Russell Chandler described the popular reflexology booths at fairs and exhibit conventions. "For $10, walk-weary sightseers can enjoy a 15-minute foot massage that does wonders for the feet—whether or not it balances their bile."[46]

An article by Sharon Fish in a 1989 *Spiritual Counterfeits Project Newsletter* recounted many instances of New Age philosophy influencing the practice of nursing. For example, she talked about Barbara Blattner's book, *Holistic Nursing*, which endorsed yoga and the chanting of a Hindu mantra. Blattner also supported psychic healing which she defined as "conducting and channeling the superconscious energy that is the source and intelligent center of all life."[47]

An organization has been started to investigate this New

Age medicine. Christians Investigating New Age Medicine (CINAM) has been founded to probe holistic health and alternative health therapies from a biblical perspective.[48]

Criteria for Discernment

A Christian can feel free to have ordinary medical problems treated with traditional medical practices without being concerned about the personal philosophy or theology of the physician. Only medical competence and convenience and cost need to be considered when consulting a physician about a broken bone, a hernia or a bad case of the flu.

The question arises: can a Christian seek nontraditional medical help? The answer is yes, if there is no occultic or pantheistic power being utilized for the cure. Otherwise, the Christian is in danger of losing faith in the one true God or in danger of coming under the influence of demonic spirits. The Christian should not become involved in self-hypnosis or altered states of consciousness. This leaves the Christian unprotected against demonic spirits.

To guide us in this extremely complex field of nontraditional medicine, Sheila Fabricant and Douglas Schoeninger have provided us 10 criteria for discernment.

> 1. *Is Jesus present in the beginning, the middle, and the end of our involvement with any method, theory or philosophy?* Are the fruits in our lives and the lives of those we minister to good or bad?

> 2. *Have I invited the Holy Spirit to speak to me through study of Scripture and church tradition in relation to this method, therapy, or philosophy?* If a healing method is of God, it will not conflict with Scripture or church tradition.

> 3. *Is there a quality of death to self-centeredness, in the sense of not seeking personal power or prestige in my use of this method, theory, or philosophy?*

> 4. *Does my use of a particular method promote appropriate care for myself and others?* Am I becoming

more sensitive to ethical concerns, fairness, repentance, forgiveness, and reconciliation?

5. *Is everyone welcome to come and learn, or does this method have a gnostic quality in the sense of an emphasis on elitist knowledge available only to a special few?*

6. *Is there a quality of the warm personal presence of Christ, rather than an exclusive emphasis on abstract truth or "energy," in this method?* Christian revelation tells us that the world has a personal center of love, incarnated in Jesus. Thus any healing method should lead us to a deeper sense of personal relationship rather than to knowledge alone.

7. *Are we open to understanding the universe in new ways, or are we rejecting a healing method out of fear of the unknown and a legalism that wants everything in its accustomed place?* Where the Holy Spirit is present, there is always something creative and surprising happening.

8. *Is my evaluation of a healing method grounded in the integrity of my personal experience?*

9. *Is my use of a particular method open to dialogue with persons of questioning or dissenting perspectives?*

10. *Does this healing method have any verifiable connection with occultism or witchcraft and, if so, is such a connection inherent in its use?* Some methods that initially appear to be occult may simply represent the misguided use of methods that can also be used in Christ-centered ways.[49]

Fabricant and Schoeninger concluded by stating that their perspectives and suggested criteria for discernment were intended only as an invitation to dialogue, not as a final or complete statement. They invited readers to comment on their article and to submit personal experiences of healing methods.

Chapter 12

Lawsuits, Dangers,
Employees' Rights,
Seven Signposts,
Widespread Influence,
Pacific Bell

Business

Continuing to explore the impact of the New Age in many areas of personal endeavor, we now come to business. New Age in the business world can be hazardous for the Christian. The Christian can get fired.

Take the case of Steve Hiatt, formerly a senior manager for Walker Chevrolet, based in Tacoma, Wash. He introduced the firm to training offered by Seattle's Pacific Institute. According to a news article by Steve Rabey in the June 17, 1988, *Christianity Today*, Hiatt and his wife, Carol, attended a facilitators' training workshop in February, 1984, designed to help him guide the firm's 60 workers through the program. On the third evening, Hiatt charged, the meetings took on a decidedly religious tone.

> The leader set a very spiritual mood and began talking about life after death and religion. He urged us to question our concepts of truth and to set spiritual goals using the program's techniques and goals. He said the real reason for the training was to save the world.[1]

The Hiatts walked out of the training session. A day later, he sent the training materials back to the Pacific Institute. This led to his being fired from a job he had held nearly 10 years. Hiatt took his problems to the Tacoma Human Rights Commission and the Seattle office of the Federal Equal Employment Opportunity Commission. Neither gave him any help. In February, 1988, he filed a civil suit against his former employer. "I just want to set a legal precedent and help stop government funding of these programs,"[2] he said.

According to the *Wall Street Journal*,[3] Jack Maichel, an attorney for Walker Chevrolet, said Hiatt was fired because of his job performance, not objections to the training program.

Christianity Today noted other New Age firings and harassment.

> * William Gleaton of Albany, Georgia, was discharged as manager of human resources at a Firestone Tire and Rubber Co. plant after objecting to a Pacific Institute training program. Firestone reached an out-of-court settlement with Gleaton.

> * James L. Baumgaertel, an inspector at the Puget Sound Naval Shipyard in Bremerton, Wash., filed a First Amendment complaint after being told to attend training using New Age techniques.

> * Employees of the DeKalb Farmers Market in Atlanta, Georgia, filed an Equal Employment Opportunity Commission complaint after being dismissed for refusing to participate in training based on Werner Erhard's *est*.[4]

The Pacific Institute contended that it has not intentionally promoted New Age thinking. " 'New Age' was a name our marketers picked back in 1979," said Jack Fitterer, president of the Pacific Institute, which had revenues of $20 million in 1987. "Now 'excellence' is the term the marketers use. We don't teach any theology. Our program is simply a cognitive psychology curriculum, similar to the curriculum that can be found on any university campus." Their "New Age Thinking" seminars have been replaced by "Investment in Excellence" programs which still contain sections on "self-image and belief" and "visualization."[5]

Christians disagreed. In his EEOC complaint, Baumgaertel asserted that his First Amendment rights had been violated because he had been ordered to attend training programs using meditation, "guided visualization" and other techniques that "can change a person's view of reality and religious beliefs." In an interview with the *New York Times*, he said: "These are psychotechnologies that are meant to induce altered states of consciousness. They are trying to reprogram the subconscious."[6]

Gleaton said he was discharged from a Firestone plant in 1984 after refusing to carry out what he described as a New Age training program offered by the Pacific Institute. He said he adhered to the Christian view that human fate is dependent upon the will of God. In contrast, he said, the course "focused everything on the self; the self was the center, the source of energy. The self had the ability to deal with any problem in life. You were capable of anything."[7]

Lawsuits

In a suit filed in federal court in December, 1988, eight former employees of the DeKalb Farmers Market, Atlanta, charged that they were fired or pressured to quit after objecting to attendance at the Forum human-potential sessions developed by Werner Erhard & Associates.[8] As we saw in Chapter Seven, the Forum is a recycling of the *est* program. "As you may have heard, we recently retired the *est* training and are offering a new program called the Forum," Werner Erhard wrote on March 27, 1985. "The Forum is all that the training was in terms of the results it produces in people's lives and, in addition, offers results produced by more than two years of intensive research on accessing the source of human effectiveness and accomplishment."[9]

According to the *Wall Street Journal*, the former DeKalb employees said the sessions, held outside of work, as well as separate programs introduced at the market by Consulting Technologies of North Miami Beach, clashed with their religious beliefs, which ranged from Christianity to Hinduism. They asked the court to enjoin the market from forcing workers to attend the sessions, which their attorneys described as "New Age." The suit sought back pay as well as damages for psychological trauma the workers say they suffered.[10]

Dong Shik Kim, a Korean-born Christian who was a supervisor at the DeKalb market, claimed in the suit that he went to the Forum sessions at his boss's behest, only to encounter "emotional confessions, psychological conditioning and programming" designed to produce a breakthrough "equivalent to being 'born again.' "[11] In the suit, Kim said that Robert Blazer, the market's owner, urged him to recruit subordinates and, when he balked, made work conditions so difficult he had to quit.

Ranjana Sampat, a bookkeeper who is a Hindu, said in the lawsuit that in another program at the market she was asked to confess intimate details of her life, including sexual relations.

Edward D. Buckley III, an attorney for the market and Blazer, contended that workers were encouraged, not coerced, to go to the Forum sessions. He claimed that ideas introduced at the market by Consulting Technologies were not religious or philosophical and did not impinge on employees' personal beliefs.

The Forum, which was not named in the suit, said it would never sanction coercing people to participate in its programs. Jan Smith, co-owner of Consulting Technologies, said the company is a "typical management consulting company" and "not at all New Age."[12]

Commenting on training programs in general, Kevin Garvey, a Hamden, Conn., consultant on psychological training, said that problems arise when the programs include controversial psychological techniques dealing with theology. Employees should be informed of the techniques beforehand, Garvey said, and allowed to choose whether to attend. "Otherwise it constitutes a forced religious conversion."[13]

The Equal Employment Opportunity Commission said it increasingly is seeing complaints about training programs that employees say infringe on their religious rights. In September, 1988, the agency issued a policy-guidance notice saying that New Age training programs can be handled under traditional guidelines of Title VII of the Civil Rights Act of 1964. If a worker challenges a training session on religious grounds, the EEOC said, employers must provide a "reasonable accommodation" unless it creates an "undue hardship"[14] on the business.

Speaking at a November 23, 1987, symposium on "Business and the New Age Movement" sponsored by the American Family Foundation, Herbert L. Rosedale, a New York attorney, warned of potential dangers to employers who impose New Age training programs.

> With the implementation of certain training programs, industry may be faced with employees claiming company liability for: emotional and physical injury arising out of training sessions; workers' compensation; necessary disclosure by employers to their carriers; and the effects of the training on the rest of the employee's life.[15]

> New Age trainings also raise broader legal issues for business: the definition of "religion" and the degree of accommodation to religious diversity required of a firm; problems arising from mandatory attendance and participation in programs; the need for advance disclosure of a program's nature and consequences; the rights of those who object to the program or aspects of it; the use of

training sessions as recruitment for additional participation in the training organization's out-of-firm activities, which may open the door to the solicitation of union organizers; the emerging limitation of at-will employment and discharge without cause; and other, derivative liability.[16]

The American Family Foundation symposium report gave other warnings about New Age training programs.

> * Carl Raschke of the University of Denver said that the New Age movement, which underpins and guides the practices of many of the training schemes now being sold to industry, aims radically to transform American society. This New Age thought, at once religious and political, holds essentially that our badly failing economic and social systems must be changed through the development of a "sharing and caring" consciousness—a new way of looking at reality, a new system of relationships among management, employees, and other factors of production. Raschke also thought that the New Age prescription for the fulfillment of this vision, with its emphasis on "we" (the converted) versus "they" (outsiders), is totalitarian.

> * Margaret Singer of the University of California, Berkeley, said that training based on New Age principles is essentially the updating of age-old techniques of social and psychological "influence" designed to create "deployable" people. The result is that the majority of trainees experience varying degrees of alienation and anomie because they were urged to give up old norms, goals, and ideals. They also suffer "culture shock" as they try to reconcile pre-training values both with what they learned in the training and with the realities of their post-training existence.

* Richard Ofshe of the University of California, Berkeley, suggested that potential consumers of New Age training programs should ask about and get satisfactory answers to inquiries about the theory behind the training in question, about how the claimed outcome is supposed to be effected. Something is wrong if the trainer cannot answer these questions; sometimes the explanation will be irrational enough to forewarn against purchase. Managers should note, Ofshe said, that low-level training in some schemes may appear harmless, but later training may well include psychologically harmful exercises. Clearly, he emphasized, managers must know exactly the content and style of the proposed training.

* Consultant Kevin Garvey talked about the case of an executive who, in the wake of a major business success, reverted to the irrational euphoria first experienced during his New Age training. This euphoric phase left him incapable of carrying out his normal daily functions. Garvey warned that involvement of persons in advanced levels of certain trainings, which tended to inhibit rational corporate activity, created "psychic time bombs" for business.[17]

Dangers

According to the American Family Foundation symposium report, Richard Watring, Chicago, personnel director for Budget Rent-a-Car, said he believed that "business should respond to the New Age movement the way it does to other external forces over which it has no control . . . by investigating, evaluating, and managing" what he characterized as "the inherent dangers in the promotion of New Age transformation." Noting that the New Age movement "is essentially spiritual, based on Eastern religion and occult mysticism," Watring contended that it "fosters a belief system that

is not compatible with the Judeo-Christian view of things."
He also warned that the New Age movement "employs techniques which alter the consciousness of those who come
under its influence without first getting their informed con-
sent."[18]

In a letter published in the April, 1987, *Training and
Development Journal,* Watring warned about the possibility of
demonic influences. "Many people ascribe to the belief in a
spiritual or supernatural realm," he wrote. "Many religious
traditions teach their adherents about such a realm, vari-
ously inhabited by angels, departed souls, demons, and the
like. Since we cannot prove either the existence of such a
realm or its nonexistence, we must be very cautious whenever we are dealing with the spiritual dimension of an
employee. For if there truly is a spiritual realm, and if we
humans are susceptible to influence from such a realm, then
teaching our employees to use their 'higher self' to improve
their performance may, in fact, be introducing them to a
form of spiritism, one involving 'occult correspondence'
where the subject is already in a heightened state of sugges-
tibility because of the trancelike state that is entered."[19]

Watring concluded an article he wrote for *Eternity* by
stating: "Private corporations that are not church-affiliated
should neither attempt to change the basic belief systems of
their employees nor should they promote the use of techniques (i.e., altered consciousness) that accelerate such
change; and while spiritual growth is important, corporations should not prescribe the methods whereby employees
grow spiritually."[20]

New Age training techniques are not "value neutral,"
asserted Ron Zemke, senior editor of *Training.* "Rather, they
are techniques inherently geared toward getting people to
adopt New Age paradigms. The problem is that the values
with which they are imbued are Eastern philosophical
views of a pantheistic, non-Christian nature. Techniques
that depend on protocols that command the learners to
project themselves into some 'other' reality and then to ex-

perience themselves as being one with all things, including God, are hardly neutral. They certainly are not neutral to Christians whose faith rests on the concept of God as an entity outside themselves . . . . In other words, there can be no such thing as a centered, self-hypnotizing, yoga-practicing meditator who is also a Bible-believing Christian. You're one or the other."[21]

Napoleon Hill is a motivational speaker and writer who is quite popular in Christian circles as well as in the general public arena. Hill's basic idea, that one can achieve financial success if one only desires it strongly enough, is very close to the New Age position that we create our own reality. "Man may become the master of himself, and of his environment, because he has the power to influence his own subconscious mind,"[22] Hill wrote in *Think and Grow Rich*. In the same book, he wrote about his practice of falling asleep while imagining a group of nine famous men meeting and talking with him in his imagination.[23] This is very similar to the practice of conjuring up demonic spirits as inner guides.

In a July 27, 1988, interview in his Berkeley office, Brooks Alexander expressed concern about the way big business is promoting New Age ideas in its training programs. "What business is interested in, business promotes. Once the New Age trainings get rooted in the financial life of this country, once the popular interest in the New Age rises to the level that it can be mass-marketed, then it's not likely to go away," he said. "I think once the New Age works its way into the corporate mentality through the influence of the trainings and once it becomes a part of the economic life of the country, then it's seriously infecting the cultural value system as a whole."[24]

In Chapter One, we quoted an article by Alexander in *Eternity* in which he said: "The end-product of New Age spirituality is a person incapable of distinguishing truth from falsehood, and programmed to ignore the issue up front." He concluded the article in this way: "It is an understatement to say that the New Age movement tends to

produce highly impressionable and therefore easily manipulated people. The ideal New Ager is truly a 'human
resource,' supple and submissive, the delight of managers,
bureaucrats and social engineers. In large numbers, a
dictator's fantasy, functional cogs for the socio-commercial-
political machine. That is the most disturbing implication of
the New Age movement—and its most likely concrete impact on our future."[25]

Employees' Rights

In a *Spiritual Counterfeits Project Newsletter* issued in 1989,
the editors gave a number of suggestions for Christian
employees and employers concerning mandatory New Age
training programs.

> 1. *Anti-discrimination law.* An employer is obligat-
> ed by law to make reasonable accommodation to
> an employee's religious beliefs. If an employee
> perceives a program to be at odds with his or her
> religious beliefs, the employer is obligated to re-
> structure the program.
>
> The Equal Employment Opportunity Commis-
> sion's policy statement made it clear: whether "the
> employer or the sponsor of a 'new age' program
> believes there is no religious basis for, or content
> to, the training or techniques used is irrelevant to
> determining the need for accommodation . . . . An
> employer may not reject an employee's request for
> accommodation on the basis that the employee's
> beliefs about 'new age' training seem unreason-
> able."
>
> Required attendance at programs that an employee
> perceives as conflicting with his or her religious
> beliefs may violate antidiscrimination laws and
> provide employees with grounds for requesting
> an investigation by the EEOC and/or filing a suit.
>
> 2. *Invasion of privacy.* The programs offered may

demand that participants contemplate or reveal details about their personal lives that are frankly nobody's business. They are particularly not the business of the sponsoring employer—another basis for litigation.

3. *Psychological damage.* The psychological fallout from New Age programs is well documented and is also grounds for filing a suit. If a company puts its employees through a program, that company is responsible for the consequences. Typically, these programs are designed to create a heightened sense of solidarity among participants by engaging in (a) high-risk activities or at least activities that are passed off or perceived as high-risk and (b) exercises that demand intimate self-disclosure. These activities are precisely the ones which have the greatest potential for taking their toll on the psychologically vulnerable.

4. *Negative results.* In spite of the claim to improve employee relationships and company productivity, New Age programs tend to do the opposite. They usually do not unify the corporate culture; they divide it.[26]

The issues for the employer "remain relatively the same even if participation in a program is considered voluntary," the article continued. "The sponsoring employer is again responsible for the consequences of the programs it introduces and endorses." The invasion of privacy and psychological damage aspects can still provide the grounds for lawsuits. The antidiscrimination law may apply if the programs are passed off as voluntary, but are really mandatory. This would be the case if employees were rewarded for attending and penalized for avoiding the programs.

Also, the article notes, fair-access laws may come into play. "If an employer introduces a voluntary program into the workplace, the door is then open for others to introduce

programs the employer may not regard with the same enthu-
siasm."[27]

Seven Signposts

Douglas Groothuis has come up with "seven signposts"
to help a Christian identify a New Age seminar. "Just because a seminar displays one of these characteristics doesn't
necessarily mean that it is New Age in orientation," he explained. "Nevertheless, it does mean that we should pro-
ceed with care, cautiously discerning the assumptions behind what is being taught."[28] His "signposts" are:

1. *Be wary of seminars that stress visualization as the
key to success.* They emphasize the purportedly
limitless power of the imagination to "create reality." What is simply a natural function of many
people's thinking is absurdly elevated to the status
of a magical principle. In some cases "guided
visualizations" may induce a hypnotic trance in
which one becomes vulnerable to suggestion. In
other cases people may feel the rush of omnipo-
tence as they measure their abilities by the vivid-
ness of their visualizations—much like balancing
one's checkbook by figuring out what one wishes
were there.

2. *Seminars that strongly emphasize positive affirma-
tions are suspect.* Believing in oneself—that is, believing only the good things and stubbornly disbe-
lieving the rest—is the key. Though blind positive
thinking is not necessarily the product of the New
Age, it is consistent with its worldview and often
used by its practitioners.

3. *Business seminars may include Eastern/occult forms
of meditation or other "psychotechnologies."* Some
seminars wear away peoples' common sense and
rational reflection through long hours of psychic
assault, resulting in an artificial and inappropriate

change of consciousness.

4. *Caution is appropriate in evaluating any business seminar that "promises you the world" or guarantees it will "change your life."* Extravagant claims in the New Age mode about total personal transformation are nothing less than religious appeals.

5. *An exorbitant cost for these miracle seminars may tip us off to their dangers.* Paying a substantial sum of (nonrefundable) money serves as a good psychological adhesive to insure that people endure the seminars even when their better judgment would normally propel them toward the door at the first few signs of aberration.

6. *Excessive secrecy about the actual content of these seminars should cause us to wonder if they are hiding something sinister instead of simply protecting a marketable commodity.* This may take the form of promoting the charisma of a particular speaker rather than divulging the content of his teaching.

7. *Seminars that involve long hours outside of the normal work schedule and/or require the spouse's attendance* may have the implicit intention of radically changing one's worldview and manner of life to fit the New Age mold.[29]

Widespread Influence

According to a May 4, 1987, *Newsweek* article, New Age consultants have been hired by such corporate giants as Pacific Bell, Procter & Gamble, TRW, Ford Motor Company and Polaroid. By one estimate, these programs account for about $4 billion in corporate spending each year.[30] American business spends about $30 billion a year in training employees. *U.S. News & World Report* linked Citibank, General Motors and General Foods to New Age training programs.[31] Human-potential seminars sponsored by the Pacific Institute—

originally called "New Age Thinking"—have attracted such clients as ABC-TV, NASA, Eastman Kodak, Peoples National Bank, McDonald's Corp., AT&T, IBM and the U.S. Army.[32]

Some of the cults we considered in Chapter Seven have adapted their teachings and are now marketing them as New Age training programs. According to Russell Chandler, New Age human-potential groups that have borrowed heavily from Scientology concepts are *est*, Lifespring and MSIA (Church of the Movement of Spiritual Inner Awareness—pronounced "Messiah"). The Los Angeles-based Church of Scientology itself has moved into management consulting through WISE, a nonprofit organization, and Sterling Management, a consulting firm. Between 1971 and 1984, Werner Erhard enrolled nearly a half-million persons in his 60-hour *est* program. When attendance began to fall off, he repackaged it as the Forum and attendance began picking up again despite the $525-per-person price tag.[33] Besides founding the Forum program, in 1984 Erhard founded Transformational Technologies, a business "designed to do for companies what *est* had done for individuals,"[34] according to *Newsweek*. In 1987, Transtech sold its services through 50 franchise operations throughout the country. Franchises sold for $20,000 and Transtech also collected 8% of all franchisees' gross receipts. Franchise billings in 1986 totaled $15 million.

It cost a lot when Erhard himself made an appearance. NASA's Goddard Space Flight Center paid $45,000 for 47 managers to attend three sessions conducted by Erhard and two associates. TRW paid the same amount for five days of training led by James Selman, Erhard's partner and Transtech's chief executive officer. Motivator Louis Tice, whose Pacific Institute was expected to gross $15 million to $20 million in 1987, charged corporations $8,000 for an appearance and $15,000 for a set of videocassettes. A company spokesman estimated that most clients paid $110 per person for Pacific Institute training. At that rate, Southern

Bell had paid by 1987 about $1.5 million to introduce 14,000 employees to the Tice method.[35]

California Business reported in 1986 that a survey of 500 company owners and presidents found that more than half had used some form of "consciousness-raising" technique. Richard Watring's 1984 survey of 780 personnel directors showed that 45% had "seen or used" one or more psycho-technologies of consciousness-raising.[36] At Stanford University's well-regarded Graduate School of Business, the syllabus for a seminar on "Creativity in Business" included chanting, meditation, "dream work," the use of Tarot cards and discussion of the "New Age Capitalist."[37]

Pacific Bell

Disgruntled employees and an angry public forced Pacific Bell of San Francisco—the state's largest utility company and the San Francisco Bay area's biggest employer—to stop its controversial "Leadership Development" training practices. The training consisted of 10 two-day sessions attended quarterly which utilized many of the ideas of Charles Krone, a student of the controversial Russian mystic G.I. Gurdjieff. According to the *San Francisco Chronicle*, Krone "devised an eclectic mixture of common sense, standard organizational development, scientific methodologies and Eastern philosophies."[38]

Jeremy Main, writing in *Fortune,* said Pac Bell hired two associates of Krone to overhaul its corporate image. "Krone," Main explained, "who often veils his ideas in impenetrable language, claims to make people rethink the way they think and hence arrive at new ways of solving problems."[39] After two years, the Krone consultants obviously made an impression on corporate culture. The 1987 corporate statement of principles, Main said, "was worded in a manner even Krone might find indecipherable. It defined 'interaction,' for example, as the 'continuous ability to engage with the connectedness and relatedness that exists and potentially exists, which is essential for the creations necessary to maintain and enhance viability of ourselves and the organization of which we are a part.' "[40]

At the American Family Foundation symposium, Main, the editor of *Fortune*, noted that the California Public Utilities Commission inquiry into the Krone training for Pac Bell (which spent $160 million on the project) revealed great employee anger and discontent over the training. (Some 15,000 of Pac Bell's 67,000 employees participated in the training.) In his *Fortune* article, Main reported that the utilities commission recommended that $25 million of the $40 million cost of the program in 1987 be charged to the stockholders, not the rate payers. Pac Bell suspended further training and ordered its own study, Main said. The company's president, Theodore Saenger, took early retirement, and his heir apparent, Executive Vice-President Lee Cox, the chief supporter of the Krone program, was demoted to the presidency of a subsidiary, Pactel Corporation.

On April 6, 1987, the *San Francisco Chronicle* ran an article by "John Hogarth," the pen name of a Pac Bell marketing manager who attended a Krone training session in 1985 and considered it a waste of time and money. The session was led by two Krone consultants who reportedly were paid $1,200 a day each. There was also a "facilitator" or member of the "thought police" among the attendees. He was a company employee who had been through the program and whose full-time job now was to guide his co-workers on the path he had trod. According to Hogarth, two full days of training came up with these directives:

Meetings should have an agenda.
Meetings should have a leader.
Meetings should have a secretary to take notes.
Meetings should have a "facilitator."

Chapter 13

Satanism,
Rock Music,
The Force,
Higher Beings,
Music

Entertainment

The New Age is very strong in the entertainment field. There are many more popular movies with New Age themes than there are with Christian themes. There are also New Age radio stations and music albums. Shirley MacLaine's television miniseries was quite popular.

Satanism

Before getting to New Age themes as such, however, I want to point out that satanism is also very rampant in the entertainment field. At a time when two-thirds of Americans do not believe a personal devil exists, teen-agers and others are flocking to movies about Satan and demonic possession. Look at the movie ads in your daily paper. If you are living in a city with more than just one or two movie theaters, there is a very good chance that you will find ads for several movies that deal with demonic influences.

Take the first *Ghostbusters* movie, for example. This was a raucous comedy, but the demonic and occultic aspects were treated seriously—at least as seriously as anything in

this wild comedy. For example, when the female lead exhibited some of the classic symptoms of possession—talking in a strange voice, levitation, the head spinning on the neck—the movie did not have to explain to the audience what was happening. They knew that an evil spirit had taken her over.

Current serious treatment of the demonic in movies probably dates back to *Rosemary's Baby* and *The Exorcist* in the late 1960s and early 1970s. Except for the unfortunate dramatic device of making the devil as powerful as or more powerful than God, these movies had a lot of real truth about Satan in them. In *The Exorcist*, for example, the girl's possession probably stemmed from a time when she played with a Ouija board—a very real spiritual danger. Her reaction to the exorcism, though quite dramatic and grotesque, was similar to reactions of possessed people exorcised by Christian missionaries.

Many of the spate of movies on the demonic feature the goat's-head god of classical satanism; they have satanic rituals and the black mass; they have chilling sacrifices of animals and humans. In short, though these movies are exaggerated and overly melodramatic, they are telling a good deal of the truth about satanism—at a time when most people say they don't believe in the devil.

Another unappetizing aspect of horror movies is the recent change in the point of view from which the movie is shot. It used to be that the camera always played the part of the victim. In the crucial scene, the monster or the killer came right at the camera. Nowadays the camera often plays the part of the mad slasher. The ghoulish audience can squeal in delight as the axe or knife or chainsaw comes into view in front of the camera as though the moviegoer were cutting up the victim. What spiritual impact does this have on the soul of the moviegoer?

The July, 1988, *Focus on the Family* published by James C. Dobson talked about the graphically violent horror films of today. The magazine reported that Americans spent $1.6 billion to rent movies in 1985 (and the figure is much higher today), with about 25% spent on horror/suspense films. Included in this figure were popular movies that depicted actual death scenes. *Faces of Death*, a ruthlessly violent film showing real and reenacted death scenes, had been viewed by 12% of Christian school students polled in a recent survey.[1]

In Chapter Eight, we talked about the satanic cult in Matamoros, Mexico, accused of killing 15 people. According to an Associated Press report, the cult members were influenced by repeated viewings of the movie *The Believers* about the time they began performing human sacrifices. The 1986 movie, starring Martin Sheen and directed by John Schlesinger, was about rich, influential families who protected their prominence with cultic rites, including human sacrifice.

"The motives of the movie's characters are chillingly similar to those of the members of the real-life cult," the AP noted. "The suspects told police that at first the cult practiced an Afro-Cuban religion which sometimes calls for the sacrifice of animals, but never humans. But the group's relatively benign rites turned sinister late last summer, about the time one of the cult's leaders began urging members to watch videotapes of *The Believers*, police said."[2]

Rock Music

There are many kinds of rock music, including folk rock and Christian rock. Only a small percentage of this broad musical style deals with blatant satanism. Here are some examples.

> * Led Zeppelin's song, "Stairway to Heaven," was actually about going to hell. The lyrics stated: "There are two ways to go, two stairways to face, one to heaven and the other to hell. Me . . . I'll take the second." There was also blatant backward masking on the song. When it is played backwards, the sound track stated quite plainly: "There's no escaping it. It's my sweet Satan. The one will be the path who makes me sad; whose power is Sa-

tan."[3]   (Occultists believe that sounds affect an individual even if the words are played backward and are unintelligible.)

* In their song, "Witchy Woman," the Eagles sang of a "restless spirit" who flies through the air with sparks flying from her fingertips. In the song, "One of Those Nights," the singer was searching for the "daughter of the devil" who possesses both desires and demons.[4]

* The British group Black Sabbath reportedly held black masses before some of their concerts. Their first album had a picture of a witch on the cover and another album depicted a nude satanic ritual with the number 666 (cf. Rev. 13:18) prominently displayed.[5]

* On one of his albums, Ozzy Osbourne, Black Sabbath's former front man, had a song entitled, "Mr. Crowley," referring to Aleister Crowley, the late satanist. Osbourne has been quoted as saying, "I don't know if I'm a medium for some outside force or not. Frankly, whatever it is, I hope it's not what I think it is—Satan."[6]

* The song "God of Thunder" by the group Kiss had these lyrics: "God of rock-n-roll will steal your mortal soul . . . . I command you to kneel before the god of thunder, the god of rock-n-roll."[7]

* An album cover of the Damned featured a woman with a crown of thorns. Undisputed Truth's "Night of the Demon" album cover showed a demon crucified on a cross. Singer Madonna told *Spin* magazine in 1985 that "crucifixes are sexy because there is a naked man on them." Spooky Tooth's album "Ceremony" depicted Jesus as a cosmic buffoon with his hand nailed into his head.[8]

* AC/DC guitarist Angus Young has said, "Some-one else is steering me—I'm just along for the ride. I become possessed when I'm on stage." Singer Joni Mitchell said she was controlled by a demon spirit, a male muse named Art. Guitarist John McLaughlin has said, "One night we were playing and suddenly the spirit entered into me, and I was playing, but it was no longer me playing."[9]

* In his column, "Light One Candle," Fr. John Catoir gave more examples of satanic lyrics from heavy-metal rock groups. In its song "The Oath," King Diamond sang: "By the symbol of the crea-tion I swear henceforth to be a faithful servant of his most persistent archangel, Prince Lucifer, whom the creator designated as his regent, and the lord of this world. Amen. I deny Jesus Christ, the deceiver, and I adjure the Christian faith, holding in contempt all of its works." In its song, "Pos-sessed," the group Venom sang: "Look at me, Satan's child, born of evil, thus defiled, brought to life through satanic birth . . . . Listen to me and I'll tell you things that will sicken your mind . . . . I drink the vomit of the priests, make love with a dying whore."[10]

* Catoir also reprinted lyrics from songs that talked about killing and depravity. "The whip is my toy. Handcuffs are your joy. You hold me down and I'm screaming for joy" was the message of Bitch's song, "Leatherbound." The Dead Kennedys were quite explicit in their song, "I Kill Children": "God told me to skin you alive . . . . I kill children. I love to see them die. I kill children. To make their moth-ers cry. I crush them under my car and I love to hear them scream. I feed them poison candy and spoil their Halloween. I kill children."[11]

You get the picture. Now on to more explicitly New Age

stuff.

The Force

"May the force be with you." Almost everybody knows what that means. This is a catchphrase the good guys used in the tremendously popular *Star Wars* movies. The underlying theology was pure New Age. There is no Creator God, no objective rules of right and wrong. There is simply this blind force which can be used by good people for good, and bad people for bad.

This force can be tapped into by suspending reason and using instinct. In the finale of the first movie, *Star Wars*, for example, Luke Skywalker was able to shoot his proton torpedo into a small opening in the Death Star only after he shut his eyes and let the force guide him.

In the second movie, *The Empire Strikes Back*, we were introduced to Yoda, who is essentially a yogi. He taught Skywalker that he could create reality—such as lifting a plane—simply by thinking. In the final movie, *Return of the Jedi*, Darth Vader became a good guy by turning to the light side of the force instead of the dark side. This was all New Age stuff. Bob Larson explained the philosophy underlying these movies.

> The *Star Wars* movie epics have been profoundly influenced by Taoistic philosophy. In conceptualizing the force, producer George Lucas has borrowed heavily from the hypothesis of a primordial, universal energy flow that is neither good nor evil. Since the motive of the individual determines the moral nature of the force, it thus possesses a duality whose positive and negative components are equivalent.

> This is, of course, not compatible with biblical theology which sees God as the omnipotent source of all that is good. Satan, the Scriptures declare, was created by God and therefore has limitations

on both his authority and power. As the source of all evil, the devil opposes the work of God, but he is not an equalizing, harmonizing opposite.

The idea of the force is from a concept found in Chinese philosophy which envisions *ch'i* (or *ki*) as a basic flow of energy sustaining all life. *Ch'i* (pronounced key) embodies the characteristics of the Tao, possessing a dual nature of yin and yang . . . .

Yin and yang are said to symbolize the complementary nature of all forces in the universe . . . . Yang is the positive force of good, light, life, and masculinity. Yin is the negative essence of evil, death, and femininity. All matter is said to contain both yin and yang, and orderly affairs are possible only when these two qualities exist in a state of proper equilibrium.[12]

The New Age also made its appearance in one of the very popular Indiana Jones movies. In Chapter Two, we talked about Tantra, or salvation through sex. Brooks Alexander saw Tantra getting wide exposure in *Indiana Jones and the Temple of Doom*. In the movie, Alexander said, "the hero combats a lefthand tantric sect for possession of a primeval *shiva-lingam* (the film's fictitious 'shankara stone'). He succeeds, and returns the tantric talisman to its rightful possessors, presumably a righthand sect which uses the same talisman in a benign and 'natural' way. Suddenly, as of 1984, millions of Americans have been introduced to the Tantra for the price of a theater ticket."[13]

Higher Beings

Another theme in contemporary movies common to the New Age is that of a more highly evolved race from outer space visiting us to improve our lives. *E.T.* and *Close Encounters of the Third Kind* were two very popular movies with this theme. This concept presupposes that humans can evolve into a higher type of existence. These outer-space beings have evolved further than we humans have and the implication is given that, with luck, we can evolve further, too. E.T. was so evolved, in fact, that he could heal people and resurrect himself from the dead. No hint was given in these movies that there is a Supreme Being, a God who created the extraterrestrials as well as the humans.

In the movie, *Cocoon*, the extraterrestrials peeled off the outer shell of human skin they were wearing and revealed themselves to be creatures of pure light—a common New Age theme. Of course, they were much wiser than the humans in the picture. The movie also went out of its way to sneer at basic Christian beliefs. According to the plot, a boatload of old people has been taken up into a space vehicle during a storm. We are informed that they will be rejuvenated through outer space medical technology and will live for several hundred more years and will fly around in the spaceship visiting lots of exciting planets and space sites.

That is nice, but the plot doesn't stop there. The movie ends with a dreary Christian memorial service by the ocean in which a minister tells the grieving relatives that the group of old people—presumed lost at sea—is now in a "much better place," that is, heaven. A young boy, the only one who knows they are actually not dead but in the space vehicle, looks up to the sky with a secret smile. He knows better. They're not in heaven, they're cruising the galaxies. The movie clearly implies that real life in a space vehicle is far superior to life in an imagined heaven. As for me, I think an eternity in heaven with God and all the angels and saints is far superior to flying around in some old space vehicle. But I'm a Christian and not a New Ager.

Douglas Groothuis found an unabashed New Age theme in the children's movie, *The Dark Crystal*, produced by Jim Henson, the creator of the Muppets. "It is essentially a fairy tale of monism," wrote Groothuis. There were two rival ruling factions in the land—the Mystics, lovable and slow-moving contemplatives, and the Skecsees, who were evil and depraved and power-hungry. As the story unfolded, a character found a lost shard once split off from the planet's magic crystal and, after many adventures, returned the lost shard to the crystal.

"With the unity of the crystal restored, we witness a major transformation," Groothuis explained. "The Mystics and the Skecsees are fused into one unified group of beings. Good and evil are transcended and cosmic unity is restored. We are told in no uncertain terms that good does not overcome evil, as in so many fairy tales; good and evil are really one and the same. The Skecsees, for all their apparent depravity, were not evil but only the dark side of the Mystics. Likewise, the Mystics were not good in themselves; they had to be reunited with the Skecsees. All is one; ultimate reality is beyond good and evil."[14]

There are many more movies with New Age themes and, of course, the New Age has also crept onto television. A *Charlie's Angels* show talked about the energy fields of the *chakras*. We had Shirley MacLaine's miniseries. Journalist Bill Moyers interviewed mythology expert Joseph Campbell for a series of programs on *The Power of Myth* on public television. Campbell, it seems, treated every myth from every culture with great respect—except for the "myths" of the Bible.

The extremely controversial movie, *The Last Temptation of Christ*, depicted Jesus as a confused wimp who doubted his messiahship and struggled with lustful temptations. Russell Chandler saw a New Age influence in the movie, which was based on Nikos Kazantzakis's 1955 novel. "Everything's a part of God," the tormented Christ declared in the movie in a decidedly pantheistic context. Chandler continued his analysis:

> On the introduction page of the script is this quotation from Kazantzakis: "It is not God who will save us—it is us who will save God, by battling, by creating and transmuting matter into spirit." In the prologue to his novel, Kazantzakis speaks of the "yearning . . . of man to attain God, or more

exactly, to return to God and identify himself with him."

The supreme purpose of the struggle between the flesh and the spirit in the book and the movie is "union with God," a very Eastern concept of the pathway to godhead and release from the cycle of birth and death into bliss.[15]

Music

New Age music is getting to be big business, reportedly grossing more than $100 million in 1987. Stemming from soft jazz and instrumental recordings of the late 1960s and early 1970s, New Age music spread to hundreds of radio stations and to popular television commercials in the 1980s. Russell Chandler noted that Windham Hill, a leading producer of New Age music "whose serene, introspective recordings first sold in health food stores in the 1970s, has parlayed an initial $300 investment into more than $35 million in sales during 1987."[16]

Chandler continued: "Critics call it 'yuppie Muzak,' 'aural wallpaper,' and 'audio valium.' Those who like it say it echoes the ambience of natural environments, helps them relax and meditate, or elicits a joy that energizes and brightens them . . . . It includes the sounds of plant vibrations, animal and nature noises, Celtic harps, gourd-shaped sitars, tunable tabla drums, drone-generating tambouras, and digital synthesizers. It can even be produced by a sheet of steel balanced on a balloon submerged in water."[17]

"As life becomes more complicated and fast-paced, people are discovering the need for peaceful sounds which they can use to create a more healing tranquil environment," New Age musicians David and Steve Gordon stated. "They use New Age music not just as background but as an integral part of their personal reality. It becomes interwoven with the fabric of their day-to-day lives, helping them to be more centered, energized and loving. Listening to New Age music is a way they can leave behind the surface intellect for a few moments and feel the unlimited peace and joy of their inner being. The essence of New Age music lies in the power of sound to actually vibrate the body's psychic energy centers and transform our awareness. To awaken within us that spark of universal love and oneness with all that is."[18]

Is New Age music dangerous? Much of what is called New Age music does not fall philosophically or theologically in the New Age movement as such. "New Age" is a popular designation. It sells records. Most New Age music really consists of light instrumentals and natural sounds like that of the surf. What harm can there be in these things?

On the other hand, harm can come because a certain percentage of New Age music is composed with the deliberate design to alter consciousness or to give the listener a pantheistic mystical experience or to open up the individual to the influence of demonic spirits. This New Age music can be very dangerous and it may be difficult to differentiate between the simply mellow New Age music and the hardcore pantheistic New Age music.

"It is generally recognized that New Age musicians indulge in various forms of occult meditation and cosmic awareness philosophies," wrote Bob Larson. "Some of them freely admit using trance channeling as a source of inspiration. Consequently, a biblical perspective would define some of the music as satanically inspired."[19]

True New Age music, then, is theologically wrong in its roots and also in the effects it hopes to achieve. "Genuine New Age music is written to alter personal reality and expose one to his supposed inner divine nature," Larson continued. "In this sense, it is a kind of musical yoga. Serious New Age composers actually believe they can vibrate the body's psychic energy centers to awaken and transform the spiritual awareness of the human spirit."[20]

Douglas Groothuis gave examples of the underlying purpose of some New Age music.

Some New Age music is intended not just to soothe the soul but to trigger a meditative change in consciousness. This could be called meditative or mystical New Age music. Steven Halpern, an innovator in New Age music with over 30 albums to his credit, has produced many albums that clearly integrate Eastern mystical practices with his music. His "Spectrum Suite" is designed to enable listeners to focus on each of the seven *chakras* (energy centers) in their body, which he thinks correspond to seven separate colors and sounds. Halpern says, "When the seventh and final selection begins, keynote B, focus your attention on the crown of your head. Visualize a violet color there and welcome the energy of divine consciousness."[21]

A tape by Robert Slap is called "Ascension to All That Is." A promotional blurb says that it is "a musical interpretation of ascending up through the astral planes to the seventh level—the Godhead, the Universal Mind . . . the All That Is."[22]

A tape with similar ethereal aspirations is "Journey Out of the Body" by David Naegles. It claims to bring the performer's own paranormal proclivities to bear on the music which is said to induce out-of-body experiences.[23]

The meditative/mystical tapes distributed under the Valley of the Sun New Age label are described as "gentle, flowing, sustained environmental music without tension or resolve" which has been (supposedly) "scientifically proven to produce dramatic changes of consciousness" and is "ideal for altered-state-of-consciousness work." Some of these tapes also contain subliminal messages thought to break into the unconscious mind to alter one's thoughts and entire life.[24]

As a final word, the Christian should be prudent in regard to New Age music. Much of it is harmless and simply relaxing. Some of it, however, can be harmful. If you're not sure it's all right, turn it off. When in doubt, throw it out!

Part 3

Christian Truth

In this section we'll suggest a forthright, doctrinally founded approach which mainline Christians can take toward the New Age. Some of your friends and relatives may be involved in some New Age practices. In your efforts to bring them back to belief in Christ, the material and resources in these chapters will prove very helpful.

Chapter **14**

Christians Respond to the New Age ____

In this chapter we'll survey the positions and publications of Christians who are concerned about the New Age. Those of you who wish a fuller treatment of specific ideas, cults or practices can follow up with materials referred to here.

Catholic Church

More than 100 years ago, the Roman Catholic Church condemned the New Age movement, in effect, when it gave a strong condemnation of pantheism in a document of the First Vatican Council, *Dogmatic Constitution on the Catholic Faith* (1870). The council condemned these five pantheistic propositions:

1. Nothing exists except matter.

2. God and all things possess one and the same substance and essence.

3. Finite things, both corporeal and spiritual, or at

least spiritual, emanated from the divine substance.

4. The divine essence becomes all things by a manifestation or evolution of itself.

5. God is universal or indefinite being, which by
determining itself makes up the universe, which is
diversified into genera, species and individuals.[1]

In 1975, Catholic theologian John A. Hardon contended
that these pantheistic ideas "pose a grave crisis in Christian
theology." He went on in his book *The Catholic Catechism* to
give the philosophical background of these five statements.

1. Materialists do not openly deny the existence of
what Christians call spirit; they simply claim that
"spirit" is a function of matter. It is not as though
there were no other reality than the dimensional;
but whatever exists, including the Christian God,
must be measured by or considered the product of
space and time.

2. Another name for pantheism is monism or sin-
gularism. It asserts that God and the universe are
ultimately identical.

3. Emanational pantheism was propounded by
Johann Fichte (1762-1814). He taught that each
human being's ego is simply an emergence of the
impersonal Absolute Ego in individual consciousness. More simply stated, we are not individual
persons really distinct from God but only individual "awarenesses" of God's knowledge of
himself or, better, of the absolute's consciousness
of itself.

4. Evolutionary pantheism of the unfolding type
was taught by Friedrich von Schelling (1775-1854).
In his theory, the whole universe (including what
believers call God) is one great organism whose

latent potencies are constantly developing by a "dynamic process." History is the progressive revelation of the absolute, which animates the world of space and time as its soul.

5. More elaborate and significant was the evolutionary pantheism of Georg Hegel (1770-1831). In the Hegelian system God exists only as the "Idea which is eternally producing itself." Unlike other evolutionists, however, Hegel postulated development through a dialectical process in which one thing (antithesis) succeeds another thing (thesis), and the resulting conflict gives rise to a third thing (synthesis). Nothing can be said simply to exist; it is still becoming. In this system, God is the universal Idea which, through incessant conflict, becomes even more perfect. Marxism has built its notion of God and the universe on Hegelianism.[2]

Interreligious Dialogue

The Catholic Church advises its members to distinguish the New Age and various cults from the major world religions. A chief spokesman for the Vatican, Cardinal Francis Arinze, acknowledges that Christians should engage in dialogue with members of major non-Christian religions with an attitude of mutual respect. He is the president of the Vatican Secretariat for Non-Christians. His office promotes dialogue with Muslims, Hindus, Buddhists, Sikhs, Taoists and other members of non-Christian religions. (Other Vatican secretariats relate with Christians who are not Catholics or with people who have no belief in God at all.) I quote some of his statements here, because I think they also will help us approach New Agers with love and concern, even though New Age ideas do not deserve the same respect as the historical religions do. While we may not agree with other people's ideas, we must respect the people and love them and be open to talking with them.

"Every human being is looking for God consciously or

unconsciously,"[3] Arinze said in a 1988 interview. "The various religions are efforts of the human soul to look for answers to the fundamental questions that touch human existence. What is the human being? Where do we come from? Who made us? What is life for? What is good? What is evil? Why suffering? Why death?"

The Roman Catholic Church wants to enter into dialogue with persons of all religious beliefs, he said. The cardinal explained that "dialogue," for him, means much more than merely academic discussion. Dialogue involves a real mutual respect of the persons involved. He referred to a 1984 document of the Secretariat for Non-Christians which was published in the Vatican newspaper *L'Osservatore Romano*. It said, in part,

> Dialogue is a manner of acting, an attitude and a spirit which guides one's conduct. It implies concern, respect and hospitality towards the other. It leaves room for the other person's identity, his modes of expression and his values. Dialogue is thus the norm and necessary manner of every form of Christian mission as well as of every aspect of it, whether one speaks of simple presence and witness, service or direct proclamation. Any sense of mission not permeated by such a dialogical spirit would go against the demands of true humanity and against the teachings of the gospel.

When you are speaking with New Agers, keep this in mind—Christians show love and concern for the salvation of others, even when they disagree with the others' positions.

In his interview, the cardinal talked about a "dialogue of life" which involves "associating together without necessarily discussing religion." Christians and non-Christians share lives in the normal contexts of home, school, store, factory or political party. "They show each other friendship. They show each other love. That is already interreligious dialogue."

The Christian does not try to hide his faith, but neither does he try to force it on others. "Even if that other person does not want to become a Christian, we just want to meet that other person as a Christian person."

"Interreligious dialogue is one of the elements of the general apostolate of the church," the cardinal said, adding that it is not the primary one. "The major element in the apostolate of the church is to preach the name of Christ." Timing and circumstances must be considered. In some countries, it is forbidden to preach the Good News. In this case, "the only thing possible for the Christian is presence in the name of Christ—what I call witness and/or dialogue."

"There comes a time when you must preach the name of Christ. You cannot do only dialogue," the cardinal continued. The Christian should propose Christianity. "A religion is proposed; it is not imposed," he stressed.

The cardinal was careful to point out that he is not saying one religion is as good as another. "This is heresy, . . . not true," he said. Persons following other religions "have handicaps. Though there are good elements in their religion, not every element is good."

The Second Vatican Council (1962-1965) discussed this matter in its *Declaration on the Relationship of the Church to Non-Christian Religions*.

> Other religions to be found everywhere strive variously to answer the restless searchings of the human heart by proposing "ways," which consist of teachings, rules of life and sacred ceremonies. The Catholic Church rejects nothing which is true and holy in these religions. She looks with sincere respect upon those ways of conduct and of life, those rules and teachings which, though differing in many particulars from what she holds and sets forth, nevertheless often reflect a ray of that Truth which enlightens all men.[4]

Seeking to understand and learn from non-Christian

philosophies and theologies is not the same as saying that all religions are equal. "The clearer God is seen in Christ, the clearer God is seen everywhere," wrote Protestant scholar Thomas C. Oden. "This does not result in a syncretism that then quickly forgets that God was made known in Christ and looks independently elsewhere. For the general revelation of God everywhere is now all the more knowable through the Revealer."[5]

"The revelation given in Christ is not therefore best understood as complementary to other revelations so that by a process of synthesis and syncretism all these revelations could be brought together in a completed way," Oden continued. "Rather, Christ is precisely the unparalleled and unrepeatable Revealer through whom other revelations are best to be understood."[6]

Catholic philosopher Peter Kreeft tackled head-on the objection: "Many roads lead up the single mountain of religion to God at the top. It is provincial, narrow-minded and blind to deny the validity of other roads than yours." He replied:

> The unproved assumption of this very common mountain analogy is that the roads go up, not down; that man makes the roads, not God; that religion is man's search for God, not God's search for man . . . . True religion is not like a cloud of incense wafting up from special spirits into the nostrils of a waiting God, but like a Father's hand thrust downward to rescue the fallen. Throughout the Bible, man-made religion fails. There is no human way up the mountain, only a divine way down. "No man has seen God at any time. The only-begotten Son who is in the bosom of the Father, he has made him known" (Jn. 1:18).[7]

Vatican Report on Cults

On May 4, 1986, the Vatican issued a *Report on Sects, Cults and New Religious Movements*.[8] The report took more than two years to prepare and was made after consultation with national conferences of bishops.

When it is talking about "sects" and "cults," the report makes it clear it is not talking about Christian denominations or churches or about major world religions such as Hinduism and Buddhism. Pseudo-Christian sects are defined as those "which, apart from the Bible, have other 'revealed' books or 'prophetic messages' or groups which exclude from the Bible certain protocanonical books or radically change their content."[9]

The Vatican report takes as its own the definition contained in one response to the questionnaire:

> For practical reasons a cult or sect is sometimes defined as "any religious group with a distinctive worldview of its own derived from, but not identical with, the teachings of a major world religion." As we are speaking here of special groups which usually pose a threat to peoples' freedom and to society in general, cults and sects have also been characterized as possessing a number of distinctive features. These often are that they are authoritarian in structure, that they exercise forms of brainwashing and mind control, that they cultivate group pressure and instill feelings of guilt and fear, etc.[10]

James J. LeBar's book, *Cults, Sects and the New Age*, gives the definition of cult developed by the New York City-based Interfaith Coalition of Concern about Cults (ICCC):

> A destructive cult has a self-appointed messianic leader who focuses followers' veneration upon himself or herself, claims divine selection and exercises autocratic control over members' lives. Deception and misrepresentation are used for purposes of recruitment, retention and fund raising. Techniques are used that are aimed at controlling individual thought and personal privacy,

frequently leading to a coerced reconstitution of personality.[11]

LeBar goes on to say that a cult can be recognized when the following characteristics are manifested by observation of the group and by the reports of former members or parents of present members:

1) An inordinate preoccupation with fundraising;

2) The use of mind-control and mind-manipulation methods in recruitment and training, which produces a severe change of personality;

3) Sudden and complete separation from friends, family and anyone else who could change a person's mind;

4) A deep-rooted hatred for anyone outside the group;

5) The exacting of total obedience from the recruit to the leader on even the lowest level;

6) The giving up of the right to leave the group.[12]

It is clear LeBar's primary concern when discussing cults is not about theology but about freedom. His basic concern is mind-control.

Christians and the Devil

As we noted in Chapter Eight, Charles W. Harris, a Catholic priest, physicist, leader in the charismatic renewal and authorized exorcist for the Archdiocese of Portland, Ore., has written a book that is proving very helpful to persons in the deliverance ministry. *Resist the Devil: A Pastoral Guide to Deliverance Prayer* is especially helpful here because it quotes official Catholic documents attesting to the existence of the devil. It also directly attacks occultism, one of the key roots of the New Age movement.

"A contrast . . . is brought out by the word 'occult,' which means 'hidden,' " Harris wrote. "Satan promises his followers knowledge and control of what is hidden: the future, the hearts of men, the secret, mysterious forces in the universe. Followers of Jesus, on the other hand, walk in faith, which is 'the assurance of things hoped for, the conviction of things not seen' (Heb. 11:1). Instead of demanding to understand and control, they trust in the wisdom and power of God."[13]

"The nature and colossal dimension of evil today may make one feel that the devil's power has been unleashed," Harris stated. "This happens whenever Christianity grows weak. However, it is important to remember that Satan is a defeated enemy whose power has been broken by the Son of God."[14]

The New Age is based on deception. This is certainly allied to the satanic. "Satan's primary weapon is . . . distortion of the truth," Harris explained. "Jesus says that the devil 'has nothing to do with the truth, because there is no truth in him. When he lies, he speaks according to his own nature, for he is a liar and the father of lies' (Jn. 8:44). Again and again the devil is identified as a liar and deceiver (1 Kgs. 22:19-23, Rev. 12:9), one who loves darkness and hates the light of God's truth (Jn. 3:19-21, Jn. 13:27-30), from whose dark kingdom people are delivered into God's light (Acts 26:18, Col. 1:13). Satan distorts the message of the kingdom and tries to take away the word of God as soon as it is received in a person's heart (Mk. 4:15)."[15]

Christians and Paganism

Peter Kreeft's *Fundamentals of the Faith* had a lot to say about the difference between Christianity and the New Age. "Modern religion is demythologized, demiracalized, dedivinized," he wrote. "God is not the Lord but 'the force,' not transcendent but immanent, not supernatural but natural. The New Paganism is a vague form of pantheism, the religion of the Blob God. It scorns traditional theism as the worship of the Snob God; in other words it confuses theism with deism. Pantheism denies transcendence; deism denies immanence; Christianity affirms both, especially by the Incarnation."[16]

Kreeft referred to the New Age movement as the New Paganism. He said it "is winning not by opposing but by infiltrating the church." He described the New Paganism as "a joining of forces by three of the enemies of theism: humanism, polytheism and pantheism. The only five possibilities for ultimate meaning and values are atheism (no God); humanism (man as God); polytheism (many gods); pantheism (one immanent God); and theism (one transcendent God)."[17] He described a demonic strategy at the root of the joining of these three enemies of the church, but he also predicted the ultimate victory of the forces of God against these enemies. "The New Paganism will one day be as dead as the Old,"[18] Kreeft promised.

Spiritual Counterfeits Project

Some Christians have founded organizations to research the cults and the New Age. The Spiritual Counterfeits Project (SCP) was founded in the early 1970s in Berkeley, Calif., by people who had left the cults and become Christians and then wanted to witness to people in the cults.[19] Brooks Alexander, an SCP cofounder along with David Fetcho, dropped out of law school in Texas in the early 1960s to drop into the drug scene in Texas, New York, Los Angeles, San Francisco and eventually Berkeley. He also became interested in Eastern mysticism and Transcendental Meditation. In Berkeley, he was confronted by a group of Christians who witnessed to him. "Alexander pledged his own life to Jesus Christ," Marcia Greene related, "and began to see the outline of the Enemy (Satan) behind the mystical and meditative emphases of the Eastern religions that had been so attractive to him while he was taking drugs."[20]

As we noted in Chapter One, Christian mysticism is to be encouraged. It is quite different from Eastern and occultic mysticism. Robert Burrows, in an SCP newsletter, defined the New Age movement as a broad and diverse cultural trend united by the worldview of occult mysticism. He further defined occult mysticism as a term designating "nonbiblical forms of mysticism that rest on the premise that humanity is divine."[21]

Fetcho came to Berkeley in 1968. For two and a half years, he was intensely involved with the Ananda Marga Yoga Society. In 1973, he committed his life to Jesus after three former yogis who had converted to Christ witnessed to him. He met Alexander in January, 1974, and they began working together in an anticult effort that led to the founding of the SCP.

Alexander, Fetcho, David Haddon and other members of the Christian World Liberation Front (CWLF) at that time began a campaign to halt the encroachment of Transcendental Meditation into the public schools and to stop the endorsement of TM by the California legislature. (For more about TM, see Chapter Seven.) A letter about TM, sent mainly to the CWLF mailing list in late 1974, was the precursor of the SCP newsletters. Alexander and Haddon also wrote articles on the cults and Eastern religions in *Right On*, a publication of the CWLF, a Berkeley Christian ministry in the late 1960s and early 1970s. The first SCP newsletter was published in February, 1975, and later that same year the SCP officially became an independent Christian nonprofit organization printing its own newsletters and tracts.

The SCP has published items at irregular intervals since then. In 1977, the SCP began publishing one or two larger works a year. These journals have considered key subjects at some length: thanatology, UFOs, holistic health, the human-potential movement, inner healing, spiritism, parapsychology and Eckankar.

SCP publications are noteworthy for accuracy, good research and fairness. Often the cult or organization under review will be allowed to give its own views, either in an unedited statement or in a fair interview. The SCP is far more interested in accurate research than in preaching. Basically, they stick to evaluations of non-Christian institutions and movements and usually do not investigate Christian churches. Besides publishing, they are an information and referral agency. They respond to written and telephone questions about the cults and the occult.

The SCP has been critical of the Christian church in general. "It will do very little good for the church to confront the cults unless we simultaneously confront our own participation in the conditions which have produced them,"[22] Alexander and Fetcho wrote in a 1976 open letter. "The ultimate spiritual counterfeit is a Christianity which has been squeezed so far into the world's mold that all distinguishing authenticity has been squeezed out of it—a Christianity which is culturally co-opted, socially irrelevant, doctrinally correct, and spiritually dead."

The purpose of the SCP, the open letter continued, involves not only a critique of the occult/metaphysical movement, but also a critique of many of the taken-for-granted institutions of Western civilization. The letter saw two possible problems resulting from the nature of the SCP literature.

> 1. The confrontive character of much of the literature can easily foster a witch-hunt mentality among zealous Christians who naively identify the main thrust of Satan's work as being in and through the cults, while ignoring the equally destructive seductions of other aspects of the "world system";

> 2. The energy of the church can be diverted into a polemic against "evil" without a corresponding development of "the good" of the kingdom which presents a living and visible alternative to spiritual counterfeits (Romans 12:21).

The letter censured the "spiritual opportunists and hucksters of anticult mania" who have not considered the whole picture. "If we conscientiously apply SCP literature to shut down every TM lecture in town, only to return home in self-satisfied alienation from the grim realities of poverty, injustice, and starvation of the world, we have been outmaneuvered by the Enemy."

In 1987, the SCP came out with a book, *The New Age Rage*,[23] which consisted of a collection of articles by various specialists. "Is the New Age movement an ominous conspiracy, a new religion, a self-help movement, or just a passing fad?," Karen C. Hoyt, one of the editors, asked in the Introduction. She did not venture a pat answer to this question, but commented that the movement was very complex and widespread. She let the various authors address these questions. The advantage of having eight individuals writing separate articles lay in the particular expertise each researcher brought to the topic. The disadvantage of a book of this type lay in the distractions of having a variety of styles and approaches and in the repetition of key points.

The New Age Rage had chapters on holistic health, science, politics, transpersonal psychology, the conspiracy theory and talking with New Agers. Brooks Alexander wrote on Tantra[24] and Alexander and Robert Burrows concluded the book by contrasting basic New Age and biblical worldviews. Here are some examples.

God

New Age: Ultimate reality (God) is one and impersonal. Being one, it contains no distinctions, is undifferentiated, without qualities or attributes. It thus unifies all dualities and transcends all values, including good and evil. It cannot be personal, since personality is a by-product of differentiation and distinction. It therefore has no will and harbors no purposes. God is pure unmanifest energy, and the cosmos is the permutations of that energy, according to strict laws of cause and effect.

Biblical: God is personal and has attributes appropriate to personality: will, purpose, values, concerns, freedom, creativity, and responsiveness. These attributes are reflected in all that God is and does. All of God's creation portrays some features of his nature, but the highest aspect of his being—personality—is specifically displayed by the highest development of his creation: humankind.

Creation

New Age: God emanates the cosmos out of its own being. The cosmos therefore is an extension of God, has the nature of God, and, in essence, is God. There ultimately is not distinction or discontinuity between God and the cosmos: *All is one*. God is creation.

Biblical: God creates the cosmos out of nothing. God transcends his creation and is distinct from it. There is a radical discontinuity between God and what he has made. The cosmos is not God and does not share his essential being. It is subordinate to God, and God is sovereign over it. God is not creation.

Humanity

New Age: Humanity also is not distinct from God. Human beings, like the rest of the cosmos, are in essence made out of God. Like ultimate reality, they are reducible to pure consciousness, featureless and impersonal. Humanity has no definite nature. Whatever nature it seems to have is illusory.

Biblical: Humanity is part of creation. We share its reality and goodness. Human beings are constructed to provide for the growth and development of personhood, precisely because God himself is personal.

Humanity's dilemma

New Age: The dilemma of humanity is a constriction of awareness. We have limited our consciousness so we do not perceive the one, but only frag-

ments of it. Our problem is metaphysical ignorance.

Biblical: The dilemma of humanity is a broken relationship with the God of creation. Our primal
ancestors were dismissed from the presence of
God. We have lost the very relationship in which
we were designed to find fulfillment.[25]

The remedy
New Age: The remedy for our dilemma is to attain
knowledge of divine reality—the one. Such knowledge is widely known and goes by many names—
gnosis, enlightenment, god-consciousness. Whatever
it is called, it represents a return to the source,
union of dualities, fusion with the one, and transcendence of human nature to self-divinity.

Biblical: The healing of our condition depends on
the restoration of our broken relationship with our
Creator. As the dilemma is personal and rela-
tional, so is its resolution. Healing is initiated by
the choice of God and is accepted by the choice of
human beings. On the human side, acceptance of
God's forgiveness is a turning or revolution. This
turning is called "repentance," or *metanoia*.[26] Repentance is simply acknowledgment of what was
previously ignored: our creatureliness and de-
pendence on God, but especially our rebellion and
hostility against God.[27]

Christian Research Institute
The Christian Research Institute (CRI) was founded by
Walter R. Martin in 1951 to provide the results of careful
research on the cults and the occult for the use of evangeliz-
ers and missionaries.

The CRI address has been for many years P.O. Box 500,
San Juan Capistrano, CA 92693-0500, but the CRI was never
actually located in that city. In the summer of 1988, a 30,000-

square-foot building in Irvine, Calif., was purchased for the CRI's international headquarters. The mailing address in San Juan Capistrano remained the same. The Irvine facility, with a staff of 40, includes studios for the one-hour daily "Bible Answer Man" radio broadcast and the offices of *Christian Research Journal*. The new facility is also the headquarters for CRI's satellite office in Sao Paulo, Brazil, and affiliate offices in Canada. Following Martin's death in 1989, CRI was continuing to operate with Hendrik H. Hanegraaff as its president.

Martin wrote 13 books, including the monumental *The Kingdom of the Cults*,[28] which has sold more than a half-million copies. He also wrote many booklets and articles. He was featured in six films and 15 videocassettes on the cults. He produced more than 60 audiocassettes on the cults, the occult and general apologetics and more than 5,000 tapes on general biblical subjects. "The Bible Answer Man" radio program, which he founded in 1965, now is broadcast six days a week. He appeared on numerous radio and television talk shows.

Martin was feisty. "Controversy for controversy's sake is sin," he said, "but controversy for truth's sake is biblical and vital to the church."[29] Besides publishing critiques of the cults, the occult and the New Age, the CRI also publishes critiques of some Christian leaders, such as those who espouse "kingdom theology" teaching. Persons being criticized are given an opportunity to respond.

The best defense against counterfeit religions is to know the true religion extremely well, Martin said in the first chapter of *The Kingdom of the Cults*. He referred to a training program of the American Banking Association, which each year sends hundreds of bank tellers to Washington to teach them to detect counterfeit money. During the entire two-week training program, no teller touches counterfeit money. Only the original is used. "The reason for this is that the American Banking Association is convinced," Martin wrote, "that if a man is thoroughly familiar with the original, he will not be deceived by the counterfeit bill, no matter how much like the original it appears."[30]

The New Age movement "is a revival of ancient occultism,"[31] Martin said in a 1985 talk in Vernon, British Columbia. The New Age movement is thus very old, but recently it "is getting organized and becoming bold and now it is penetrating all areas of our culture." Martin defined occultism as "the practice of hidden, secret, mysterious, esoteric things." It is energized with satanic power. Martin said he had been lecturing on the occult since the early 1950s, but until recently the various occultic groups wouldn't even talk with one another. After the occultic explosion of the mid-1970s, however, the groups were beginning to form networks and cooperate.

"The New Age movement has been from its very beginning out to get Christianity, to destroy the revelation of God as it is given to us in the Old and New Testaments," Martin charged in his talk. He contended that the core of the New Age is a refusal "to acknowledge the God of the Bible" and to acknowledge monotheism. Martin summarized the New Age proclamation as: "We will integrate all religions and all practices and all mythologies and all superstition and all of the evils of the world including the Cabala, but we will refuse to bow our knees and worship the God of creation."

Martin's 13th book, *The New Age Cult*, appeared shortly before his death.

> This is a very difficult book to write . . . because so many people, Christian and non-Christian alike, know so little about the evils of New Age thinking. It is also difficult because almost 35 years ago I warned of the New Age movement and correctly predicted the growth of the occult. I wish I had been wrong!

> There can be little doubt that in the wake of the New Age holocaust, the time for action is *now* and we must be prepared to "give an answer to every

man that asketh you of the hope that is in you" (1
Pt. 3:15) .... The challenge is here, the time is now!
By divine grace we still have time to confront and
evangelize those in the New Age cult. The cult is
the world of occultic darkness and spiritual danger beyond belief.[32]

Martin, in his talk, identified the god of the New Age, the
"ever unknowable" god, as Lucifer, the prince of devils. The
New Age philosophy "draws its power from another dimension," Martin charged. He noted that New Age pundits are
always claiming wisdom from so-called ascended masters or
avatars or messengers from the other side. "These avatars
are the representatives of Satan," Martin said.

Its fascination with avatars points out similiarities of the
New Age movement with the cults, but there are differences.
"The New Age movement is not a cult by any accepted
sociological definition of the term,"[33] Elliot Miller wrote in
the first of a series of six articles on the New Age. "Although
there are several cults which could be classified within it (for
example, the Rajneeshees, Transcendental Meditation, and
the Divine Light Mission), most are on the movement's
periphery. Some, like the Movement of Spiritual Inner
Awareness and the Sufi Order in the West, are more in its
mainstream, but only because they are *less* exclusive, and
their leadership *less* authoritarian than most cults. Cult
membership is by far the exception, and not the rule, for New
Agers."[34]

Summarizing the fundamental danger of the New Age,
Miller wrote in the fourth of his series of articles: "The most
serious error underlying New Age mythology is the unwarranted assumption (based in monistic subjectivism) that
there are not truths 'out there' that we need to be concerned
about. If, as Christians argue, the Bible is a trustworthy
divine revelation, such thinking is grievously false, for God
is an objective, not subjective, reality as far as humanity is
concerned. Therefore, certain propositions are objectively
true, and others objectively false."[35]

Cornerstone

This bimonthly publication aimed at a countercultural audience frequently carries articles on the cults and current trends such as the New Age movement. The magazine has reprinted some of the more popular articles as tracts. Cornerstone Press publishes books, including the annual *Directory of Cult Research Organizations*, edited by Eric Pement.[36] The 1988 directory, for example, gave the names, addresses and phone numbers of 305 evangelical countercult ministries and 43 nonevangelical research or information groups.

Cornerstone and these other projects are endeavors of Jesus People USA, a Christian community in the Uptown section of Chicago which has its roots in the early Jesus movement in the late 1960s and early 1970s. Other community outreaches include the Christian rock band, REZ, Streetlight Theater and a Crisis Pregnancy Center. The community has a feeding program for the poor and works with refugees, the elderly and youth. It has a thrift store, a remodeling business and a moving business.

Douglas Groothuis

Two of the best books on the New Age movement from a Christian perspective have been written by Douglas Groothuis: *Unmasking the New Age* (1986) and *Confronting the New Age* (1988). In his first book, Groothuis talked about the demise of secular humanism. "With God evacuated, the universe lost its ultimate purpose, meaning and value," he wrote. "Morality was severed from its absolute universal reference to God; instead it was determined by the whims of humanity—relativism." People with sensitivity began to realize that atheism was exacting a price. Humanism devoid of God was tending toward nihilism—the belief that everything is meaningless and absurd. While humanity was exalting itself as the measure of all things, people were beginning to find themselves "the lords of nothing—nothing but a meaningless universe with no direction, destiny or purpose."[37]

Disillusioned with secular humanism and frightened of nihilism, humanity turned back to the supernatural, back to a search for God. People in the West, however, instead of returning to their Judeo-Christian heritage, turned to the East and its pantheism and monism. This was a disastrous mistake, primarily because they were turning away from God's revealed truth, but also because they were importing a belief system quite different even in simple human terms.

Gordon R. Lewis of Denver, a former visiting professor in India, wrote about the effects of centuries of a monistic worldview in that country in the Foreword to *Unmasking the New Age*. "In a rural area of that poverty-stricken culture, human life was cheap. I could see how difficult it is to evangelize pantheists who believe that they are already divine, have endless potential for self-improvement, are not inherently sinful, and not in need of the gracious, once-for-all provision of Jesus Christ's atonement," Lewis wrote. "I began to understand why after 200 years of missionary work, only some 4 percent of the world's second largest population is in any sense of the word Christian."[38] (See also the section on Hinduism in Chapter Two.)

New Age philosophy is a combination of pantheism and occultism. The latter has its special dangers. Groothuis, relying especially on the writings of the late Kurt Koch, a Christian theologian and occult counselor for 45 years, listed a number of spiritual maladies caused by occult involvement.

> 1. *Mediumistic affinity.* Those who open themselves up to the occult in any form may develop mediumistic powers that subject them to malignant spiritual influences.

> 2. *Resistance to the things of God.* Those ensnared by the occult often find it difficult to turn from their practices and to God. The lowerarchy often doesn't relinquish its prisoners easily.

3. *Character and emotional disorders.* Koch says that occult healings, for instance, often result in "compulsive lying, compulsive stealing (kleptomania), and compulsive arson (pyromania)."[39]

4. *Breeding ground for mental illness.* From his extensive counseling experience, Koch believes that occult activity makes one vulnerable to mental illness. In a newspaper article entitled "Witches in Wisconsin," Johnathan, the high priest of a coven in Madison, says that he has encountered four people who turned psychotic because they were not prepared for the occultic overload from involvement in witchcraft.[40]

5. *Oppression of descendants.* Koch's writings often stress the reality of generational curses whereby descendants sometimes inherit a predilection for occult phenomena.

6. *Suicide.* Since Satan's supreme strategy is to kill and destroy (Jn. 10:10), it isn't surprising that his charms would lead to self-slaughter. In addition to examples given by Koch, psychic H.H. Bro states that persons who try to develop psychic powers for the wrong reasons "embark on a course of increasingly distraught behavior, compulsive actions, alienation from friends and relatives, and finally multiple personality symptoms [possession] or suicide."[41]

7. *Ghosts and poltergeists.* Poltergeists are particularly noisy or disruptive spirits and ghosts are less openly obnoxious, but nevertheless demonic, entities. Koch says that "in all cases of spooks which I have been able to investigate, occult practices lay at the root of spook phenomena."[42]

8. *Frequent diseases.* Koch warns that, while not all illness is directly demonic, "people who come

under the curse of sins of sorcery are frequently plagued with illness of every sort."[43, 44]

Groothuis is associate director of Probe Center Northwest, Seattle, located near the University of Washington. The center's outreach to the university includes study groups, personal tutoring and sponsoring such campus events as lectures, films and forums.

Russell Chandler

Russell Chandler, the award-winning religion writer for the *Los Angeles Times*, took eight months off in 1987-88 to write a book, *Understanding the New Age*.[45] The book was a great asset to literature probing the New Age for a number of reasons. Chandler brought a great deal of expertise and prestige to his critique of the New Age. He was very thorough. He covered almost every aspect of the multifaceted New Age. He delved into the background of some of the key players on the scene. He combined solid journalistic standards with an up-front Christian faith.

Toward the end of his book, Chandler shifted somewhat from the perspective of an impartial journalist to that of a Christian apologist. (He has a master of divinity degree from Princeton Theological Seminary and was ordained a Presbyterian minister.) "The Tower of Babel, described in the Old Testament (Gen. 11:1-9), was probably a cosmic temple connected with the occult religion of astrology, as was the Babylonian ziggurat built later on the same site,"[46] Chandler wrote. God was not pleased with this effort of human beings to consider themselves divine and so God confounded the people's language. Thus, from earliest times, "humanity has sought to organize itself around an instrument of its own creation," Chandler observed. "This search for self-realization has ascended to the pinnacle of self-idolatry—and has been flattened beneath the righteous hammer blows of a Higher God."

In an attempt to make gods of themselves, on the other hand, contemporary individuals are more likely to look inside themselves rather than build a tower in the sky. "If you desire wisdom greater than your own, you can find it inside you," stated New Age-allied psychiatrist M. Scott Peck. "To put it plainly, our unconscious is God . . . . The goal of spiritual growth [is] . . . the attainment of godhead by the conscious self. It is for the individual to become totally, wholly God."[47]

Science-fiction writer Ray Bradbury is another person who believes humans are divine: "The living God is not out there. He is here. God did not create us. Man, living too close to himself, could not see that he was the godhead, that he was the Lord and himself Christ . . . . We are more than water, we are more than earth, we are more than sun. We are God giving himself a reason for being."[48]

Chandler found this view dangerous:

> According to Bradbury, the biblical God is dead; man is God. Man has all glory and honor and power. And this is the insidious danger inherent in the New Age. The New Age worldview is that the self is all there is, that right and wrong are mere projections of whatever seems permissible to one at the time. From this perspective there are no rules or absolute moral imperatives, and therefore one is ultimately not responsible for one's actions.[49]

A rather comprehensive treatment of basic worldviews was contained in James W. Sire's *The Universe Next Door.*[50] The chapters focus on Christian theism, deism, naturalism, nihilism, existentialism, Eastern pantheistic monism and the New Age.

In their search for God, some people look not to a tower in the sky or to the unconscious, but to Jesus. Many of these, however, do not look to the Jesus of the Bible. "To Eastern-oriented religious groups, Jesus is an avatar—one of the many incarnations of God," Sire explained. "To Christian Scientists, he is the Great Healer; to political revolutionaries, he is the Great Liberator; to Spiritualists, he is a first-rate medium; to one new consciousness philosopher, he is the prototype of Carlos Castaneda's Don Juan, a sorcerer who can restructure events in the world by mental exercise. Everyone, it seems, wants Jesus for themselves."[51]

Some people may find Bob Larson's *Straight Answers on the New Age* particularly helpful because of its format. It has a lot of brief definitions and some sections are written in question and answer form. It also has a fairly extensive index.

Ruth A. Tucker's *Another Gospel: Alternative Religions and the New Age Movement* actually spent much more time on such longstanding cults as the Mormons, Jehovah's Witnesses, Children of God, Unification Church and Hare Krishnas, etc., than it did on the New Age movement. This was a big book, however, with much material on the New Age, along with an index and an extensive bibliography.

World religions and cults are regularly probed on the weekly half-hour television program, "The John Ankerberg Show."[52] Using an informal debate format, Christians and representatives of non-Christian religions and cults discuss their beliefs.

Jeremiah Films has made a 103-minute videocassette, *Gods of the New Age*, as well as a number of other videocassettes on the Mormons and other cults.[53]

Chapter 15

God,
Human Beings,
Spirits

Basic Christian Teaching

This is the chapter you've been waiting for. Here we talk about the truth.

We can trust our senses. This is taken for granted almost everywhere, including in the literature of developmental psychology. If a child cannot rely on one of the senses, there is probably something wrong with the way the sense organ is working. "Emotionally speaking," stated Karen C. Hoyt, "it takes massive denial to negate sense perception, or it could indicate the actual presence of hallucinations or illusions. In other words, when we cannot rely on our sense perceptions, we are either mentally or physically ill. In this state, we cannot distinguish between what is coming in through our senses and what is manufactured in our mind."[1]

Christians and other persons of common sense use logical thinking processes to correlate the information received through sensory impressions and to abstract ideas from them. They are thus able to interact with one another and with the external world in an orderly and meaningful way.

New Agers, on the other hand, block the reasoning

process through such psychotechnologies as chanting, meditation and creative visualization. These techniques for altering consciousness, said Elliot Miller, "are capable of interrupting or even bringing to a halt one's normal patterns of conceptual thought *without* extinguishing or diminishing consciousness itself."[2] One can only understand reality through a mystical experience, New Agers say.

"Although New Agers do not generally repudiate normal reasoning processes, they do believe that they have experienced something that transcends them," Miller continued. "Thus it is very difficult for rational arguments (such as concerning the dangers of subjectivism) to penetrate their mindset: they simply assume that the one challenging the experience has not had it—or he also would 'know.' "[3]

Reason, in itself, can lead to a certain limited understanding of God, but this is quite inadequate. J. Rodman Williams has written: "Although God does reveal himself in nature, humanity, and history and exhibits therein his deity, power, benevolence, and righteousness so that all people basically know God, this knowledge is suppressed. Rather than leading them to glorifying and thanking God, . . . this knowledge is spurned by people so that all their thinking about God becomes vain and futile . . . . The wine of God's knowledge has become the vinegar of human confusion."[4]

There is objective truth because God has created an objectively true universe. Futhermore, God has revealed objective truths about himself. Writing from a Roman Catholic perspective, John A. Hardon said that, because Christianity "looks upon reality, it is not monistic, since the universe is not either God or the world; it is God *and* the world. Jesus Christ is not either God or man; he is God *and* man . . . . Our conduct is not either all good because everyone is saved or all bad because everyone is depraved, but it is good *and* bad because we can either cooperate with God's will or reject the advances of his love."[5]

So, how do we know about God? Through revelation. God tells us about himself. To grasp this revelation, we need the gift of faith. Education, by itself, is not enough.

Peter Kreeft, a professor of philosophy at Boston College, the nation's second largest Catholic university, talked about the deplorable state of Christian education.

> Fewer than 5 percent of my Catholic-educated students can explain why it is not a contradiction to call God both one and three, or Christ both divine and human. They have never even heard of the distinction between person and nature. Many are astonished at the very idea of giving proofs for the existence of God or for the immortality of the soul. Most shocking of all, well over three-quarters of all the "educated" Catholic college students I have taught do not know, after 12 years of catechism classes, how to get to heaven! . . . They rarely even mention Jesus when asked that question.[6]

When Christians do know their faith, however, and do try to witness to others, they run into two big problems. The typical modern mind "does not believe in objective truth and it does not believe in objective values," Kreeft asserted. "When the gospel is preached to this mind, its response is likely to be not 'What you say is not true,' but rather 'What you say may be true for you but it is not true for me; what right do you have to impose your personal beliefs on me?' And when you talk about Christian morality, it almost always seems to modern people like a cafeteria choice, like an optional aisle in the supermarket of lifestyles, like a choice of style in clothing or cars. They have never heard the words, 'thus saith the Lord.' "[7]

Proper reasoning is not enough. Christian education is not enough. Faith is needed and faith is a supernatural gift from God. The *New Catholic Encyclopedia* explained this point.

> Faith is truly the work of God . . . . No man can come to Christ unless he be drawn unto him. On the purely natural level (the practical apologist) un-

derstands that one will not believe unless one
wishes to believe. He thus realizes most clearly
that he cannot force a man by purely logical reasons to place an act of supernatural faith, any more
than Christ himself could do so by making claims
and actually proving them by miracles. His, in
short, remains the task of offering the rational
foundation for a supernatural, superrational edi-
fice.[8]

The reality of Jesus' life, death and bodily resurrection is
fundamental to the Christian faith. "There is good warrant
in Scripture for saying that our faith should be consonant
with reason," commented Hardon. "St. Paul tells the Romans to worship God 'in a way that is worthy of thinking
beings' (Rom. 12:1). And the Corinthians are told that 'if
Christ has not been raised then our preaching is useless and
your believing is useless' (1 Cor. 15:14). From Peter's Pente-
cost homily on through the apostolic age, Christ's bodily resurrection was the primary evidence offered to the Mediter-
ranean world that there is no other name than Jesus by which
humans are to be saved."[9]

The principal source of Christian teaching is the Bible.
How do we know the Bible is true? Because the Bible says it
is true and says that God will give guidance and the gift of
faith to those who ask. The seeker needs to pray to receive
this gift. The second letter to Timothy (3:16-17) says: "All
Scripture is inspired by God and profitable for teaching, for
reproof, for correction, and for training in righteousness,
that the man of God may be complete, equipped for every
good work."

In John's Gospel (14:18), Jesus says: "I will not leave you
desolate; I will come to you." The book of Proverbs (3:6)
encourages us: "In all your ways acknowledge him and he
will make straight your paths."[10]

Christian truths can also be learned from the church and
from the mature discernment of Christian leaders. "Where
there is no guidance, a people falls; but in an abundance of

counselors there is safety," says Proverbs (11:14).

In his letter to the Ephesians (4:11-14), Paul talks about the leadership gifts God has given his church:

> And his gifts were that some should be apostles, some prophets, some evangelists, some pastors and teachers, to equip the saints for the work of ministry, for building up the body of Christ, until we all attain to the unity of the faith and of the knowledge of the Son of God, to mature manhood, to the measure of the stature of the fullness of Christ; so that we may no longer be children, tossed to and fro and carried about with every wind of doctrine, by the cunning of men, by their craftiness in deceitful wiles.

This book is written for all Christians and especially Roman Catholics and mainline Protestants. It is important that Christians work together to witness to a world starving for true religious teaching about the one true God and the one true Savior of all human beings, Jesus Christ. Can we work together? The various Christian denominations are divided among themselves by different views on various aspects of Christianity. Many Protestants, proclaiming *sola scriptura* ("only Scripture"), stress the Bible as the sole font of the faith. Catholics revere the Bible, but also give importance to the authoritative teaching of the church. Perhaps the Catholic philosopher, Peter Kreeft, can help us out.

> There are not two rival horses in the authority race, but one rider (the church) on one horse (Scripture). The church as writer, canonizer, and interpreter of Scripture is not another source of revelation but the author and guardian and teacher of the one source, Scripture. We are not taught by a teacher without a book or by a book without a teacher, but by one teacher, the church, with one book, Scripture.[11]

The basics of Christianity are in the Nicene Creed, which consists of elements of doctrine contained in an early baptismal creed of Jerusalem and enactments of the Council of Nicaea (325) and the Council of Constantinople (381). The creed reads as follows.

> We believe in one God, the Father, the Almighty, maker of heaven and earth, of all that is seen and unseen.

> We believe in one Lord, Jesus Christ, the only Son of God, eternally begotten of the Father, God from God, Light from Light, true God from true God, begotten, not made, one in Being with the Father. Through him all things were made. For us men and for our salvation he came down from heaven: by the power of the Holy Spirit he was born of the Virgin Mary, and became man. For our sake he was crucified under Pontius Pilate; he suffered, died, and was buried. On the third day he rose again in fulfillment of the Scriptures; he ascended into heaven and is seated at the right hand of the Father. He will come again in glory to judge the living and the dead, and his kingdom will have no end.

> We believe in the Holy Spirit, the Lord, the giver of life, who proceeds from the Father and the Son. With the Father and the Son he is worshiped and glorified. He has spoken through the prophets. We believe in one holy catholic and apostolic church. We acknowledge one baptism for the forgiveness of sins. We look for the resurrection of the dead, and the life of the world to come. Amen.[12]

God

You might want to refer back to Chapter Fourteen and the section taken from *The New Age Rage* in which Brooks Alexander and Robert Burrows contrasted the New Age and biblical views of God, creation, humanity and salvation.

"All attempts at discussion of God are dubious if God is completely unrevealed mystery and absolutely unknowable," wrote Protestant theologian Thomas C. Oden. "Rather than taking that extreme position, Christian teaching has argued that God is reliably and sufficiently knowable, even if incomprehensible."[13]

God freely created the universe. "God is at liberty to create either this world or some other world—or no world," Oden explained. "Christian teaching has continued to reject both emanationism, the notion that the physical world emanates from the being of God, and an evolutionary idealism that holds that creation is proceeding progressively on its own apart from God as Creator."[14]

The First Vatican Council, in its *Dogmatic Constitution on the Catholic Faith*, described God in this way:

> The holy, Catholic, apostolic Roman Church believes and professes that there is one true and living God, the Creator and Lord of heaven and earth. He is almighty, eternal, beyond measure, incomprehensible, and infinite in intellect, will and in every perfection.
>
> Since he is one unique spiritual substance, entirely simple and unchangeable, he must be declared really and essentially distinct from the world, perfectly happy in himself and by his very nature, and inexpressibly exalted over all things that exist or can be conceived other than himself.[15]

Douglas Groothuis, quoting Walter Martin, pointed out that in the Bible God performs the acts of a personal being.

> God hears (Exodus 2:24); God sees (Genesis 1:4); God creates (Genesis 1:1); God knows (2 Timothy 2:19, Jeremiah 29:11); God has a will (1 John 2:17); God is a cognizant reflectable ego, i.e., a personal being, "I AM that I AM" (Exodus 3:14, Genesis

17:1). This is the God of Christianity, an omnipotent, omniscient, and omnipresent Personality,
who manifests every attribute of a personality.[16]

There is only one God, but there are three Persons in God.
This is the mystery of the Trinity. This is the way catechist
Alan Schreck described this mystery.

God is one because he possesses a single divine
nature, the nature of God. Nature, in this sense, is
what makes something what it is . . . .

The one God exists as three persons who are distinct but undivided, since each person fully possesses the same divine nature, the nature of God . . . .

In God, the persons are distinct, and yet are united in a far deeper way than any human persons
because of the perfection and integrity (unity) of
the divine nature, the being of God. The unity of
the three persons of God is so great and profound
that it is incorrect to say they are divided in any
way.[17]

Jesus Christ is the Son of God, true God and true man. He
lived, died and rose from the dead nearly 2,000 years ago.
"Jesus possesses two distinct but inseparable natures, the
divine and the human, united in one person," Schreck explained. "Jesus' human nature and human will were so
conformed to his divine nature and divine will that the two
were joined into an inseparable harmony so that we can truly
say that Jesus was one person, not two, but composed of a
divine and a human nature."[18]

The Holy Spirit is God. He is a distinct Person of the
Blessed Trinity, coeternal and coequal with the Father and
the Son. "The Spirit is sent by the eternal Father and by Jesus
to give light, comfort, and strength, and to stir up within us
a newness of life," the book, *The Teaching of Christ*, stated.
"The Holy Spirit seals our friendship with God (see 2 Corinthians 1:22), and he unites us with one another by the divine

love he pours forth in our hearts (see Romans 5:5)."[19]

Human Beings

All human beings are creatures of God. They have a body and an immortal soul. After death, they are judged by Jesus Christ and are destined for an eternity of happiness in heaven or an eternity of punishment in hell. The body will be resurrected and reunited with the soul for an eternity of blessedness or damnation.

Death is certain. If you don't believe in death, you're hopelessly out of touch with reality. "Death is our one certainty in an age of skepticism," wrote Peter Kreeft, "our one absolute in an age of relativism, our one inescapable brush with otherworldliness in an age of *this*-worldliness, our last link with the sacred in an age of secularism. To secularize death, as our culture is doing, is the last blasphemy."[20]

What happens after death? Polls show that nearly 70% of Americans believe in life after death. Regionally, New England had the lowest percentage of believers in life after death (56%) and the upper Midwest had the highest (79%). More Protestants (76%) expressed such belief than Catholics (68%) or Jews (17%).[21]

What is this life after death? According to a *Newsweek* poll taken in December, 1988, 77% of Americans believed in heaven and 76% thought they had a good or excellent chance of getting there. On the other hand, 58% believed there is a hell and only 6% thought they had a good or excellent chance of getting there.[22]

If there is no heaven or hell, the value of human life and human actions is greatly diminished. "In rejecting heaven and hell, the rationalistic modern consciousness also rejects the awesome seriousness of moral and immoral behavior," Kenneth L. Woodward wrote. "But for those who take God seriously, human freedom means the capacity to make moral decisions which have radical and enduring consequences. Hell, then, is not a place created by a God bent on getting even, but the alienation we choose for ourselves. Heaven, on

the other hand, is for lovers—of others and of God. 'Thou
has made us for thyself,' wrote Saint Augustine nearly 17
centuries ago, 'and our hearts are restless, till they rest in
thee.' "[23]

In his book, *Everything You Ever Wanted to Know About
Heaven but Never Dreamed of Asking*, Peter Kreeft wrote:
"Even Jesus' most popular, compassionate, and loving saying talks about hell: John 3:16—'For God so loved the world
that he gave his only Son, that whoever believes in him
should not perish but have eternal life.' Hell is five times
mentioned in the sermon on the mount. If there is no hell, or
even if there are only a tiny few in it so that there is very little
practical danger for ordinary people, then Jesus is scaring us
just for the hell of it, and is a bad teacher, not a good one."[24]

"Eternal life with God is an absolutely free gift. There is
nothing that any person could do to merit, earn, or deserve
an eternity of happiness with God," Alan Schreck explained.
"Salvation is also a gift that must be accepted through our cooperation with God's grace and our freely given response to
the work of the Holy Spirit in our lives. From this perspective, eternal life or salvation is not simply a gift that we
receive at the end of our lives when we die. Eternal life begins
now as we choose to accept God's grace and his gift of the
Holy Spirit."[25]

The Bible talks of the finality of death and judgment. Its
teachings contradict those who espouse out-of-body experiences or reincarnation.

> It is appointed for men to die once, and after that
> comes judgment (Heb. 9:27).

> For as the body apart from the spirit is dead, so
> faith apart from works is dead (Jas. 2:26).

> We would rather be away from the body and at
> home with the Lord . . . . For we must all appear
> before the judgment seat of Christ, so that each
> one may receive good or evil, according to what he
> has done in the body (2 Cor. 5:8,10).

> And as they were stoning Stephen, he prayed, "Lord Jesus, receive my spirit" (Acts 7:59).

> [The penitent thief at the crucifixion] said, "Jesus, remember me when you come into your kingdom." And he said to him, "Truly, I say to you, today you will be with me in Paradise" (Lk. 23:42-43).

> The dust returns to the earth as it was, and the spirit returns to God who gave it (Eccles. 12:7).

> As he passed by, he saw a man blind from his birth. And his disciples asked him, "Rabbi, who sinned, this man or his parents, that he was born blind?" Jesus answered, "It was not that this man sinned, or his parents, but that the works of God might be made manifest in him" (Jn. 9:1-3). (Repudiating the doctrine of karma.)

Scripture texts "indicate that reincarnation and the Bible are mutually exclusive," stated Bob Larson. "No false claim of countless opportunities of reformation can stand alongside the finished work of Christ's redemption."[26]

The Christian view of death gives an added importance to life. "Christianity is not pessimistic," wrote Hardon. "The work of God, and the work of man, are objects of great importance in the Christian economy . . . . Measured by time, this life is short, whereas eternity is long. Measured by moral standards, this life should be seen in all its terrifying, and exciting, potential for deciding our immortal destiny."[27] (Chapters Two and Three have lengthy treatments of reincarnation and the law of karma.)

Spirits

In the satanism section of Chapter Eight, we saw that a recent poll revealed that only 34% of Americans believe in a personal devil. In a September, 1988, talk, Karl Strader of Lakeland, Fla., reported that 73% of United States clergy do not believe in a personal devil, according to another poll. "That's why so many clergymen are getting clobbered," he said.

A Catholic priest in Lafayette, La., Joseph Brennan, on the other hand, has been doing something about the spread of satanism. A September, 1989, newspaper article reported that he has been counseling victims of ritualistic abuse and satanic cults for the past three years. He estimated that there are 8,000 satanic covens in the United States with 100,000 members nationwide.[28]

If some Catholic priests do not believe in a personal devil, it is clear that they have not been listening to their leaders. At a November 15, 1972, general audience in the Vatican, Pope Paul VI called "defense from the evil which is called the devil" as being one of the greatest needs of the church today. "Evil is not merely a lack of something, but an effective agent, a living, spiritual being, perverted and perverting," he said, ". . . a terrible reality. Mysterious and frightening. It is contrary to the teaching of the Bible and the church to refuse to recognize the existence of such a reality."[29]

He went on to express regret that contemporary theology lacked an awareness of this problem: "It would be very important to return to a study of Catholic teaching on the devil and the influence he is able to wield, but nowadays little attention is paid to it."[30]

Likewise, Pope John Paul II, in a talk August 20, 1986, discussed, among other things, the devil, good and bad angels, and their relationship to good and evil in Christian life. Satan's power is "not infinite," he said, but nevertheless it causes serious damage and in some cases might require exorcism. "The existence of bad angels requires of us a sense of vigilance, so we will not give in to their flattery." The devil, as "head of the demons," is a real power but has been dethroned by Christ with the assurance that good will triumph over evil.[31]

"To maintain today that Jesus' words about Satan express only a teaching borrowed from his culture and are unimportant for the faith of other believers is evidently to show little understanding either of the Master's character or of his age," the Vatican's Sacred Congregation for the Doctrine of the Faith asserted in 1975. "If Jesus used this kind of language and, above all, if he translated it into practice during his ministry, it was because it expressed a doctrine that was to some extent essential to the idea and reality of the salvation he was bringing."[32]

Cardinal John O'Connor of New York takes satanism seriously. "You are the salvific movement against satanism," he told 5,300 Catholic charismatics at a national conference in June, 1989, at the University of Notre Dame. Satanism is "a movement that is bringing an almost indescribable poison into the world. And only your holiness, only your goodness, only your prayer can adequately counter that movement."

Norman Geisler listed a number of Bible passages that talk about the devil.

> The devil's first appearance in Scripture is as a subtle serpent who tempts Eve and precipitates man's fall into sin (Genesis 3:1 ff.). Later, it becomes clear that he has cohorts in his crime called "demons" (Deuteronomy 32:17) who lead men into idolatry, immorality (Leviticus 17:7), and even child sacrifice (Psalm 106:37). Over and over again in the Bible demons appear, sometimes to lie (1 Kings 22:21), often to encourage idolatry (Deuteronomy 32:17), and always in opposition to God's plan and people (Daniel 10:13-20).
>
> In the New Testament the appearance of Christ on earth seems to stir the legions of darkness. Jesus gave his disciples special power over demons (Matthew 10:1). The apostles rebuked evil spirits for their work of divination (Acts 16:16-18). They cause sickness (Matthew 12:22-24) and produce violent seizures in some of their captives (Mat-

thew 17:18). They are said to "possess" certain people (Matthew 12:22-24) and even speak from within them (Mark 5:8-9; Luke 4:33).[33]

All angels were created by God. Some of them sinned and were cast out of God's presence. The devil is Satan or Lucifer, the principal fallen angel, and evil spirits are other fallen angels.

> Now war arose in heaven, Michael and his angels fighting against the dragon; and the dragon and his angels fought, but they were defeated and there was no longer any place for them in heaven. And the great dragon was thrown down, that ancient serpent, who is called the Devil and Satan, the deceiver of the whole world—he was thrown down to earth, and his angels were thrown down with him (Rev. 12:7-9).

Some Christian writers have seen some verses of Isaiah 14 as recounting the fall of Lucifer. The literal meaning of the passage is a prophecy about the king of Babylon. Using an accommodated sense of Scripture, the writers see the text as also referring to Satan. Some translations have "Lucifer" instead of "Day Star."

> How you are fallen from heaven, O Day Star, son of Dawn! How you are cut down to the ground, you who laid the nations low! You said in your heart, "I will ascend to heaven; above the stars of God I will set my throne on high; I will sit on the mount of assembly in the far north; I will ascend above the heights of the clouds, I will make myself like the Most High." But you are brought down to Sheol, to the depths of the pit (Is. 14:12-15).

The devil may be fallen but he's still an angel and angels by nature are more powerful than humans. The second letter of Peter (2:11) calls angels "greater in might and power" than humans. The devil, the most powerful of the fallen angels, is called the "ruler of this world" (Jn. 12:31) for he is more powerful than any creature on earth. We humans are no match for this powerful enemy if we rely only on our natural powers or on human wisdom.

> For we are not contending against flesh and blood, but against the principalities, against the powers, against the world rulers of this present darkness, against the spiritual hosts of wickedness in the heavenly places (Eph. 6:12).

Christians have nothing to fear, however. Jesus' death on the cross gives us victory over the devil and his works. Thus, in any given temptation, God provides us with the grace to resist and overcome the temptation.

> God is faithful, and he will not let you be tempted beyond your strength, but with the temptation will also provide the way of escape, that you may be able to endure it (1 Cor. 10:13).

> Submit yourselves therefore to God. Resist the devil and he will flee from you (Jas. 4:7).[34]

Let us not forget that there are good angels, too. Angels often "appeared at highly important moments in biblical history," J. Rodman Williams noted, "for example, in the New Testament at the birth of Jesus, at his resurrection, and at his ascension, and they will appear at his future return. Angels never call attention to themselves but invariably point to something else—often mysterious, even incomprehensible. They always seem to be a part of God's action and have their existence alongside or in relation to him. The being of angels is a matter of little biblical interest; their activity is much more a matter of interest."[35]

The New Age is false and it is banal. Christianity is true and infinitely beautiful. There is no comparison between the two. The next chapter will have some tips on witnessing to New Agers about the truth and beauty of Christianity.

Chapter 16

Evangelizing
New Agers

When relating with New Agers, perhaps the best offense is a good defense. Before studying the New Age in detail, the Christian first should study the Bible and sound theology books. Before confronting New Agers in a public forum, the Christian needs to repent of personal sin and seek forgiveness. The Christian needs to draw close to Jesus through prayer and Christian meditation.

After the Christian's own house is in order, perhaps the next step will be to see that the houses of neighboring Christians are in order. Are these nominal Christians practicing their faith? Are they well-instructed in their religion? Are their children being taught orthodox Christianity? Perhaps a prayer group or a Bible study group needs to be established in the neighborhood.

Are there problems of doctrine or practice in the local church? How can these be resolved so that Christians can unite to face the common danger of the New Age?

Cults

Before his death in 1989, Walter Martin had been studying the cults and debating with cult leaders since 1950. In his book, *The New Age Cult*, Martin talked about witnessing effectively to people involved in cults. "The Christian will learn almost immediately that after he witnesses to the truthfulness of the gospel message, he will have to introduce Christian apologetics, a reasoned defense of the validity of Christian truth."[1] He gave some advice for the Christian witness who is using the techniques of evangelism and apologetics.

> *Preparation of prayer.* Pray that God will open the eyes and ears and soul and mind of the person you are going to witness to.
>
> *Repeat and reword.* Grow in patience and learn to state your position at least three times in different words. People frequently simply do not "hear" the first time, but need the reinforcement of repetition. Remember that it is difficult to accept the truth of the gospel.
>
> *Communicate your love.* Whenever possible, communicate your spiritual concern for the person and go beyond the desire to make a statistic out of the person for some local congregation. New Agers are particularly sensitive to sincere love and concern for their well-being.
>
> *Seek common ground.* Find a common ground from which you can approach the controversial issues. Whatever helps establish an amicable relationship facilitates communication, particularly if it is in the realm of spiritual values.
>
> *Define terminology.* Define your terminology in an inoffensive way. When the New Ager is talking about God, love, Jesus Christ, salvation or reincarnation, ask him to explain what he means. Try to arrive at a dictionary definition rather than a subjective judgment.

Question, don't teach. Do not try to teach a New
Ager or cultist, for the moment you don the teacher's garment, he will "tune out" just as he has been
programmed to do. People are threatened by others who intimidate them with a professorial attitude that communicates an air of superiority,
whether it is real or imagined. Jesus questioned
the Pharisees, the Sadducees, the scribes, the He-
rodians, and even common men on subjects for
which they had no real answers of enduring value.
If incarnate Truth was that tactful, we can use a
little sanctified tact ourselves.

Read the Bible. Wherever possible, use your Bible
and ask the New Ager to read the specific passages
under discussion. [Martin calls] this technique
"falling on the sword." Since the Bible is called the
sword of the Spirit (Eph. 6), we need only position
the sword properly as they read and it will penetrate, even where all of our arguments and reasoning have failed.

Avoid criticism. Avoid attacking New Age cult
leaders or founders of specific groups, for even if
the New Ager knows that you are correct, he will
remain true to human nature and defend against
what he considers to be unloving criticism.

Commend. Praise the zeal, dedication and (wherever possible) the goals of the New Age movement
because its basic nature is both messianic and
millennial. The New Age cult is seeking the right
things, but with the wrong methods and with
wrong reasons, sometimes merely because their
vision is impaired by sin.

Study the New Age. When dealing with New Age
thinking, be sure that you can accurately cite New
Age leaders and writings. If you do not under-

stand or have not read what your opponent is talking about, make it a point to check it out before you talk with him again.

Define "Jesus." Ask the New Age believer if he can explain the difference between the Jesus found in the Bible and the Jesus who appears in New Age literature. Let him see that the name "Jesus" means nothing unless it is defined within the context of New Testament revelation.

Reveal the weakness of moral relativism. By asking questions, show the New Ager how logically flawed it is to allow subjectivism and moral relativism to lead him. Help him understand that he cannot live consistently with these principles. For instance, ask: "If your truth is your truth and my truth is my truth, how can we be certain about anything?"

Show the Bible to be reliable. It is important to set forth the historic reliability of the Bible when discussing the concept of absolute truth with New Agers. We can benefit from a study of biblical history and archeology to add credibility to our position.

Reveal the inconsistency of the New Age worldview. The worldview of the New Age movement is a monistic pantheistic concept. Monistic pantheism teaches that all is one and all is divine. It makes no division between God and his creation. This is inconsistent with logic and experience since billions of people can speak the personal pronoun "I" from the context of their own experience and lives. Each person is different from all the other persons. Mankind cannot even collectively account for the earth, life or the problem of evil apart from divine revelation.

Provide books or tapes. Refer the New Ager to some good Christian books, tapes, videocassettes, audiocassettes, booklets, or tracts addressing New Age thinking. Or you might give him one.

A note of warning. In dealing with the New Age cult, we are in reality dealing with spiritual warfare against the forces of darkness, and we are told by God to put on the whole armor of heaven so that we will be able to withstand the forces of Satan (see Eph. 6:11).[2]

In his article, "Evangelizing New Agers," Doug Groothuis gave similar advice and also pointed out two more weaknesses of the New Age viewpoint that can be used in a discussion with a New Ager. "The New Age view of the divinity of humanity must neglect the reality of human evil," he wrote. "The biblical view of our finitude and our fallenness as sinners better explains the human condition than the New Age idea that we are all really God."

Groothuis continued: "The concept of an impersonal God is unsatisfying because it allows no ultimate personal relationship. Tuning in to 'the Force' pales in comparison with loving and being loved by our Heavenly Father. Jesus Christ should be exalted as the supreme revelation of God's love."[3]

Gordon R. Lewis, a professor of theology and philosophy at Denver Seminary and the founder of Evangelical Ministries to New Religions, said he goes out of his way to talk to New Agers. "In an increasingly polarized and violent world, I desire to promote understanding and just relationships among my 'neighbors.' Even though some people may be involved to some degree in New Age thought and practice, they are still image-bearers of God and so of inestimable worth. I respect their inherent rights and treat them as I would want them to treat me. Like foreign missionaries, we need contacts with the people we seek to reach," Lewis said.

"Evangelism is the ultimate goal of Christian outreach.

After seeking to remove roadblocks in the way of faith, I invite people to believe the gospel and trust Christ. If they do not immediately receive the Messiah, I hope that in God's providence they will have taken a step in that direction."[4]

Patience

Eric Pement counseled that a Christian wishing to witness to someone involved in a cult or the New Age movement should be very patient. He suggested that the Christian set aside at least five or six hours for conversation.

> Forty-five minutes is not enough time to discuss the philosophy governing another's life. . . . Get to know one another at a meal to discover similarities and your mutual humanness, and avoid stereotyping or making false assumptions. Then, after the meal, you can share with sensitivity and tact. Yes, be blunt about heresy, sin and deception. But don't be harsh.[5]

Pement noted that the Christian witness should have a strong personal sense of salvation and a biblical worldview. "Your worldview should include an understanding of the Creator, creation, the fall (of humans), evil, the atonement and the church."[6] The Christian must have a knowledge of the Bible that is accurate, quick and broad and must have an active prayer life. "You must learn the beliefs of those people before you ever meet them,"[7] Pement added.

He suggested that the conversation be personal as well as intellectual. The Christian can describe his or her own personal conversion to Christ. The Christian can offer to spend some time in leisure activities with the cultist so they can come to know each other better. As a final note, he suggested that the Christian schedule a time for further conversation with the cultist.

> People are seldom won in the first conversation, or even in the tenth. Choose a specific date before you leave. It took nine months of witnessing by a few

determined Christians before my own stubborn-
ness broke and I came to Christ, after being born
and raised a Reorganized Latter Day Saint
[Mormon].[8]

Elitism

When Christians claim that only they have the complete
religious truth, they are attacked as elitist. "All religions are
the same, deep down," people charge. Peter Kreeft answered this objection this way.

This is simply factually untrue. No one ever makes this
claim unless he is

1. abysmally ignorant of what the different religions of
the world actually teach or

2. intellectually irresponsible in understanding these
teachings in the vaguest and woolliest way or

3. morally irresponsible in being indifferent to them.

The objector's implicit assumption is that the distinctive
teachings of the world's religions are unimportant, that the
essential business of religion is not truth but something else:
transformation of consciousness or sharing and caring or
culture and comfort or something of that sort—not conversion but conversation. Christianity teaches many things no
other religion teaches, and some of them directly contradict
those others.[9]

Why Witness?

Evangelizing is a matter of love. We love people and we
want to see that they have the very best. Knowing Jesus as
Lord and Savior is the very best thing they can have.

For the Christian, evangelization is not something optional. Jesus commands his followers to evangelize. "And
Jesus came and said to them, 'All authority in heaven and on
earth has been given to me. Go therefore and make disciples
of all nations, baptizing them in the name of the Father and
of the Son and of the Holy Spirit, teaching them to observe
all that I have commanded you' " (Mt. 28:18-20).

We don't know the future. We don't know how many more years we will live. We don't know how long our friends have to live. If we don't effectively share the gospel with those we know, perhaps no one ever will. We can't be sure someone else will come along and witness to them. It could be a matter of our friends' eternal salvation, a matter of heaven or hell.

St. Paul writes: "For, 'everyone who calls upon the name of the Lord will be saved.' But how are men to call upon him in whom they have not believed? And how are they to believe in him of whom they have never heard?" (Rom. 10:13-14).

Jesus desires to give all men and women what he has given us Christians. "For God so loved the world that he gave his only Son, that whoever believes in him should not perish but have eternal life. For God sent the Son into the world, not to condemn the world, but that the world might be saved through him" (Jn. 3:16-17).

Furthermore, if we Christians don't share the gospel, we will dry up spiritually. When we share our faith, our faith comes alive. We need to pour out God's love to others in order to receive it more abundantly. "So everyone who acknowledges me before men, I also will acknowledge before my Father who is in heaven; but whoever denies me before men, I also will deny before my Father who is in heaven" (Mt. 10:32-33).[10]

Appendix

Anticult Groups and Contacts ─────

   Chapters One and Fourteen have a great deal of information about Christian and nonreligious anticult organizations. Helpful books and periodicals are listed in these two chapters and in many footnotes in other chapters.

   Listed here are the principal organizations you can contact for more information about cults or the New Age movement. You might also want to check the very helpful *Directory of Cult Research Organizations*, edited by Eric Pement.

Christian Organizations

Spiritual Counterfeits Project
PO Box 4308
Berkeley, CA 94704
(415) 540-0300 (office, Mon.-Fri. 8:30-5)
(415) 540-5767 (Access Info Line, Monday and Wednesday 10-4)
(Generally does not analyze other Christian bodies.)

Christian Research Institute
PO Box 500
San Juan Capistrano, CA 92693
(714) 855-9926 (Tuesday through Friday, 10 to noon)
(Sometimes analyzes "aberrant" Christian groups.)

Jesus People USA; Cornerstone Press
Eric Pement, research coordinator
4707 N. Malden
Chicago, IL 60640
(312) 989-2080 (cult information, Tuesday through Saturday)
(312) 561-2450 (main switchboard, 24 hours)
(Publishes the annual *Directory of Cult Research Organizations.* The 1988 directory listed 305 evangelical countercult ministries and 43 nonevangelical research and information groups.)

Probe Center Northwest
Doug Groothuis, research associate
4750 18th Avenue NE
Seattle, WA 98105
(206) 523-2170

Christian Apologetics: Research and Information Service (CARIS)
PO Box 1659
Milwaukee, WI 53201
(414) 771-7379 (Monday through Thursday)

Nonreligious Organizations

These organizations are not concerned about the orthodox theology of any group. They are looking at the group either academically or from a strictly mind-control aspect.

Institute for the Study of American Religion (ISAR)
PO Box 90709
Santa Barbara, CA 93190-0709
(805) 961-8133

Cult Awareness Network (CAN)
2421 W. Pratt Boulevard #1173
Chicago, IL 60645
(312) 267-7777 (24-hour hotline)

American Family Foundation (AFF)
PO Box 336
Weston, MA 02193
(617) 893-0930

Focus
Carol Giambalvo, national coordinator
2567 Columbus Avenue
Oceanside, NY 11572
(516) 764-4584

Notes ———————————————

Chapter 1

1. See F. LaGard Smith, *Crystal Lies: Choices and the New Age* (Ann Arbor, MI: Servant Publications, 1989), pp. 23-25.
2. St. Augustine, *Confessions*, tr. John K. Ryan (Garden City, NY: Doubleday Image Book, 1960), p. 254.
3. Johannes Quasten, *Patrology Vol. III: The Golden Age of Greek Patristic Literature* (Westminster, MD: Newman Press, 1960), pp. 292-295.
4. Regarding the differences among Roman Catholics and Protestants on this topic, see my comments in note 25 of Chapter 14.
5. *A Complete Guide to the Tarot* (New York: Crown Publishers, 1970), p. 148.
6. Elliot Miller, "The New Age Movement: What Is It?" in *Forward* (summer, 1985), p. 18. The series of articles continued in the issues for fall, 1985, winter, 1986, spring-summer, 1986, fall, 1986, and in *Christian Research Journal* (winter-spring, 1987). Both magazines are published by the Christian Research Institute. One magazine is a successor to the other. Miller was the editor of the magazines. To contact CRI, see Appendix. The articles have also been made into a book: Elliot Miller, *A Crash Course on the New Age Movement* (Grand Rapids, MI: Baker Book House, 1989).
7. Ibid.

8. Ibid.
9. *National and International Religion Report* (Apr. 25, 1988), p. 6. Brooks is the cofounder and executive director of the Spiritual Counterfeits Project, Berkeley, CA. See Appendix for the address of SCP.
10. Ibid., p. 7.
11. Brooks Alexander, "The New Age Movement Is Nothing New," *Eternity* (Feb., 1988), p. 34.
12. Ibid.
13. Douglas Groothuis, *Confronting the New Age* (Downers Grove, IL: Intervarsity Press, 1988), pp. 20-32.
14. Ibid., p. 43, citing Andrew Greeley, "Mysticism Goes Mainstream," *American Health* (Jan.-Feb., 1987), p. 48.
15. Russell Chandler, *Understanding the New Age* (Dallas: Word Publishing, 1988), pp. 20-21.
16. Karen Hoyt and J. Isamu Yamamoto, ed., *The New Age Rage* (Old Tappan, NJ: Fleming H. Revell Co., 1987), p. 11.
17. Anna Madezyk, "New Age: Is This the Dawning of a New Spiritual Awakening?," *Daily Herald* (Palatine, IL: Dec. 17, 1987).
18. *Intercessors for America Newsletter* (Reston, VA: June, 1988), p. 4.
19. Walter Martin, *The Kingdom of the Cults* (Minneapolis: Bethany House Publishers, 1985), p. 401.
20. *Time*, "New Age Harmonies" (Dec. 7, 1987), pp. 62-72.
21. See Robert M. Bowman, Jr., "Cult Update: Trends in New Religions," in *Christian Research Journal* (fall, 1987), p. 21, and Chandler, *Understanding the New Age*, pp. 96-97.
22. See *1st Century Messenger* (Apr.-June, 1988), p. 1.
23. See Groothuis, *Confronting the New Age*, pp. 72-74.
24. Hoyt, Introduction, *The New Age Rage*, p. 12.
25. Miller, "Tracking the Aquarian Conspiracy: Part Two," *Christian Research Journal* (winter-spring, 1987), p. 17.
26. David Spangler, *Emergence: Rebirth of the Sacred* (Forres, Scotland: Findhorn Publications, n.d.), p. 144; cited in *Passport Magazine* (Oct.-Nov., 1987), p. 6, quoted by Chandler, *Understanding the New Age*, p. 288.
27. George Craig McMillan, "Laya Yoga and Enlightenment," *Life Times*, Vol. 1, No. 3, p. 43, quoted by Chandler, *Understanding the New Age*, p. 289.
28. M. Scott Peck, *The Road Less Traveled: A New Psychology of Love, Traditional Values and Spiritual Growth* (New York: Simon & Schuster, 1978), pp. 281, 283, quoted by Chandler, *Understanding the New Age*, p. 297.
29. Chandler, *Understanding the New Age*, p. 279. Henry was quoted in George W. Cornell, "Paganism Seen Ruin of Western Civilization,"

Los Angeles Times (July 11, 1987), pt. 2, p. 6.
30. Quoted by Chandler, ibid.
31. Ralph Rath, "A Scholar's Scary Report on the Occult," *Oakland Tribune* (May 23, 1973), p. 20A.
32. Chandler, *Understanding the New Age*, p. 32.
33. Ibid. Marilyn Ferguson was the author of *The Aquarian Conspiracy*.
34. James W. Sire, *The Universe Next Door* (Downers Grove, IL: Intervarsity Press, 1988), pp. 203-204.
35. Groothuis, *Confronting the New Age*, p. 77, quoting H. Reiker, *The Yoga of Light* (Los Angeles: Dawn House, 1974), p. 9; quoted in John Weldon and Clifford Wilson, *Occult Shock and Psychic Forces* (San Diego: Master, 1980), p. 72.
36. Ibid., pp. 77-78. See Weldon and Wilson, *Occult Shock*, pp. 71-74.
37. Elliot Miller, "The New Myth: A Critique of New Age Ideology," *Forward* (spring-summer, 1986), p. 27.
38. Douglas Groothuis, "Confronting the New Age Counterfeit," in *Equipping the Saints* (fall, 1988), p. 2.
39. Brooks Alexander, "The Coming World Religion," in the *Spiritual Counterfeits Project Journal* (winter, 1984), pp. 20-23. Introduction by the editor-in-chief, J. Isamu Yamamoto, p. 5.
40. Ibid.
41. Ibid, pp. 22-23. Contact the Spiritual Counterfeits Project for the complete text of this article. See Appendix for the SCP address.

Chapter 2

1. J. Isamu Yamamoto, "Different Religions, Different Goals," *Spiritual Counterfeits Project Journal* (winter, 1984), p. 37.
2. Ibid.
3. Sire, *The Universe Next Door*, p. 152.
4. Alexander, "Occult Philosophy and Mystical Experience," *Spiritual Counterfeits Project Journal* (winter, 1984), p. 14.
5. Miller, "The New Age Movement: What Is It?," p. 20.
6. Walpola Rahula, *What the Buddha Taught* (New York: Grove Press, 1974), p. 12.
7. K.M. Sen, *Hinduism* (Baltimore: Penguin, 1962), p. 7, quoted by Walter Martin, *The New Cults* (Santa Ana, CA: Vision House, 1980), p. 80.
8. Martin, *The New Cults*, pp. 80-81.
9. See Josh McDowell and Don Stewart, *Understanding Non-Christian Religions* (San Bernardino, CA: Here's Life Publishers, 1982), p. 20.
10. Martin, *The New Cults*, p. 82.
11. John P. Newport, *Christ and the New Consciousness* (Nashville:

Broadman Press, 1978), pp. 14-18.
12. Vishal Mangalwadi, *Yoga* (Chicago: Cornerstone Press, 1984).
13. Huston Smith, *The Religions of Man* (New York: Harper and Row Perennial Library, 1958, 1965), pp. 33-34.
14. Newport, *Christ and the New Consciousness*, p. 18.
15. See Appendix for the address of Cornerstone Press to order Mangalwadi's leaflet.
16. Bob Larson, *Larson's Book of Cults* (Wheaton, IL: Tyndale House Publishers, 1982), p. 74.
17. Gandhi, *For Pacifists* (Ahmedabad: Navajivan Publishing House, 1949), p. 74.
18. Ibid., pp. 3, 64.
19. Larson, *Larson's Book of Cults*, pp. 75-76.
20. Ibid., p. 79.
21. Ibid.
22. Tal Brooke, *The Other Side of Death: Does Death Seal Your Destiny?* (Chattanooga, TN: The John Ankerberg Show, 1979), p. 76.
23. Smith, *The Religions of Man*, p. 15.
24. David G. Bradley, *A Guide to the World's Religions* (Englewood Cliffs, NJ: Prentice-Hall, 1963), p. 108.
25. Larson, *Larson's Book of Cults*, p. 84.
26. Ibid., p. 85.
27. Ibid., pp. 85-86.
28. Ibid., p. 88.
29. Ibid., p. 90.
30. Newport, *Christ and the New Consciousness*, p. 53.
31. Mark R. Mullins, "The Worldview of Zen," *Update: A Quarterly Journal of New Religious Movements* (Dec., 1983), p. 50, quoted by Chandler, *Understanding the New Age*, p. 44.
32. Larson, *Larson's Book of Cults*, p. 98.
33. Ibid., p. 92.
34. Ibid., p. 93.
35. Ibid.
36. Jacob Needleman, *The New Religions* (New York: Pocket Books, 1970, 1972), p. 37.
37. Chandler, *Understanding the New Age*, p. 45, quoting Robert Anton Wilson, *The Cosmic Trigger: Final Secret of the Illuminati*, cited by Christopher Lasch, "Soul of a New Age," *Omni* (Oct., 1987), p. 85.
38. See Chandler, *Understanding the New Age*, p. 205.
39. Ibid., p. 46.
40. Robert J.L. Burrows, "The Coming of the New Age," in Hoyt and Yamamoto, ed., *The New Age Rage*, p. 23.
41. Nina Easton, "Shirley MacLaine's Mysticism for the Masses," *Los*

Angeles Times Magazine (Sept. 6, 1987), p. 10, quoted by Chandler, *Understanding the New Age*, p. 47.

42. Chandler, *Understanding the New Age*, p. 47.
43. See Burrows, "The Coming of the New Age," p. 24.
44. Ibid., p. 31.
45. Marilyn Ferguson, *The Aquarian Conspiracy: Personal and Social Transformation in Our Time* (Los Angeles: Jeremy P. Tarcher, 1980), p. 26. See also Chapter Six of this book.
46. Irving Hexham and Karla Poewe-Hexham, "The Soul of the New Age," *Christianity Today* (Sept. 2, 1988), p. 20.
47. Miller, "The New Age Movement: What Is It?," p. 19.
48. Brooks Alexander and Robert Burrows, "New Age and Biblical Worldviews," *Equipping the Saints* (fall, 1988), pp. 6-7.
49. C.S. Lewis, *Miracles* (New York: Macmillan, 1947), pp. 84-85, quoted by Alexander, "Occult Philosophy and Mystical Experience," p. 15.

Chapter 3

1. *The World Almanac and Book of Facts 1987* (New York: Pharos Books, 1986), p. 544.
2. Bruce Goldberg, *Past Lives, Future Lives* (New York: Ballantine Books, 1982), p. 270.
3. Ibid., p. 265.
4. Dick Sutphen, *Pre-Destined Love* (New York: Pocket Books, 1988), pp. 220-222.
5. Larson, *Larson's Book of Cults*, p. 56.
6. Norman L. Geisler and J. Yutaka Amano, *The Reincarnation Sensation* (Wheaton, IL: Tyndale House Publishers, 1986), p. 108.
7. See Bradley, *A Guide to the World's Religions*, p. 106.
8. Hammalawa Saddhatissa, *Buddhist Ethics: The Path to Nirvana* (London: Wisdom Publications, 1987), p. 83.
9. Ibid., p. 45.
10. Ibid., p. 21.
11. Rahula, *What the Buddha Taught*, p. 43.
12. Larson, *Larson's Book of Cults*, p. 58.
13. See Chapter 15 of this book.
14. Joe Fisher, *The Case for Reincarnation* (Garden City, NY: Doubleday, 1984), quoted in *The New Age Catalogue* (New York: Doubleday Dolphin Book, 1988), p. 106.
15. Shirley MacLaine, *Out on a Limb* (New York: Bantam Books, 1983), p. 205, cited by Groothuis, *Confronting the New Age*, p. 103.
16. Chandler, *Understanding the New Age*, p. 268.

17. Joseph P. Gudel, Robert M. Bowman, Jr., and Dan R. Schlesinger, "Reincarnation—Did the Church Suppress It?," *Christian Research Journal* (summer, 1987), p. 12.
18. Larson, *Larson's Book of Cults*, p. 59.
19. Jane E. Brody, "Near-Death Experience Leaves Lasting Impact on Millions of People," N.Y. Times News Service, *South Bend Tribune* (Nov. 27, 1988), p. S12.
20. Goldberg, *Past Lives, Future Lives*, p. 260.
21. Ibid.
22. Rodney Clapp, "Rumors of Heaven," *Christianity Today* (Oct. 7, 1988), p. 19.
23. Ibid.
24. Floyd C. McElveen, *The Beautiful Side of Death* (Grand Rapids, MI: Gospel Truths Ministries, n.d.), p. 83. Material adapted from Maurice Rawlings, *Beyond Death's Door* (Nashville: Thomas Nelson, 1978), pp. 102-120.
25. Ibid., p. 86.
26. Ibid., pp. 88-89.
27. Ibid., p. 90.
28. Ibid., p. 91.
29. Ruth Montgomery, *A World Beyond* (Westminster, MD: Random House, 1971), quoted in *The New Age Catalogue*, p. 10.
30. Lynn Smith, "The New, Chic Metaphysical Fad of Channeling," *Los Angeles Times* (Dec. 5, 1986), Part V, quoted by Elliot Miller, "Channeling: Spiritistic Revelations for the New Age," *Christian Research Journal* (fall, 1987), p. 14.
31. Brooks Alexander, "Theology From the Twilight Zone," *Christianity Today* (Sept. 18, 1987), pp. 22-26.
32. See Miller, "Channeling," p. 15.
33. Alexander, "Twilight Zone," p. 26.
34. Chandler, *Understanding the New Age*, pp. 81-82.
35. Ibid., p. 82, citing Dick Roraback, "An Artist's Brush With Immortality," *Los Angeles Times* (Apr. 19, 1988).
36. Jane Roberts, *Seth Speaks: The Eternal Validity of the Soul* (Englewood Cliffs, NJ: Prentice-Hall, 1972).
37. Ramtha, *Ramtha*, ed. Steven Lee Weinberg (Eastsound, WA: Sovereignty, 1986).
38. Alexander, "Twilight Zone," p. 24.
39. Miller, "Channeling," p. 17. See note 30.
40. Ibid., citing Alice A. Bailey, *Telepathy* (New York: Lucis Publishing Co., 1950), pp. 75-77, quoted by Jon Klimo, *Channeling* (Los Angeles: Jeremy P. Tarcher, 1987), p. 321.
41. Ibid., citing Joey Crinita, *The Medium Touch: A New Approach to*

Mediumship (Norfolk, VA: Unilaw Library/Donning Co., 1982), p. 45, quoted in Klimo, *Channeling*, p. 22.

42. Ibid., p. 22.
43. M.D. Griffin, "Spiritism," in *New Catholic Encyclopedia* (Washington, DC: Catholic University of America, 1967), p. 577.
44. Edward A. Pace, "Spiritism," in *Catholic Encyclopedia* (New York: Robert Appleton, 1909), p. 223.
45. Ibid., p. 224.

Chapter 4

1. Chandler, *Understanding the New Age*, p. 239, citing Reuter's News Service (May 5, 1988).
2. See ibid., citing the AP (May 3, 1988).
3. Donald T. Regan, *For the Record*, book excerpt in *Time* (May 16, 1988), p. 26.
4. Ibid., p. 41.
5. See Larson, *Larson's Book of Cults*, p. 254.
6. John Ankerberg and John Weldon, *The Facts on Astrology* (Eugene, OR: Harvest House Publishers, 1988), p. 8, citing Lawrence E. Jerome, *Astrology Disproved* (Buffalo, NY: Prometheus Books, 1977), p. 1.
7. Ibid., p. 8, citing Bernard Gittelson, *Intangible Evidence* (New York: Simon & Schuster, 1987), p. 338.
8. Ibid., p. 9, citing Derek and Julia Parker, *The Compleat Astrology* (New York: Bantam Books, 1978), p. 178.
9. J.J. Leonard, "Count Me In" (advertisement/article), *Parade Magazine* (Nov. 19, 1989), pp. 22-23.
10. Chandler, *Understanding the New Age*, p. 239, citing the AP (May 3, 1988).
11. Ankerberg and Weldon, *The Facts on Astrology*, p. 3, citing *The Los Angeles Times* (Sept. 3, 1975), pp. 1, 30.
12. Josh McDowell and Don Stewart, *Understanding the Occult* (San Bernardino, CA: Here's Life Publishers, 1982), p. 29.
13. Roger B. Culver and Philip A. Ianna, *Astrology: True or False? A Scientific Evaluation* (Buffalo, NY: Prometheus Books, 1988), pp. ix-x.
14. Ibid., pp. 210-211.
15. Ankerberg and Weldon, *The Facts on Astrology*, p. 6.
16. See ibid., pp. 30-38; Larson, *Larson's Book of Cults*, pp. 254-257; McDowell and Stewart, *Understanding the Occult*, pp. 26-30.
17. Charles Strohmer, *What Your Horoscope Doesn't Tell You* (Wheaton, IL: Tyndale House Publishers, 1988).

18. Brooks Alexander, book review, *Spiritual Counterfeits Project Journal*, Vol. 8, No. 1, p. 67.
19. Charles R. Strohmer, "A Journey From the New Age to the New Birth," *Equipping the Saints* (fall, 1988), p. 13.
20. Randall N. and Vicki V. Baer, *The Crystal Connection: A Guidebook for Personal and Planetary Ascension* (San Francisco: Harper and Row, 1987), Preface and Introduction.
21. Katrina Raphaell, *Crystal Enlightenment: The Transforming Properties of Crystals and Healing Stones* (Santa Fe: Aurora Press, 1985), quoted in *The New Age Catalogue*, p. 20.
22. Otto Friedrich, "New Age Harmonies," *Time* (Dec. 7, 1987), p. 64.
23. Chandler, *Understanding the New Age*, p. 103.
24. Ibid., p. 105.
25. Ibid., pp. 136-137.
26. Eric Pement, "The Cry for Crystals," *Cornerstone*, Issue 86, pp. 5-6.
27. Chandler, *Understanding the New Age*, p. 237.
28. Pement, "The Cry for Crystals," p. 6, citing *Omni* (Oct., 1987), p. 96.
29. Chandler, *Understanding the New Age*, p. 106.
30. Ibid., p. 137.
31. Ibid., p. 90, citing Bill Lawren, "UFO Poll," *Omni* (Oct., 1987), p. 144.
32. Larson, *Larson's Book of Cults*, p. 344.
33. Paris Flammonde, *UFO Exist!* (New York: Ballantine Books, 1976), pp. 424-445.
34. Mark Albrecht and Brooks Alexander, "UFOs: Is Science Fiction Coming True?," *Spiritual Counterfeits Project Journal* (Aug., 1977), pp. 12-23.
35. Ibid., p. 14.
36. Chandler, *Understanding the New Age*, p. 94.
37. Ibid., quoting Martin Gardner, *New Age: Notes of a Fringe-Watcher* (Buffalo, NY: Prometheus Books, 1988), p. 213.
38. Mark Albrecht, "NASA and the Search for ETI," *Spiritual Counterfeits Project Journal* (Aug., 1977), p. 24. ("ETI" is extraterrestrial intelligence.)
39. Thomas C. Oden, *The Living God: Systematic Theology Volume 1* (New York: Harper & Row, 1987), pp. 268-269.
40. Clifford Wilson, *The Alien Agenda* (New York: New American Library, 1988), p. 220.
41. John White, "What's Out There? UFOs and the Search for Higher Consciousness," *New Realities* (Nov.-Dec., 1987), p. 46.
42. Albrecht and Alexander, "UFOs," p. 19, citing Lynn G. Catoe, *UFOs and Related Subjects: An Annotated Bibliography* (prepared for the USAF Office of Scientific Research).

43. Ibid., citing Janet Gregory, "Similarities in UFO and Demon Lore," *Flying Saucer Review*, Vol. 17, No. 2, p. 31.

44. Ibid., citing John Keel, *UFOs: Operation Trojan Horse* (New York: G.P. Putnam's Sons, 1970), p. 44.

45. Larson, *Larson's Book of Cults*, p. 348.

46. John Weldon and Clifford Wilson, "Close Encounters With UFO Occupants," an unpublished manuscript cited by Albrecht and Alexander, "UFOs," p. 23.

47. Jon Klimo, *Channeling: Investigations on Receiving Information From Paranormal Sources* (Los Angeles: Jeremy P. Tarcher, 1987), p. 42, quoted by Sire, *The Universe Next Door*, p. 191.

48. Shirley MacLaine, *It's All in the Playing* (New York: Bantam Books, 1987), p. 172, quoted by Sire, *The Universe Next Door*, pp. 191-192.

49. *Time* (Dec. 7, 1987), p. 72.

50. MacLaine, *It's All in the Playing*, quoted in *The New Age Catalogue*, p. 40.

51. Douglas Groothuis, book review, *Christian Research Journal* (fall, 1987), p. 28.

52. Brooks Alexander, book review, *Spiritual Counterfeits Project Journal*, Vol. 7, No. 1 (1987), p. 37.

53. Shirley MacLaine, *Going Within: A Guide for Inner Transformation* (New York: Bantam Books, 1989).

54. *Shirley MacLaine's Inner Workout* (Stamford, CT: Vestron Video, 1988).

55. Martin Gardner, *New Age: Notes of a Fringe-Watcher* (Buffalo, NY: Prometheus Books, 1988), pp. 36, 188, quoted by Chandler, *Understanding the New Age*, pp. 52-53.

56. Dennis Livingston, "Taking on Shirley MacLaine," *New Age Journal* (Nov.-Dec., 1987), p. 79, quoted by Chandler, *Understanding the New Age*, p. 53.

57. Groothuis, *Christian Research Journal*, p. 28.

58. Smith, *Crystal Lies*, p. 16.

59. MacLaine, *Going Within*, p. 8.

60. Ibid., p. 17.

61. Ibid., p. 223.

62. Ibid., p. 204.

63. MacLaine, *Dancing in the Light* (New York: Bantam Books, 1985), pp. 341-342.

64. Groothuis, *Christian Research Journal*, p. 28.

Chapter 5

1. Jeremy Tarcher, "New Age as Perennial Philosophy," *New Realities*

326 THE NEW AGE: A Christian Critique

(May-June, 1988), pp. 27-28. Also published in *Los Angeles Times* (Feb. 7, 1988).
2. Published as a winter, 1988, supplement to the *New Age Journal*.
3. Volkswagen ad in *Time* (Oct. 17, 1988).
4. Volkswagen ad in *Time* (Nov. 14, 1988).
5. See Chapter Three, note 14.
6. Ibid., "Why Publish a New Age Catalogue?," p. ix.
7. Ibid., p. 16. Jonathan Parker, *Pathways to Mastership* (Ojai, CA: Institute for Human Development, 1986).
8. Ibid., p. 25. David and Lucy Pond, *The Metaphysical Handbook* (Port Ludlow, WA: Reflecting Pond Publications, 1985).
9. Ibid., p. 28. Julia Line, *The Numerology Workbook* (New York: Sterling Publishers, 1985).
10. Ibid., p. 56. James Allen, *Become the Master of Your Own Destiny* (San Rafael, CA: Whatever Publishing, 1987).
11. Ibid., p. 57. Marcus Allen, *Tantra for the West* (San Rafael, CA: Whatever Publishing, 1981).
12. Ibid., p. 55. Dick Sutphen, *Master of Life Manual* (Agoura Hills, CA: Valley of the Sun, 1987).
13. Ibid., p. 64. American Research Team, *Astral Sounds*, a 60-minute cassette (Grand Rapids, MI: Potentials Unlimited, 1973).
14. Ibid., p. 65.
15. Ibid., p. 72. Gavin and Yvonne Frost, *Astral Travel* (York Beach, ME: Samuel Weiser, 1982).
16. Ibid., p. 73.
17. Ibid., p. 97. Cai Inderhill, "The Divine Triangle," from *Life Times Magazine*.
18. Ibid., p. 112.
19. Ibid., p. 118.
20. Ibid., p. 130.
21. Ibid., p. 138.
22. Published in San Anselmo, CA. The issue I have is #56 (summer, 1988).
23. *The Llewellyn New Times,* St. Paul, MN (Sept.-Oct., 1988), p. 24.
24. (Brighton, MA: Rising Star Associates).

Chapter 6

1. David Fetcho and Brooks Alexander, "SCP Response to John Todd Inquiries," *Spiritual Counterfeits Project Newsletter* (Sept., 1978), p. 3.
2. Ibid.
3. Ibid.
4. Ad in *Los Angeles Times* (Apr. 25, 1982), part 1, p. 31. Reproduced in

Media Spotlight Special Report (1982), p. 16.

5. Ad in *Los Angeles Times* (May 2, 1982), part 1, p. 27. Reproduced in *Media Spotlight Special Report*, p. 16.

6. *Media Spotlight Special Report*, p. 9.

7. For an excellent treament of Constance Cumbey, see Eric Pement's leaflet, "The New Age Movement: Consensus or Conspiracy?" (Chicago: Cornerstone Press, 1988), updated from a 1983 article in *Cornerstone*. Cumbey's books are *The Hidden Dangers of the Rainbow: The New Age Movement and Our Coming Age of Barbarism* (Shreveport, LA: Huntington House, 1983) and *A Planned Deception: The Staging of a New Age "Messiah"* (East Detroit, MI: Pointe Publishers, 1985).

8. Cumbey, *The Hidden Dangers of the Rainbow*, Introduction, unpaginated.

9. See previous note and Elliot Miller, two book reviews, *Christian Research Journal* (summer, 1987), pp. 25-29.

10. Pement, "Consensus or Conspiracy?," pp. 10-11.

11. Ibid., p. 11.

12. Miller, book reviews, p. 26.

13. Cited by Pement, "Consensus or Conspiracy," p. 12. David Spangler, *Reflections on the Christ* (Findhorn, Moray, Scotland: Findhorn Publications, 1981, third ed.), pp. 44-45.

14. Ibid., p. 12.

15. Ibid., quoting Alice A. Bailey, *The Externalisation of the Hierarchy* (New York: Lucis Publishing Co., 1957), p. 548.

16. See Appendix for the address of the Christian Research Institute.

17. See *Christianity Today* (Jan. 13, 1989), p. 58; (Feb. 17, 1989), p. 45.

18. M. Basilea Schlink, *New Age From a Biblical Viewpoint* (Darmstadt-Eberstadt, West Germany: Evangelical Sisterhood of Mary, 1987). English edition, 1988, p. 6.

19. Miller, book reviews, p. 25.

20. Texe Marrs, *Dark Secrets of the New Age: Satan's Plan for a One World Religion* (Westchester, IL: Crossway Books, 1987), back cover.

21. Ibid., pp. viii and ix.

22. Ibid., p. 204.

23. Texe Marrs, *Mystery Mark of the New Age: Satan's Design for World Domination* (Westchester, IL: Crossway Books, 1988), p. 13.

24. Ibid., pp. 236-237.

25. Ibid., pp. 157, 161.

26. Ibid., p. 165.

27. Elissa Lindsey McClain, *Rest From the Quest* (Shreveport, LA: Huntington House, 1984), Preface, quoted in Chandler, *Understanding the New Age*, p. 228.

28. Chandler, *Understanding the New Age*, p. 229.

29. Dave Hunt and T.A. McMahon, *The Seduction of Christianity: Spiritual Discernment in the Last Days* (Eugene, OR: Harvest House Publishers, 1985), pp. 7-8.
30. Ibid., p. 213.
31. Ibid., p. 12.
32. Dave Hunt, *Beyond Seduction: A Return to Biblical Christianity* (Eugene, OR: Harvest House Publishers, 1987), pp. 2-3.
33. Dave Hunt, *A Study Guide for the Cult Explosion* (Eugene, OR: Harvest House Publishers, 1981), p. 26, quoted by Eric Pement, "Consensus or Conspiracy?," p. 15.
34. Dave Hunt, *Peace, Prosperity and the Coming Holocaust* (Eugene, OR: Harvest House Publishers, 1983), p. 47, quoted by Hoyt and Yamamoto, *The New Age Rage*, p. 189.
35. Chandler, *Understanding the New Age*, p. 231.
36. Bob and Gretchen Passantino, book review, *Forward* (fall, 1986), p. 28.
37. See Chapter Two, note 45.
38. Ibid., pp. 18-19.
39. See ibid., p. 26.
40. Mark Albrecht, book review, *Spiritual Counterfeits Project Newsletter* (Apr.-May, 1982), p. 6.
41. See Hoyt and Yamamoto, *The New Age Rage*, pp. 185-201.
42. Spiritual Counterfeits Project staff, "The Final Threat: Cosmic Conspiracy and End Times Speculation," in Hoyt and Yamamoto, *The New Age Rage*, p. 200.
43. Douglas Groothuis, *Unmasking the New Age* (Downers Grove, IL: Intervarsity Press, 1986), p. 35.
44. Groothuis, *Confronting the New Age*, pp. 199-200, referring to Anthony Downs, "They Sell Sizzle, But Their Predictions Fizzle," *Wall Street Journal* (Apr. 6, 1983).
45. Chandler, *Understanding the New Age*, p. 225.
46. Ibid., p. 233, quoting Maurice Smith, "Understanding and Responding to the New Age Movements" (Interfaith Witness Department, Home Mission Board, Southern Baptist Convention, 1985), p. 8.
47. Pement, "Consensus or Conspiracy?," p. 18.

Chapter 7

1. Josh McDowell and Don Stewart, *Understanding the Cults* (San Bernardino, CA: Here's Life Publishers, 1982), pp. 17, 29.
2. Ruth A. Tucker, *Another Gospel: Alternative Religions and the New Age Movement* (Grand Rapids, MI: Zondervan Publishing House, 1989),

p. 16.

3. Larson, *Larson's Book of Cults*, p. 28.
4. See Chandler, *Understanding the New Age*, p. 69.
5. Denise Denniston and Peter McWilliams, *The Transcendental Meditation TM Book: How To Enjoy the Rest of Your Life* (Allen Park, MI: Three Rivers Press, 1975), pp. 14-15.
6. See *TM in Court: The Complete Text of the Federal Court's Opinion in the Case of* Malnak *v.* Maharishi Mahesh Yogi (Berkeley, CA: Spiritual Counterfeits Project, 1978). For background information, consult the Foreword by Michael J. Woodruff.
7. Ibid., p. 74.
8. Ibid., p. 37.
9. Copy of Randolph's affidavit provided by the Spiritual Counterfeits Project.
10. Douglas Shah, *The Meditators* (Plainfield, NJ: Logos International, 1975), p. 98.
11. David Haddon and Vail Hamilton, *TM Wants You! A Christian Response to Transcendental Meditation* (Grand Rapids, MI: Baker Book House, 1976), pp. 67-68.
12. Wilson and Weldon, *Occult Shock*, p. 50. They cite *Journal of Transpersonal Psychology*, "On the Meaning of Transpersonal: Some Metaphysical Perspectives" (1971, #1), pp. 39-40.
13. Ibid., p. 51.
14. Jose Silva and Philip Miele, *The Silva Mind Control Method* (New York: Pocket Books, 1977).
15. Sid Roth and Irene Harrell, *Something for Nothing: The Spiritual Rebirth of a Jew* (Plainfield, NJ: Logos International, 1976), pp. 103-104.
16. This incident indicates that the counselors are demonic, but it also raises the problem that demons are not God and cannot predict the future. Perhaps there were other indications that Roth was leaning to Christianity even though he was not conscious of this at the time.
17. Elmer Green and Alyce Green, "How Safe Is 'Mind Training'?," in Martin Ebon, ed., *The Satan Trap* (Garden City, NY: Doubleday & Co., 1976), pp. 249, 251, quoted by Newport, *Christ and the New Consciousness*, p. 103.
18. Newport, *Christ and the New Consciousness*, p. 103.
19. Ibid., citing Ebon, *The Satan Trap*, pp. 255 ff.
20. Ibid., p. 105, citing Harry McKnight, *Silva Mind Control Through Psychorientology* (Laredo, TX: Institute of Psychorientology, Inc., 1972), pp. 77-78.
21. *Time* (Apr. 5, 1976), pp. 56-67, quoted in a leaflet, *Cult of the Month—*

Scientology: Pandora's Box (Chicago: Cornerstone Press, n.d.), p. 1.
22. See *Pandora's Box*, p. 1.
23. Larson, *Larson's Book of Cults*, p. 313.
24. Ibid.
25. See ibid. and *Pandora's Box*, p. 4.
26. See *Pandora's Box*, pp. 6-7.
27. Brooks Alexander, "Scientology: Human Potential Bellwether," *Spiritual Counterfeits Project Journal* (winter, 1981-82), p. 27.
28. See *Spiritual Counterfeits Project Journal: Eckankar: A Hard Look at a New Religion* (Berkeley, CA: Spiritual Counterfeits Project, Sept., 1979), pp. 45-47. See Appendix for SCP address to obtain this journal.
29. See Larson, *Larson's Book of Cults*, p. 271.
30. Ibid.
31. Chandler, *Understanding the New Age*, pp. 74-75.
32. *Spiritual Counterfeits Project Journal: Eckankar*, p. 5.
33. Ibid., p. 40.
34. Mark Albrecht, "Guru Ma Comes to Town," *Spiritual Counterfeits Project Newsletter* (Jan.-Feb., 1979), p. 3.
35. Robert Burrows, "Church Universal and Triumphant: The Summit Lighthouse," *Spiritual Counterfeits Project Journal* (winter, 1984), p. 63. For more information on the I AM movement, see Martin, *The New Cults*, pp. 203-236.
36. Michael P. Harris, "Paradise Under Siege," *Time* (Aug. 28, 1989), p. 61.
37. Burrows, "Church Universal," p. 63.
38. Church Universal promotional flyer.
39. Burrows, "Church Universal," p. 68.
40. Larson, *Larson's Book of Cults*, p. 267.
41. Martin, *The New Cults*, p. 106, citing R.C. Heck and J.L. Thompson, "EST: Salvation or Swindle," in *San Francisco Magazine* (Jan., 1976), p. 70. (Martin places the year of Erhard's abandonment of his first wife as 1960.)
42. Some good sources on Werner Erhard include: Martin, *The New Cults*, pp. 105-142; Newport, *Christ and the New Consciousness*, pp. 106-117; Larson, *Larson's Book of Cults*, pp. 275-279; Cornerstone Press leaflet, "est: Getting it or Losing it" (1982); *Spiritual Counterfeits Project Journal* (winter, 1981-82), pp. 19-23, and Vol. 8, No. 1 (1988), pp. 32-56.
43. Carol Giambalvo and Robert Burrows, "The Hunger Project Inside Out," *Spiritual Counterfeits Project Journal*, Vol. 8, No. 1 (1988), p. 36, citing W.W. Bartley, III, *Werner Erhard: The Transformation of a Man* (New York: Clarkson N. Potter, 1978), pp. 166-168.

44. Ibid., p. 36.
45. Stanley Dokupil and Brooks Alexander, "*est:* The Philosophy of Self-Worship," *Spiritual Counterfeits Project Journal* (winter, 1981-82), p. 21, citing *The Graduate Review* (magazine of the *est* organization) (Nov., 1976), pp. 3-4.
46. Ibid.
47. "*est:* Getting it or Losing it," p. 3.
48. Ibid.
49. Ibid.
50. Ibid., pp. 2-3, quoting Mark Brewer, "We're Gonna Tear You Down and Put You Back Together," *Psychology Today* (Aug., 1975), p. 39.
51. *Spiritual Counterfeits Project Journal,* Vol. 8, No. 1, p. 45.

Chapter 8

1. Batavia, IL: Lion Publishing Corp., 1986.
2. Ibid., p. 7.
3. Tal Brooke, "Sai Baba: Lord of the Air," *Spiritual Counterfeits Project Newsletter* (summer, 1985), p. 16.
4. Ibid.
5. The way I look at things, only God or angels using God's power can work true miracles, but demonic forces can perform paranormal acts which may seem like miracles.
6. Brooke, *Riders,* p. 20.
7. Ibid., p. 21.
8. Ibid., p. 41, quoting Swami Muktananda, *Play of Consciousness* (San Francisco: Harper & Row, 1978), pp. 75-78.
9. Ibid., p. 44, quoting Muktananda, *Play,* pp. 88-89.
10. Ibid., pp. 117-120, quoting Rajneesh, *The Discipline of Transcendence: Discourses on the 42 Sutras of Buddha, Vol. 2* (Poona: Rajneesh Foundation, 1978), pp. 301-310.
11. Ibid., p. 171.
12. Ibid., p. 172.
13. See Chandler, *Understanding the New Age,* pp. 60-61. (Chandler says 5,000 followers; *Time* says 10,000.)
14. *Time* (Jan. 16, 1989), p. 78.
15. Brooke, *Riders,* pp. 187-188.
16. Ibid., p. 202.
17. See Norman Geisler, *Signs and Wonders* (Wheaton, IL: Tyndale House Publishers, 1988), p. 95.
18. C.S. Lewis, *Screwtape Letters* (New York: Macmillan, 1961), Preface, quoted by Chandler, *Understanding the New Age,* p. 277.

19. Charles W. Harris, *Resist the Devil: A Pastoral Guide to Deliverance Prayer* (South Bend, IN: Greenlawn Press, 1989), p. 7.
20. Ibid., pp. 8-9.
21. Ibid., pp. 36-39.
22. Matthew and Dennis Linn, ed., *Deliverance Prayer: Experiential, Psychological and Theological Approaches* (New York: Paulist Press, 1981).
23. Randy Cirner and Michael Scanlan, *Deliverance from Evil Spirits: A Weapon for Spiritual Warfare* (Ann Arbor, MI: Servant Books, 1980); Michael Harper, *Spiritual Warfare: Defeating Satan in the Christian Life* (South Plainfield, NJ: Bridge Publishing, 1970); Don Basham, *A Manual for Spiritual Warfare* (Greensburg, PA: Manna Books, 1974).
24. Christopher Nugent, *Masks of Satan: The Demonic in History* (Westminster, MD: Christian Classics, 1983, 1989).
25. Charles J. Gans, "Hospital Team Aims To Wean Teens From Devil Worship," *South Bend Tribune* (Sept. 7, 1989), p. A6.
26. Richard Woodbury, "Cult of the Red-Haired Devil," *Time* (Apr. 24, 1989), p. 30.
27. Information on the cult came from many AP stories.
28. See Lisa Levitt Ryckman, AP national writer, "Satanic Cults Ravage Teens," *Elkhart [IN] Truth* (Feb. 14, 1988).
29. AP story, "Satanism Blamed in Murder-Suicide," *South Bend Tribune* (Jan. 11, 1988).
30. Robert Larson, *Satanism: The Seduction of America's Youth* (Nashville: Thomas Nelson Publishers, 1989), p. 22.
31. See Bob Olmstead, "Detective Sees Crime, Satanism Link," *National Catholic Register* (May 22, 1988), front and back pages.
32. Ibid., p. 1.
33. Ryckman, "Satanic Cults."
34. See Brian Peterson, "Satanic Crime in America," *Charisma & Christian Life* (Oct., 1988), p. 34.
35. See Katherine Kam, "Ritual Killings Have Satanic Overtones," *Christianity Today* (Sept. 2, 1988), p. 52.
36. Olmstead, "Detective," back page.
37. Michelle Smith and Lawrence Pazder, M.D., *Michelle Remembers* (New York: Simon & Shuster Pocket Books, 1980), abstract distributed by *Spiritual Discernment Series*, Shelburne, VT.
38. See Kam, "Ritual Killings," p. 52.
39. Office of the Attorney General, State of California, "Report on the Kern County Child Abuse Investigation," p. 71, quoted by Lauren Stratford, *Satan's Underground* (Eugene, OR: Harvest House, 1988), p. 202, quoted by Bruce G. Frederickson, *How To Respond to*

Satanism (St. Louis, MO: Concordia Publishing House, 1988), p. 6.
40. Frederickson, *How To Respond to Satanism*, p. 6.
41. See Kam, "Ritual Killings," p. 52.
42. Unsigned article, "Ritual Abuse and the Occult," *Spiritual Counterfeits Project Newsletter*, Vol. 14, No. 4 (1989), p. 3.
43. Kam, "Ritual Killings," p. 53.
44. *National & International Religion Report* (Nov. 7, 1988), p. 8. The report was written by physicist Shawn Carlson of the Lawrence Berkeley Laboratories and Gerald Larue, emeritus professor of religion at the University of Southern California.
45. See "Satan in the News?," *Religion Newswriters Association Newsletter* (July-Aug., 1989), p. 4.
46. Craig S. Hawkins, "The Many Faces of Satanism," *Forward* (fall, 1986), pp. 18-20.
47. Ibid., p. 21.
48. Ibid.
49. Chandler, *Understanding the New Age*, p. 272.
50. Ibid., pp. 123-124.
51. Ibid., p. 124.
52. Jeffrey Burton Russell, *Witchcraft in the Middle Ages* (Ithaca, NY: Cornell University Press, 1972), p. 17.
53. Ibid., p. 18.
54. Ibid., p. 19.
55. Ibid., p. 22.
56. See ibid., pp. 87-88.
57. See McDowell and Stewart, *Understanding the Occult*, pp. 175-181.
58. See Chandler, *Understanding the New Age*, p. 124.
59. Ibid., citing J. Gordon Melton, *Encyclopedic Handbook of Cults in America* (New York and London: Garland Publishing, 1986), p. 211.
60. Ibid.
61. Ibid., p. 123.
62. Starhawk, *The Spiral Dance: A Rebirth of the Ancient Religion of the Great Goddess* (Hagerstown, MD: Harper & Row, 1979), quoted in *The New Age Catalogue*, p. 138.
63. Colin Wilson, *The Occult* (New York: Random House Vintage Books, 1971, 1973), p. 415.
64. See Chandler, *Understanding the New Age*, p. 197.
65. Ibid., p. 121.
66. Charlene Spretnak, "Ecofeminism: Our Roots & Flowering," *Ecology Center Newsletter* (Nov., 1987), pp. 1-2, quoted by Chandler, *Understanding the New Age*, p. 122.
67. Rosemary Curb and Nancy Manahan, ed., *Lesbian Nuns: Breaking*

Silence (Tallahassee, FL: Naiad Press, 1985), pp. xxx-xxxi, cited by Chandler, *Understanding the New Age*, p. 122.

68. Robert J.L. Burrows, "A Vision for a New Humanity," in Hoyt and Yamamoto, *The New Age Rage*, p. 45, quoting Deena Metzger, "Re-Vamping the World: On the Return of the Holy Prostitute," *Utne Reader* (Aug.-Sept., 1985), p. 123.

69. Sire, *The Universe Next Door*, p. 166.

70. Ibid., p. 167, quoting Eugene Nida and William A. Smalley, *Introducing Animism* (New York: Friendship Press, 1959), p. 50.

71. Ibid.

72. Ibid., p. 162.

73. Brooks Alexander, "A Generation of Wizards: Shamanism and Contemporary Culture, Part II," *Spiritual Counterfeits Project Newsletter* (Mar.-Apr., 1983), p. 2, quoting Michael Harner, *The Way of the Shaman: A Guide to Power and Healing* (San Francisco: Harper & Row, 1980), p. 138.

74. Jose Stevens and Lena S. Stevens, *Secrets of Shamanism: Tapping the Spirit Power Within You* (New York: Avon Books, 1988), p. 6.

Chapter 9

1. Robert H. Schuller, *Peace of Mind Through Possibility Thinking* (Garden City, NY: Doubleday, 1977), p. 115.

2. Laurie Petrie, Scripps Howard News Service, "Cardinal Criticizes Theologian for Views on Christ," *South Bend Tribune* (Nov. 3, 1988), p. A12. The cardinal was referring to Knitter's book *No Other Name?* and a book he edited, *The Myth of Christian Uniqueness: Toward a Pluralistic Theology of Religions*.

3. Ibid.

4. Matthew Fox, *The Coming of the Cosmic Christ* (San Francisco: Harper & Row, 1988).

5. Ibid., p. 228.

6. Ibid., p. 235.

7. Ibid., p. 176.

8. Ibid., pp. 239-240.

9. Ibid., p. 238.

10. Ibid., p. 137.

11. Ibid., p. 79.

12. Richard Cimino, "Matthew Fox's 'Creation Spirituality,'" *National Catholic Reporter* (Apr. 28, 1989).

13. Peter Kreeft, review of *The Coming of the Cosmic Christ* in the *National Catholic Register* (Apr. 2, 1989), p. 8.

14. Dorothy Ranaghan, "Enneagrams: Shrouded History and Dangerous Guides," *New Heaven/New Earth* (Oct., 1988), pp. 8-9.
15. Ibid., p. 8.
16. Ibid.
17. Ibid.
18. Dorothy Garrity Ranaghan, *A Closer Look at the Enneagram* (South Bend, IN: Greenlawn Press, 1989), p. 34.
19. Ibid., p. 36, citing P.D. Ouspensky, *In Search of the Miraculous* (Saddlebrook, NJ: Harcourt, Brace, 1949).
20. Maria Beesing, Robert J. Nogosek and Patrick H. O'Leary, *The Enneagram: A Journey of Self Discovery* (Denville, NJ: Dimension Books, 1985), p. 5.
21. Don Richard Riso, *Personality Types: Using the Enneagram for Self-Discovery* (Boston: Houghton-Mifflin Co., 1987), p. 8.
22. Ranaghan, *A Closer Look*, pp. 24-25, citing Sister Mary Helen Kelley, O.S.C., *The Human Trinity* (Memphis, TN: Monastery of St. Clare), Tape Nine, Side One, and Sister Barbara Metz, S.N.D. deN., and Father John Burchell, O.P., *The Enneagram and Prayer: Discovering Our True Selves Before God* (Denville, NJ: Dimension Books, 1987), p. 93.
23. Larson, *Larson's Book of Cults*, p. 141.
24. Ibid.
25. News report by unnamed writer, *Christian Research Journal* (summer, 1988), p. 27.
26. Ibid.
27. Ron Rhodes, "The Christ of the New Age Movement," *Christian Research Journal* (summer, 1989), p. 12, quoting David Spangler, *Reflections on the Christ*, p. 107, and *Conversations with John* (Middleton, WI: Lorian Press, 1983), p. 5.
28. William M. Alnor, "Santeria: Rapid Growth in Urban America," *Christian Research Journal* (summer, 1989), p. 5.
29. Edmond C. Gruss, "A Summary Critique: *God Calling*," *Christian Research Journal* (summer, 1988), pp. 29-30.
30. Miller, "The New Age Movement: What Is It?," p. 23.
31. Chandler, *Understanding the New Age*, pp. 204-205, quoting Jeffrey A. Trachtenberg and Edward Giltenan, "Mainstream Metaphysics," *Forbes Magazine* (June 1, 1987), p. 156.
32. Ibid., pp. 208-209, quoting Dialogue House/National Intensive Journal Workshop, Los Angeles (May 15, 1981).
33. Marianne S. Andersen and Louis M. Savary, *Passages: A Guide for Pilgrims of the Mind* (New York: Harper & Row, 1973).
34. Louis M. Savary and Patricia H. Berne, *Kything: The Art of Spiritual Presence* (New York: Paulist Press, 1988).

35. Ibid., p. 23.
36. Peter A. Campbell and Edwin M. McMahon, *Bio-Spirituality: Focusing as a Way to Grow* (Chicago: Loyola University Press, 1985), pp. v-vi.
37. Donna M. Steichen, "Eastern Mysticism Invades Religious Life," *The Forum* (Aug., 1989), p. 9.
38. Ibid.
39. Ray Stanford, *Fatima Prophecy: A Psychic Channels the Controversial Prophecy of Fatima for the New Age* (New York: Ballantine Books, 1987, 1988).
40. George Cornell, AP religion writer, "Religion, UFOs Linked: Minister," *South Bend Tribune* (Apr. 22, 1989), p. A7.
41. See Harry James Cargas, "Priest-Ecumenist-Secularist Sees Hope in Trinity," *National Catholic Reporter* (May 12, 1989), p. 11.
42. Gianni Valente, "Deep Prayer: Deep Void," *30 Days* (Sept., 1989), p. 6.
43. Ibid.
44. Ibid., p. 8.
45. Quoted by ibid., p. 13.
46. Massimo Introvigne, "The Latest Fashion Comes From Japan," *30 Days* (Sept., 1989), pp. 12-13.
47. Valente, "Deep Prayer," pp. 13-14.
48. Ibid., pp. 14-15.
49. Ibid., quoting from the 1986 book *From the Ganges' Banks to the Jordan's Edge.*
50. See Frances Adeney, "Re-visioning Reality," *Spiritual Counterfeits Project Newsletter* (June-July, 1981), p.1; John Koffend, "The Gospel According to Helen," *Psychology Today* (Sept., 1980), pp. 74-90; Miller, "Channeling," p. 11; *Spiritual Counterfeits Journal*, Vol. 7, No. 1 (1987) (three articles).
51. Dean C. Halverson, "*A Course in Miracles:* Seeing Yourself as Sinless," *Spiritual Counterfeits Project Journal*, Vol. 7, No. 1 (1987), pp. 18, 20.
52. "A Matter of *Course:* Conversation With Kenneth Wapnick," *Spiritual Counterfeits Project Journal*, Vol. 7, No. 1 (1987), p. 15.
53. Miller, "Channeling," p. 11.
54. See Dean Halverson, "Urantia . . . the Brotherhood, the Book," *Spiritual Counterfeits Project Newsletter* (Aug., 1981).

Chapter 10

1. Chandler, Understanding the New Age, citing Suzanna Little, "Children in the New Age Bookstore," *Publishers Weekly* (Sept. 25,

1987), p. 72.
2. See ibid., pp. 153, 154, 156.
3. Published by Eagle Education Fund, 1623 W. 102 Ave., Denver, CO 80221.
4. Samantha Smith, "New Age Goes to College," *Eagle Forum* (winter, 1988), p. 1.
5. Johanna Michaelsen, "The Spirit of Halloween," *Charisma & Christian Life* (Oct., 1989), p. 48, reprinted from her book, *Like Lambs to the Slaughter* (Eugene, OR: Harvest House Publishers, 1989).
6. Groothuis, *Confronting the New Age*, quoting Dick Sutphen, "Infiltrating the New Age Into Society," *What Is* (summer, 1986), p. 14.
7. Ibid., pp. 142-143.
8. Frances Adeney, "Educators Look East," *Spiritual Counterfeits Project Journal* (winter, 1981-82), p. 30. The article was reprinted from *Radix* magazine (Nov.-Dec., 1980).
9. Ibid., p. 29.
10. Ibid., p. 31.
11. Chandler, *Understanding the New Age*, pp. 154-155.
12. Helen Hull Hitchcock, "Catholic Education Goes Over the Rainbow: The NCEA and the New Age," *Fidelity* (Aug., 1985), p. 26.
13. Ibid., p. 30.
14. Bob Larson, *Straight Answers on the New Age* (Nashville: Thomas Nelson Publishers, 1989), p. 238.
15. Elliot Miller, "Tracking the 'Aquarian Conspiracy' Part One," *Forward* (fall, 1986), p. 15.
16. Richard A. Baer, Jr., "Parents, Schools and Values Clarification," *Wall Street Journal* (Apr. 12, 1982), quoted by Miller, "Tracking," pp. 15 and 27.
17. Groothuis, *Confronting the New Age*, p. 133.
18. Phyllis Schlafly, *Child Abuse in the Classroom: Excerpts From Official Transcript of Proceedings Before the U.S. Department of Education* (Alton, IL: Pere Marquette Press, 1984), pp. 27-36.
19. Ibid., pp. 138-142.
20. W.R. Coulson, "Founder of 'Value-Free' Education Says He Owes Parents an Apology," *Journal of the American Family Association* (Apr., 1989), p. 21.
21. Groothuis, *Confronting the New Age*, p. 135.
22. Ibid., pp. 135-136, citing Gregg L. Cunningham, *Globalism in the Schools: Independence Issue Paper* (Golden, CO: Independence Institute, 1986), p. 3.
23. Ibid., p. 136.
24. Citing Andre Ryerson, "The Scandal of 'Peace Education,'" *Commentary* (June, 1986), p. 44.

25. Groothuis, *Confronting the New Age*, pp. 136-140.
26. Chandler, *Understanding the New Age*, pp. 32-33.
27. Ibid., p. 33.
28. Miller, "Tracking the Aquarian Conspiracy Part Two," *Christian Research Journal* (winter-spring, 1987), p. 13.
29. Paul McGuire, *Evangelizing the New Age* (Ann Arbor, MI: Servant Publications, 1989), pp. 26-27, quoting Ruth C. Clark, "Pentagon Meditation Club," *Meditation* (fall, 1988), p. 7.
30. Ibid., p. 27, quoting Clark, p. 7.
31. See "Beware of the Hunger Project," *Spiritual Counterfeits Project Newsletter* (Apr.-May, 1979), p. 2. The unsigned article quotes extensively from Suzanne Gordon, "Let Them Eat Est," *Mother Jones* (Dec., 1978), pp. 42-52.
32. Larson, *Straight Answers*, p. 245, citing "Hunger Project Feeds Itself," *The Cult Observer* (Apr., 1985), p. 15.
33. Giambalvo and Burrows, "The Hunger Project Inside Out," p. 43.
34. Fritjof Capra, *The Turning Point* (Toronto: Bantam Books, 1982), p. 78, quoted by Miller, *Crash Course*, p. 42.
35. Ibid., p. 43.
36. Fritjof Capra, *The Tao of Physics* (Berkeley: Shambhala, 1975), p. 11, quoted by Mark Albrecht and Brooks Alexander, "The Sellout of Science," *Spiritual Counterfeits Project Journal* (Aug., 1978), p. 26.
37. Albrecht and Alexander, "Sellout," p. 26.
38. See Capra, *Tao of Physics*, p. xv.
39. Dean C. Halverson, "Science: Quantum Physics and Quantum Leaps," in Hoyt and Yamamoto, *The New Age Rage*, p. 88.

Chapter 11

1. *New Age Journal* (Mar.-Apr., 1988), p. 46.
2. Martin L. Rossman, "The Healing Power of Imagery," *New Age Journal* (Mar.-Apr., 1988), pp. 54-56.
3. C. Norman Shealy, "New Medicine: Does Modern Medicine Heal?," *New Realities* (Nov.-Dec., 1987), p. 7.
4. Ibid.
5. Marilyn Ferguson, *The Aquarian Conspiracy*, p. 242.
6. Ibid.
7. Chandler, *Understanding the New Age*, p. 162, quoting Jack Gordon, "Training Terms: What Does Wholistic Mean?," *Training* (Sept., 1987), p. 66.
8. Ibid.
9. Miller, "Tracking," p. 13, quoting Jerry Driessen, "Health Sharing: Comments on the Characteristics of Holistic Health" (fact sheet)

(Holistic Health Education—Association for Holistic Health, May, 1978).

10. See Chandler, *Understanding the New Age*, p. 163.

11. Miller, "Tracking," p. 13.

12. Ibid., quoting Dana Ullman, "Holistic Health: Friend and Foe of Progressive Health Care," *International Journal of Holistic Health and Medicine* (winter, 1984), p. 22.

13. Ibid.

14. *Journal of Christian Healing* was founded in 1979 by The Association of Christian Therapists. In 1982, its publication was turned over to the Institute for Christian Healing. Contact: *Journal of Christian Healing*, 103 Dudley Ave., Narberth, PA 19072.

15. Sheila Fabricant and Douglas Schoeninger, "Evaluating Methods and Theories of Healing," *Journal of Christian Healing* (spring, 1987), p. 35.

16. Ibid., pp. 35-39.

17. Paul C. Reisser, Teri K. Reisser and John Weldon, *New Age Medicine: A Christian Perspective on Holistic Health* (Downers Grove, IL: Intervarsity Press, 1987), pp. 108-112.

18. Chandler, *Understanding the New Age*, p. 169.

19. John G. Fuller, *Arigo: Surgeon of the Rusty Knife* (New York: Thomas Y. Crowell, 1974).

20. Reisser *et al.*, *New Age Medicine*, p. 108.

21. Ibid., pp. 109-110, quoting Fuller, *Arigo*, pp. 18-19.

22. Ibid., p. 110.

23. Ibid., pp. 111-112.

24. McDowell and Stewart, *Understanding the Occult*, p. 113, quoting Kurt Koch, *Occult ABC* (Grand Rapids, MI: International Publishers, n.d.), p. 238.

25. Reisser *et al.*, *New Age Medicine*, pp. 112-113.

26. Ibid., p. 117, citing Hugh Lynn Cayce, *Venture Inward* (New York: Harper & Row, 1964), p. 11.

27. Ibid., p. 113.

28. See Reba Ann Karp, *Edgar Cayce Encyclopedia of Healing* (New York: Warner Books, 1986), p. 3.

29. Wilson and Weldon, *Occult Shock and Psychic Forces*, p. 71.

30. Ibid., p. 22, quoting H. Rieker, *The Yoga of Light* (Los Angeles: Dawn House, 1974), pp. 9, 134.

31. Ibid., p. 75.

32. Paul C. Reisser, "Holistic Health: Marcus Welby Enters the New Age," in Hoyt and Yamamoto, *The New Age Rage*, pp. 68-69.

33. Reisser *et al.*, *New Age Medicine*, p. 45, quoting Dolores Krieger, *The Therapeutic Touch: How To Use Your Hands To Help or Heal* (Engle-

wood Cliffs, NJ: Prentice-Hall, 1979), p. 13.

34. See Chandler, *Understanding the New Age*, p. 165, and Miller, "Tracking," p. 14.

35. Reisser *et al.*, *New Age Medicine*, p. 47.

36. Janet Quinn, "Therapeutic Touch: The Empowerment of Love," *New Realities* (May-June, 1987), p. 23.

37. Chandler, *Understanding the New Age*, p. 249.

38. Ibid., p. 168.

39. Paul C. Reisser, book review, *Spiritual Counterfeits Project Journal*, Vol. 8, No. 1, p. 58, quoting Bernie S. Siegel, *Love, Medicine & Miracles* (New York: Harper & Row, 1987), pp. 19-20.

40. Reisser *et al.*, *New Age Medicine*, p. 126.

41. Groothuis, *Confronting the New Age*, p. 183.

42. See Reisser in Hoyt and Yamamoto, *The New Age Rage*, pp. 70-71.

43. Reisser *et al.*, *New Age Medicine*, p. 137.

44. Groothuis, *Confronting the New Age*, pp. 188-189, quoting Kenneth R. Pelletier, *Mind as Healer, Mind as Slayer* (New York: Dell, 1977), pp. 297-298.

45. See Reisser in Hoyt and Yamamoto, *The New Age Rage*, p. 65.

46. Chandler, *Understanding the New Age*, p. 166.

47. Sharon Fish, "Nursing's New Age," *Spiritual Counterfeits Project Newsletter*, Vol. 14, No. 3 (1989), pp. 4-5, quoting Barbara Blattner, *Holistic Nursing* (Englewood Cliffs, NJ: Prentice-Hall, 1981), pp. 84-85.

48. Contact CINAM at P.O. Box 16855, Asheville, NC 28816.

49. See Fabricant and Schoeninger, "Evaluating Methods," pp. 39-41.

Chapter 12

1. Steve Rabey, "Karma for Cash: A 'New Age' for Workers?," *Christianity Today* (June 17, 1988), p. 69.

2. Ibid., p. 71.

3. Martha Brannigan, "Employers' 'New Age' Training Programs Lead to Lawsuits Over Workers' Rights," *Wall Street Journal* (Jan. 9, 1989), p. B1.

4. Rabey, "Karma for Cash," p. 71.

5. Ibid., p. 74.

6. Robert Lindsey, "Gurus Hired To Motivate Workers Are Raising Fears of 'Mind Control,' " *New York Times* (Apr. 17, 1987).

7. Ibid.

8. Brannigan, "New Age Training Programs," p. B1.

9. Quoted by Carol Giambalvo, "The Forum: *est* in the Heir," *Spiritual Counterfeits Project Journal*, Vol. 8, No. 1, p. 47.

10. See Brannigan, "New Age Training Programs," p. B1.
11. Ibid.
12. Ibid.
13. Ibid.
14. Ibid.
15. American Family Foundation, "Business and the New Age Movement: A Symposium" (Nov. 23, 1987), p. 4. Contact AFF, Box 336, Weston, MA 02193.
16. Ibid.
17. Ibid., pp. 1-3.
18. Ibid., pp. 3-4.
19. Richard Watring, letter, *Training and Development Journal* (Apr., 1987), p. 8.
20. Richard Watring, "New Age Training in Business: Mind Control in Upper Management?," *Eternity* (Feb., 1988), p. 32.
21. Ron Zemke, "What's New in the New Age?," *Training* (Sept. 26, 1987), p. 30.
22. Napoleon Hill, *Think and Grow Rich* (New York: Fawcett-Crest Books, 1960), p. 72.
23. Ibid., pp. 215-219.
24. Quotes from a transcript of the interview.
25. Alexander, "Nothing New," p. 34.
26. Unsigned article, "New Age in Business: What You and Your Employer Should Know," *Spiritual Counterfeits Project Newsletter*, Vol. 14, No. 1 (1988), pp. 1, 8.
27. Ibid.
28. Groothuis, *Confronting the New Age*, p. 163.
29. Ibid., pp. 163-165.
30. Annetta Miller and Pamela Abramson, "Corporate Mind Control," *Newsweek* (May 4, 1987), p. 38.
31. *U.S. News & World Report* (Feb. 9, 1987), p. 68.
32. Groothuis, *Confronting the New Age*, p. 161.
33. Chandler, *Understanding the New Age*, pp. 72-73.
34. Miller and Abramson, "Corporate Mind Control," p. 39.
35. See Peter Waldman, "Companies Seeking Advice Spawn Host of Consultants," *Wall Street Journal* (July 24, 1987), p. 19.
36. See Chandler, *Understanding the New Age*, p. 148.
37. Robert Lindsey, "Spiritual Concepts Drawing a Different Breed of Adherent," *New York Times* (Sept. 29, 1986), p. B12.
38. Groothuis, *Confronting the New Age*, p. 162, quoting Kathleen Pender, "Pac Bell's New Way To Think," *San Francisco Chronicle* (Mar. 23, 1987), p. 6.
39. Jeremy Main, "Trying to Bend Managers' Minds," *Fortune* (Nov.

Chapter 13

23, 1987), p. 100.

40. Ibid.

Chapter 13

1. "Today's Horror Films Make Hitchcock Fare Seem Tame," *Focus on the Family* (July, 1988), p. 11.
2. AP, "Film Influenced Matamoros Cult," *South Bend Tribune* (Apr. 16, 1989), p. A6.
3. James J. LeBar *et al., Cults, Sects, and the New Age* (Huntington, IN: Our Sunday Visitor, 1989), p. 148.
4. Ibid., pp. 147-148, citing Bob Larson, *Rock for Those Who Listen to the Words and Don't Like What They Hear* (Wheaton, IL: Tyndale House, 1986), p. 40.
5. Ibid., p. 148.
6. Ibid., citing *Hit Parader* (Feb., 1978), p. 24.
7. Michael Keating, "More Than Meets the Ear," *Pastoral Renewal* (July-Aug., 1987), p. 7.
8. Leilani Corpus, "The Force Behind Rock," *The Forerunner* (May, 1989), p. 13.
9. Ibid., p. 12.
10. John Catoir, "Light One Candle: Some Heavy Metal 'Lyrics,' " *The Criterion* (Oct. 27, 1989), p. 5.
11. Ibid.
12. Larson, *Larson's Book of Cults,* pp. 100, 98.
13. Alexander, "Tantra," p. 12.
14. Groothuis, *Unmasking,* p. 19.
15. Chandler, *Understanding the New Age,* p. 22, citing American Family Association (Tupelo, MS), "Script Sheet on the Movie 'The Last Temptation of Christ,' A Sampling of Scenes and Quotes From the Script," and citing Nikos Kazantzakis, *The Last Temptation of Christ,* tr. P.A. Bien (New York: Simon & Shuster, 1960), pp. 1-2.
16. Ibid., p. 158.
17. Ibid., citing Otto Friedrich *et al.,* "New Age Harmonies," *Time* (Dec. 7, 1987), p. 69.
18. David and Steve Gordon, "The True Spirit of New Age Music," in *The New Age Catalogue,* p. 207.
19. Larson, *Straight Answers,* p. 176.
20. Ibid., p. 177.
21. Groothuis, *Confronting the New Age,* p. 191, citing Steven Halpern and Louis Savary, *Sound Health* (San Francisco: Harper & Row, 1985), p. 186.
22. Ibid., p. 192, quoting *Master of Life,* Issue 35, p. 2.

23. Ibid., quoting *Master of Life*, p. 39.
24. Ibid., pp. 192-193.

Chapter 14

1. Quoted by John A. Hardon in *The Catholic Catechism* (Garden City, NY: Doubleday, 1975), p. 58.
2. Ibid., pp. 59-60.
3. See my article, "Dialogue with Non-Christians: Mutual Respect," *AD 2000 Together* (fall, 1988), pp. 6-7.
4. Walter M. Abbott, ed., *The Documents of Vatican II* (New York: America Press, 1966), pp. 660-663.
5. Oden, *The Living God*, pp. 22-23.
6. Ibid.
7. Peter Kreeft, *Fundamentals of the Faith: Essays in Christian Apologetics* (San Francisco: Ignatius Press, 1988), pp. 76-77.
8. The entire text of the Vatican's *Report on Sects, Cults and New Religious Movements* as well as an Introduction and Commentary can be found in *Origins* (May 22, 1986), pp. 1-10.
9. Ibid., p. 3. Note: Protestant churches which exclude certain deutero-canonical (apocryphal) books are not considered sects.
10. Ibid. The report refers to the book by Dave Breese, *Know the Marks of the Cults* (Wheaton, IL: Victor Books, 1985).
11. LeBar, *Cults, Sects and the New Age*, p. 15.
12. Ibid., p. 17.
13. Harris, *Resist the Devil*, p. 31.
14. Ibid., p. 30.
15. Ibid., p. 33.
16. Kreeft, *Fundamentals*, p. 104.
17. Ibid., p. 105.
18. Ibid., p. 106.
19. See the *Spiritual Counterfeits Project Special Collection Journal* (winter, 1984) and an article by Marcia Greene, "Spiritual Counterfeits Project," *PCC Renewal News* (May-June, 1981). This magazine serves Presbyterian charismatics. See Appendix for the address and phone number of the SCP and other organizations knowledgeable about the New Age.
20. Greene, "Spiritual Counterfeits Project," p. 12.
21. Robert Burrows, "New Age Movement: Self-Deification in a Secular Culture," *Spiritual Counterfeits Project Newsletter* (winter, 1984-85), pp. 4, 8.
22. Brooks Alexander and David Fetcho, "Spiritual Counterfeits in Context: An Open Letter," *Spiritual Counterfeits Project Journal* (winter, 1984), pp. 9-12, reprinted from *Spiritual Counterfeits Project*

Newsletter (Sept., 1976).
23. See Chapter 1, note 16.
24. See Chapter Two of this book.
25. We are trying to contrast New Age beliefs with Christian beliefs without fragmenting the Christian position. In general, Protestants would be more inclined to see the fall of our first parents as causing a destruction of our relationship with God while Roman Catholics would be more inclined to call this only a wounding of the relationship.
26. Catholics generally repent of their sins and seek forgiveness from God through the sacraments of Reconciliation and Anointing of the Sick.
27. See *The New Age Rage*, pp. 248-255, for a complete comparison.
28. Minneapolis: Bethany Fellowship, many editions. I have used the 15th printing (1974) of the 1965 edition.
29. Quoted by Elliot Miller in an editorial, *Christian Research Journal* (winter-spring, 1988), p. 3.
30. Martin, *The Kingdom of the Cults*, p. 16.
31. Walter Martin, "The New Age Movement," cassette tape C-107, Christian Research Institute. See Appendix for information on CRI.
32. Walter Martin, *The New Age Cult* (Minneapolis: Bethany House Publishers, 1989), pp. 7-8.
33. Miller, "The New Age Movement: What Is It?," p. 18. *Forward* was published by the Christian Research Institute. See Chapter One, note 6, for more information on Miller's articles and Appendix for the CRI address.
34. Miller seems to be using the term "cult" with the connotation of a tight organization with strict teaching and controls. Martin seems to use "cult" more as denoting something involved with the occult.
35. Miller, "The New Myth," *Forward* (spring-summer, 1986), p. 27.
36. See Appendix for more information on Jesus People USA and Cornerstone Press.
37. Groothuis, *Unmasking*, pp. 40-41.
38. Ibid., in Foreword by Gordon R. Lewis, p. 10.
39. Kurt Koch, *Occult ABC* (Grand Rapids, MI: Literature Mission Aglasterhausen, 1983), p. 40.
40. Mette Hammer, "Witches in Wisconsin: Magic Is the Medium for Area Practitioners of Wicca," *Isthmus* (July 25-31, 1986), p. 10.
41. H.H. Bro, *Fate* (Feb., 1971), pp. 102-3, quoted in Wilson and Weldon, *Occult Shock and Psychic Forces*, p. 443.
42. Kurt Koch, *Christian Counseling and Occultism* (Grand Rapids, MI: Kregel, 1981), p. 181.

43. Koch, *Occult ABC*, p. 280.
44. Groothius, *Confronting the New Age*, pp. 80-83.
45. See Chapter 1, note 15.
46. Chandler, *Understanding the New Age*, pp. 295-6.
47. Peck, *The Road Less Traveled*, pp. 281, 283, quoted by Chandler, *Understanding the New Age*, p. 297.
48. Quoted by Chandler, *Understanding the New Age*, p. 319.
49. Ibid., p. 320.
50. See Chapter 1, note 34.
51. James W. Sire, *Scripture Twisting* (Downers Grove, IL: Intervarsity Press, 1980), p. 24, quoted by Chandler, *Understanding the New Age*, pp. 317-8.
52. For information write: The John Ankerberg Show, PO Box 8977, Chattanooga, TN 37411.
53. Contact Jeremiah Films at PO Box 1710, Hemet, CA 92343. (800) 828-2290 or (800) 633-0869 in California.

Chapter 15

1. Karen C. Hoyt, "Personal Growth: Finding or Losing the Self," in Hoyt and Yamamoto, *The New Age Rage*, pp. 170-171.
2. Elliot Miller, "A 'New Age' of Science: An Inquiry into the Influence of Mysticism on Science," *Forward* (fall, 1985), p. 10.
3. Ibid.
4. J. Rodman Williams, *Renewal Theology: Systematic Theology From a Charismatic Perspective* (Grand Rapids, MI: Zondervan, 1988), p. 35.
5. Hardon, *The Catholic Catechism*, p. 24.
6. Kreeft, *Fundamentals*, p. 15.
7. Ibid., p. 19.
8. G.K. Malone, "Apologetics, Practical," *New Catholic Encyclopedia*, Vol. 1, p. 677.
9. Hardon, *The Catholic Catechism*, p. 38.
10. For more on this point, see my book, *God Is at Work in You: A Practical Guide to Growth in the Spirit* (South Bend, IN: Greenlawn Press, 1989), pp. 21-23.
11. Kreeft, *Fundamentals*, pp. 274-275.
12. See Felician A. Foy, O.F.M., ed., *1989 Catholic Almanac* (Huntington, IN: Our Sunday Visitor, 1988), pp. 200-201.
13. Oden, *The Living God*, p. 44.
14. Ibid., p. 266.
15. First Vatican Council, *Dogmatic Constitution on the Catholic Faith*, cited by Hardon, *The Catholic Catechism* (Garden City, NY: Doubleday, 1975), p. 55.

16. Groothuis, *Confronting the New Age,* p. 109, citing Martin, *Kingdom of the Cults,* 1974 ed., p. 284.
17. Alan Schreck, *Basics of the Faith: A Catholic Catechism* (Ann Arbor, MI: Servant Books, 1987), pp. 11-12.
18. Ibid., p. 55.
19. Ronald Lawler, O.F.M.Cap., Donald W. Wuerl and Thomas Comerford Lawler, *The Teaching of Christ: A Catholic Catechism for Adults* (Huntington, IN: Our Sunday Visitor, 1976, 1983), p. 150.
20. Kreeft, *Fundamentals,* p. 153.
21. *National & International Religion Report* (May 22, 1989), p. 8, citing research by Robert C. Bolin and Daniel Kenow of North Dakota State University published in *Omega.*
22. "Vision of Eternity," *Newsweek* (Mar. 27, 1989), p. 53.
23. Kenneth L. Woodward, "Heaven," *Newsweek* (Mar. 27, 1989), p. 55.
24. Peter J. Kreeft, *Everything You Ever Wanted To Know About Heaven, but Never Dreamed of Asking* (San Francisco: Harper & Row, 1982), p. 123.
25. Schreck, *Basics of the Faith,* p. 294.
26. Larson, *Larson's Book of Cults,* p. 61.
27. Hardon, *Catholic Catechism,* pp. 257-258.
28. *National Catholic Register* (Sept. 10, 1989), p. 2.
29. See *L'Osservatore Romano* (Nov. 23, 1972).
30. See Joseph Cardinal Ratzinger with Vittorio Messori, *The Ratzinger Report* (San Francisco: Ignatius Press, 1985), p. 137.
31. See "News Events," *1987 Catholic Almanac,* p. 101.
32. Sacred Congregation for the Doctrine of the Faith, *Les formes multiples de la superstition* (1975), quoted by Harris, *Resist the Devil,* p. 105.
33. Norman Geisler, *Signs and Wonders* (Wheaton, IL: Tyndale House, 1988), p. 96.
34. See Rath, *God Is at Work in You,* pp. 48-58.
35. Williams, *Renewal Theology,* p. 172.

Chapter 16

1. Martin, *The New Age Cult,* p. 97.
2. Ibid., pp. 98-108.
3. Douglas Groothuis, "Evangelizing New Agers," *Christian Research Journal* (winter-spring, 1987), p. 7.
4. Gordon R. Lewis, "Why I Talk With New Agers," *Christian Research Journal* (summer, 1989), p. 7.
5. Eric Pement, "Witnessing to People in Cults," *Spiritual Counterfeits Project Newsletter* (Nov.-Dec., 1983), p. 10.

6. Ibid., p. 9.
7. Ibid.
8. Ibid., p. 10.
9. Kreeft, *Fundamentals,* p. 75.
10. This section was adapted from my book, *God Is at Work in You,* pp. 75-76.

FOR YOU: Books of related interest
from Greenlawn Press

A Closer Look at the Enneagram
By Dorothy Garrity Ranaghan

Despite the enneagram's growing popularity in some Christian circles, *A Closer Look* cautions against its use by Christians. Mrs. Ranaghan documents its roots in the occult and in distortions of Christian doctrine. This brief yet thorough booklet is essential reading for pastoral leaders and those who use the enneagram.
Order # GRNL9105, $3.75, paperback

Resist the Devil
A Pastoral Guide to Deliverance Prayer
By Rev. Charles W. Harris, C.S.C.

This powerful book shows you methods of deliverance prayer and discernment that are spiritually and psychologically sound. Rev. Harris, an authorized diocesan exorcist, enlightens you with case histories of real and imagined evil spiritual influences.
Order # GRNL9075, $5.95, paperback

God Is at Work in You
A Practical Guide to Growth in the Spirit
By Ralph Rath

The author of *The New Age: A Christian Critique* gives you a treasury of time-tested practices for strong, authentic Christian living. *God Is at Work in You* gives you inspiring advice on daily prayer, discerning God's will, sharing the gospel, and more. Scripture readings and real-life examples enrich each chapter. Prayer-group leaders—and others in pastoral ministry—can find solid teaching material here!
Order # GRNL9113, $4.95 paperback

Order these books today from your local Christian bookstore or from:
    Greenlawn Press, Dept. R, 107 S. Greenlawn Ave.,
    South Bend, IN 46617
    (Please add $1.50 for shipping and handling.)

● ●

Cassette tapes available

You can purchase a two-hour overview of *The New Age: A Christian Critique* on a set of two casette tapes. These talks by Ralph Rath are available—at a cost of $9.95 plus $1.50 for shipping and handling—from Resurrection Tapes, 1203 E. Lake St., Minneapolis, MN 55407.

BLADE
OF THE IMMORTAL

Cry of the Worm

publisher
Mike Richardson

series editor
Dave Chipps

collection editor
Suzanne Taylor

collection designers
Harald Graham
& Amy Arendts

art director
Mark Cox

**English version produced by Studio Proteus
for Dark Horse Comics, Inc.**

BLADE OF THE IMMORTAL Vol. 2: CRY OF THE WORM
Blade of the Immortal copyright © 1996, 1997, 1998 by Hiroaki Samura.
All rights reserved. First published in Japan in 1994 by Kodansha
Ltd., Tokyo. English translation rights arranged through Kodansha
Ltd. This English-language edition © 1998 by Studio Proteus and
Dark Horse Comics, Inc. All other material © 1998 by Dark Horse
Comics, Inc. All rights reserved. No portion of this publication may
be reproduced by any means without written permission from the
copyright holders. The stories, characters, and incidents in this
publication are entirely fictional. Dark Horse Comics® is a trademark
of Dark Horse Comics, Inc. All rights reserved.

This volume collects issues seven through eleven
of the Dark Horse comic-book series,
Blade of the Immortal.

Published by
Dark Horse Comics, Inc.
10956 SE Main Street
Milwaukie, OR 97222

First edition: March 1998
ISBN: 1-56971-300-6

7 9 10 8

Printed in Canada

OF THE IMMORTAL

art and story
HIROAKI SAMURA

translation
Dana Lewis & Toren Smith

lettering and retouch
Wayne Truman & Tomoko Saito

Cry of the Worm

DARK HORSE COMICS®

ABOUT THE TRANSLATION

The Swastika

The main character in *Blade of the Immortal*, Manji, has taken the "crux gammata" as both his name and his personal symbol. This symbol is also known as the *swastika*, a name derived from the Sanskrit *svastika* (meaning "welfare," from *su* — "well" + *asti* "he is"). As a symbol of prosperity and good fortune, the swastika was widely used throughout the ancient world (for example, appearing often on Mesopotamian coinage), including North and South America and has been used in Japan as a symbol of Buddhism since ancient times. To be precise, the symbol generally used by Japanese Buddhists is the *sauvastika*, which moves in a counterclockwise direction, and is called the *manji* in Japanese. The *sauvastika* generally stands for night, and often for magical practices. The *swastika*, whose arms point in a clockwise direction, is generally considered a solar symbol. It was this version (the *hakenkreuz*) that was perverted by the Nazis and used as their symbol. It is important that readers understand that the *swastika* has ancient and honorable origins and it is those that apply to this story, which takes place in the 18th century (ca. 1782-3). *There is no anti-Semitic or pro-Nazi meaning behind the use of the symbol in this story. Those meanings did not exist until after 1910.*

The Artwork

The creator of *Blade of the Immortal* requested that we make an effort to avoid mirror-imaging his artwork. Normally, all of our manga are first copied in a mirror-image in order to facilitate the left-to-right reading of the pages. However, Mr. Samura decided that he would rather see his pages reversed via the technique of cutting up the panels and re-pasting them in reverse order. While we feel that this often leads to problems in panel-to-panel continuity, we place primary importance on the wishes of the creator. Therefore, most of *Blade of the Immortal* has been produced using the "cut and paste" technique. There are, of course, some sequences where it was impossible to do this, and mirror-imaged panels or pages were used.

The Sound Effects & Dialogue

Since some of Mr. Samura's sound effects are integral parts of the artwork, we decided to leave those in their original Japanese. We hope readers will view the unretouched sound effects as essential portions of Mr. Samura's extraordinary artwork. In addition, Mr. Samura's treatment of dialogue is quite different from that featured in average samurai manga and is considered to be one of the things that has made *Blade* such a hit in Japan. Mr. Samura has mixed a variety of linguistic styles in this fantasy story, where some characters speak in the mannered style of old Japan, while others speak as if they were street-corner punks from a bad area of modern-day Tokyo. The anachronistic slang used by some of the characters in the English translation reflects the unusual mix of speech patterns from the original Japanese text.

FANATIC

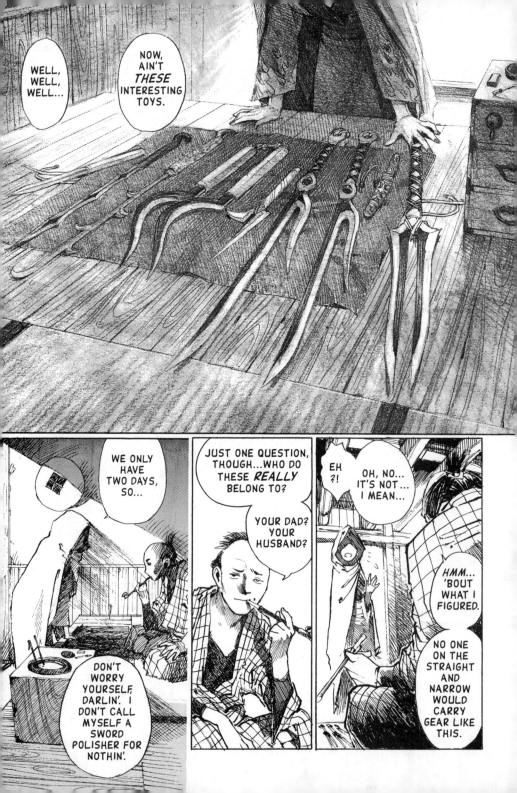

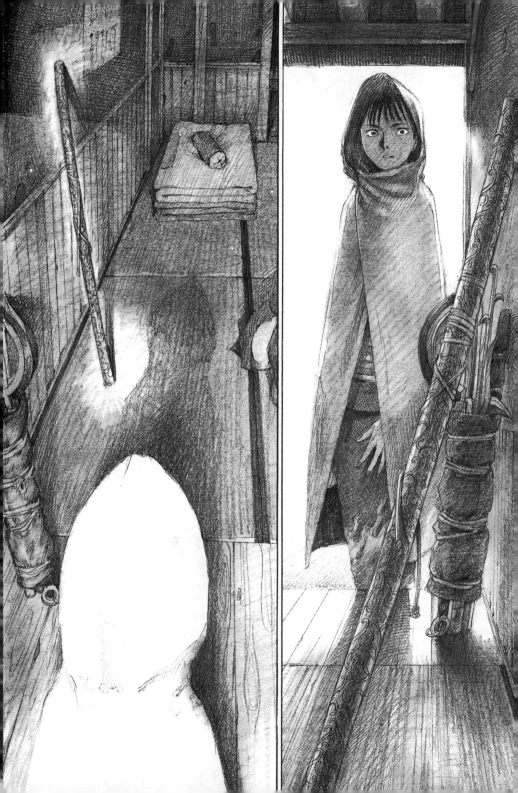

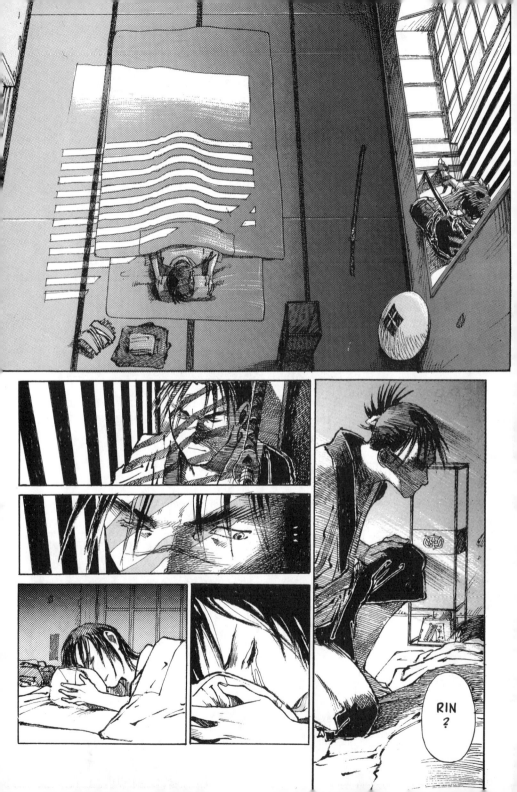

CRY OF THE WORM
Part 1: Path of Fire

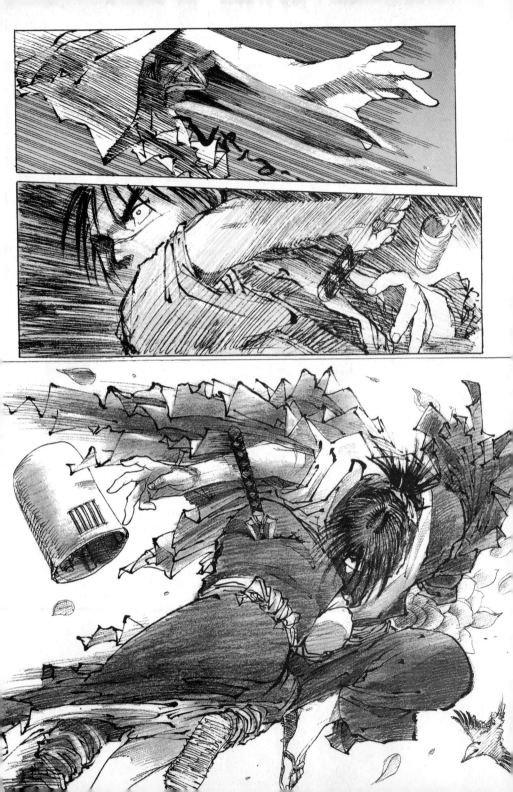

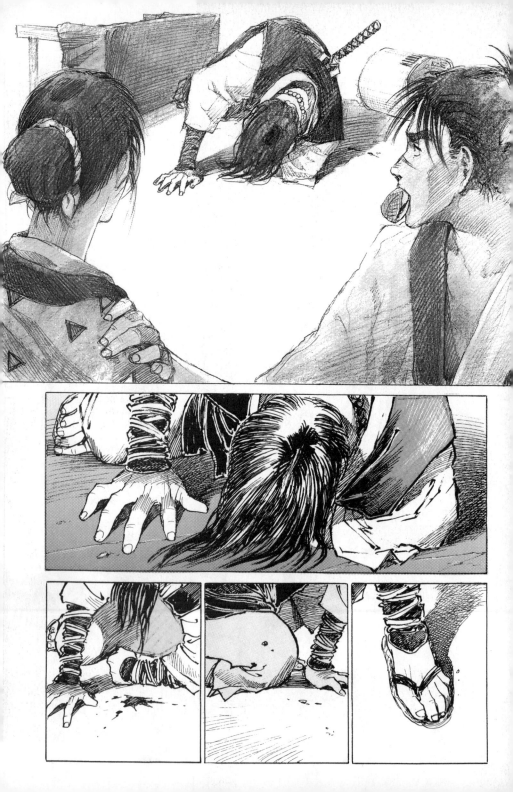

I...
I'LL
SAY
IT...

...ONE
MORE
TIME.

砂利....

YOU
AND I...
WE SHOULD
UNDERSTAND
EACH
OTHER.

....
....!

CRY OF THE WORM
Part 2: Path of Blood

POK

MANJI—TAKE THESE.

UNGG...

?

IT'S AN *ANTIDOTE* I LEARNED ABOUT FROM MY MOTHER.

THEY'RE PILLS ROLLED FROM *DOSEI-MOTSUKŌ* AND *RENGYŌ*.

"GONE TO HOT SPRINGS FOR VACATION. NO EXAMINATIONS UNTIL THE WEEKEND. --KAKUSHIN, TOWN DOCTOR"

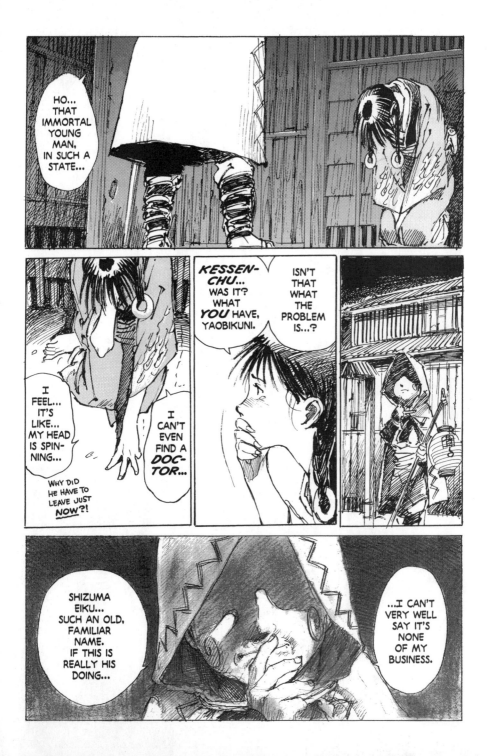

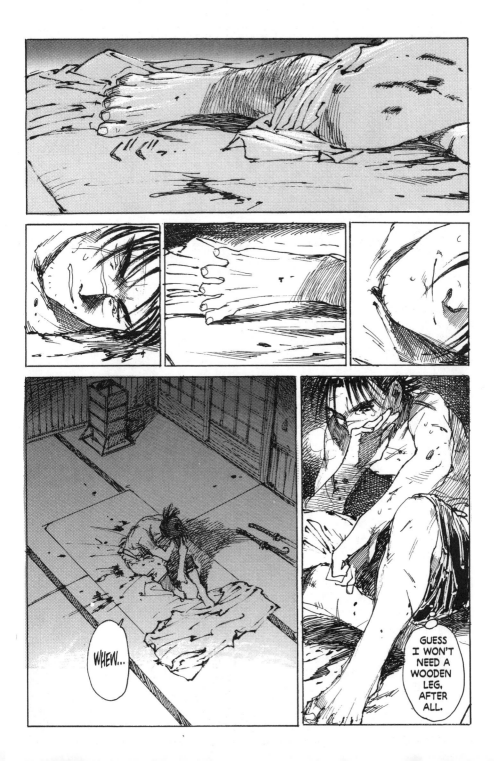

WHEW...

GUESS I WON'T NEED A WOODEN LEG, AFTER ALL.

THE BANKS OF THE
YOTSUYA OUTER MOAT.
I'M WAITING.
　　--SHIZUMA EIKU

SO...I RAN OUT LIKE AN IDIOT AND GOT CAUGHT... FOR *NOTHING*.

AAA...!

THERE WAS NO CHOICE-- I HAD *NO* CHOICE!

I'M SORRY! I AM SO *SORRY*, YOUNG MISS!

HE THREATENED TO KILL MY *GRANDSON*!

AND I DIDN'T *KNOW* WHAT HE'D DO--

I GUESS YOU'RE STILL IN YOUR FORTIES. IN THE DARK I COULDN'T TELL.

I'M A FOOL.

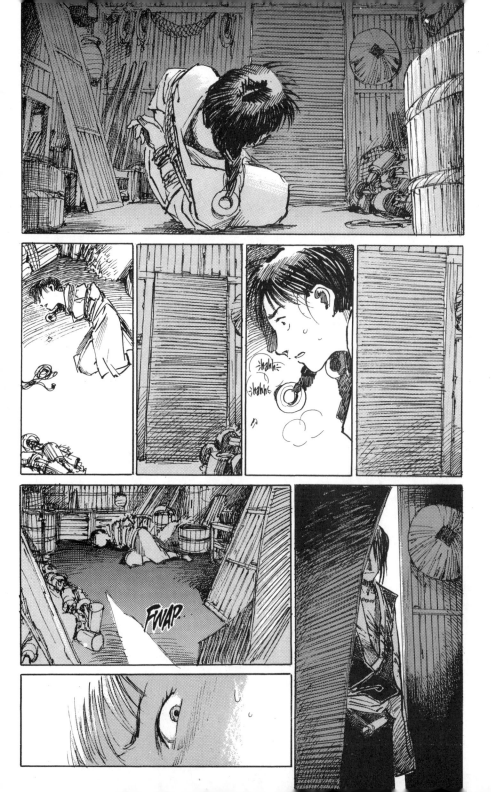

......!
....!

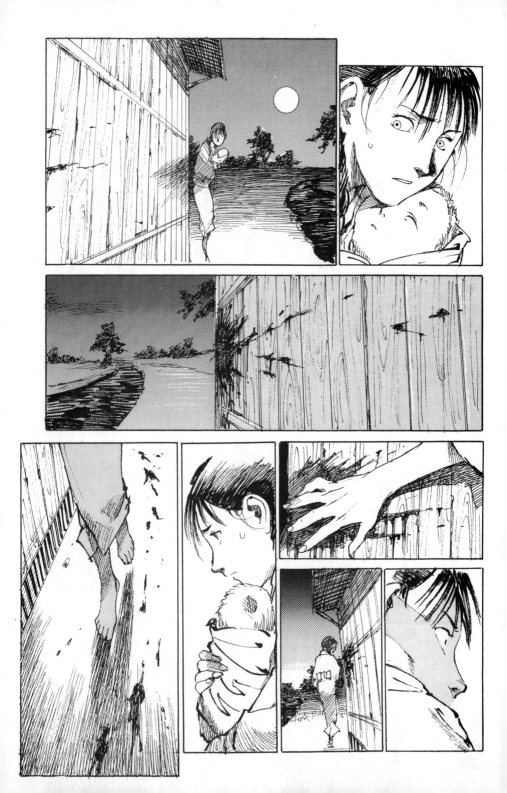

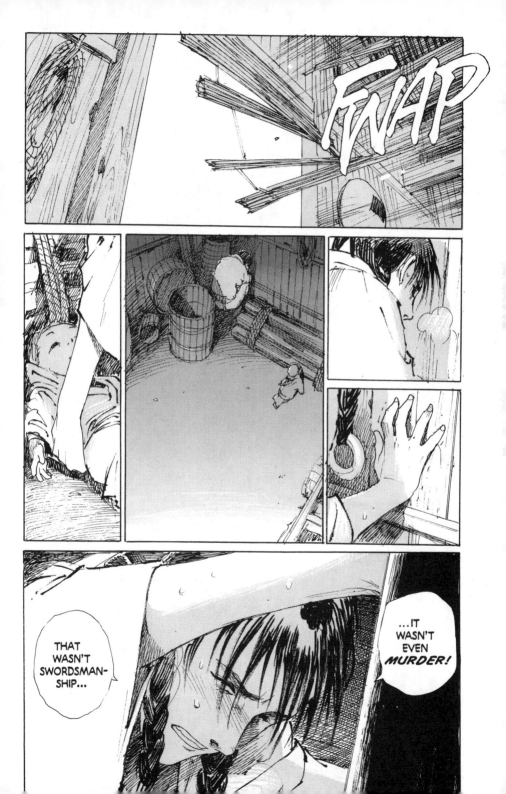

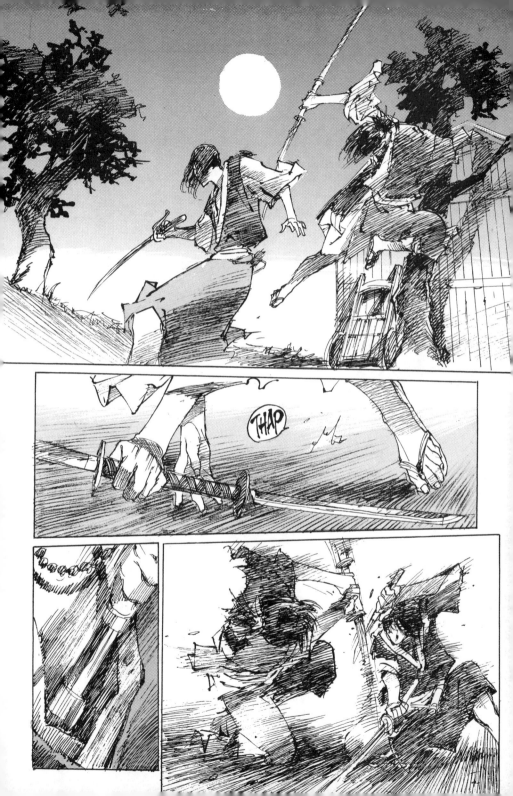

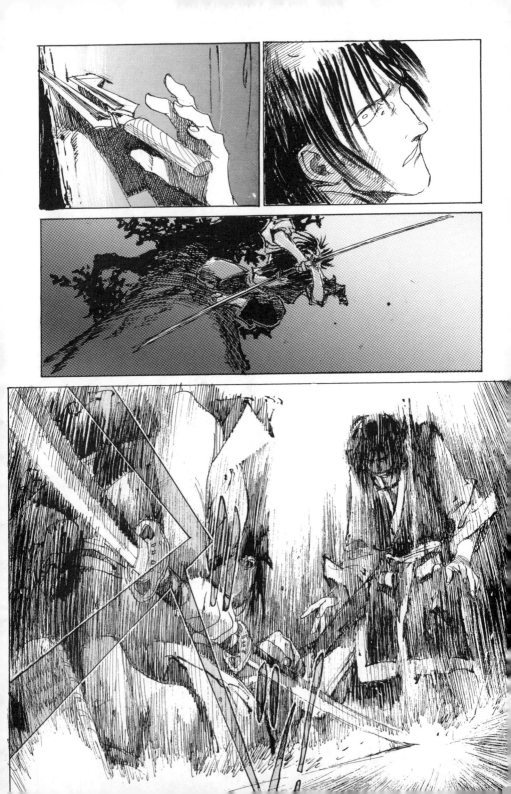

GLOSSARY

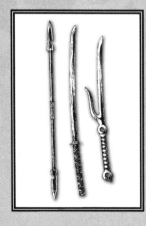

Daimyō: Ruler of a feudal fiefdom.

Dōjō: Training centers. Here, centers for swordsmanship.

Doseimotsukō, Rengyō: These plants (Dutchman's Pipe and Forsythia) can alleviate some types of poisoning when boiled and consumed.

Edo: Capital of pre-modern Japan. Later renamed Tokyo.

Ezo: Hokkaido and the other islands north of Japan. At the time, they were still controlled by the indigenous Ainu peoples and were a perilous back door into closed Japan for foreign goods and people.

Itto-ryū: The radical sword tradition led by Anotsu.

Kenshi: A swordsman, not necessarily born into the samurai caste.

Kessen-chu: The "sacred bloodworms." A person infected by them cannot die but feels pain like a mortal.

Kessen-satsu: "Bloodworm killer."

Magatsu: A ronin with Rin's enemy, Anotsu.

Muromachi: The reign of the Ashikaga shoguns in Kyoto, A.D. 1338-1573. The last period of

social stability in Japan before two centuries of civil war and the rise of the Tokugawa Shogunate.

Mutenichi-ryū: The sword tradition taught by Rin's father.

Ryō: A high-value gold coin.

Sangin: An official trip to the capital. Daimyo of outlying fiefdoms were required to spend one year in three in Edo, allowing the Shogun to keep them under tight control.

Sakura-mochi: A delicacy made from pounded sweet rice paste and cherry-tree leaves.

Sanzu no Kawa: River of the Dead. Analogous to the River Styx in Greek mythology. Crossed by the dead on their way to the underworld.

Satori: The state of intuitive illumination sought by followers of Zen Buddhism; the movement of such enlightenment.

Toyotomi: Toyotomi Hideyoshi, A.D. 1536-1598, the first warlord to unify Japan. After he died of an illness, his empire collapsed and his son and heir was killed by the Tokugawa family, who rule Japan at the time of our story.

Uji: An area near Kyoto.

Warabi: An edible plant (bracken or fernbrake).

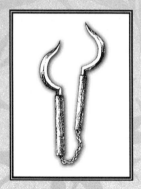

COVER GALLERY

The following are Hiroaki Samura's covers from issues eight, seven, ten, and eleven of the *Blade of the Immortal* comics series. Issues nine through eleven of *Blade of the Immortal* also included pinups by many of the industry's finest artists. We chose to feature those of Gene Ha and Gary Gianni.

pinup by Gene Ha

pinup by Gary Gianni